The Complete
Best of Bridge
Cookbooks

VOLUME 1

All 350 Recipes from
The Best of Bridge and *Enjoy!*

Robert
ROSE

The Complete Best of Bridge Cookbooks, Volume 1
Text copyright © 2008, 1980 by Karen Brimacombe, Mary Halpen, Helen Miles, Valerie Robinson and Joan Wilson
Photographs copyright © 2008 by Robert Rose Inc.
Cover and text design copyright © 2008 by Robert Rose Inc.

The recipes in this book were previously published in *The Best of Bridge: Royal Treats for Entertaining*, published in 1980 by Best of Bridge Publishing Ltd., or in *Enjoy! More Recipes from The Best of Bridge*, published in 1980 by Best of Bridge Publishing Ltd.

For complete cataloguing information, see page 372.

Cover design and page layout: PageWave Graphics, Inc.
Indexer: Belle Wong
Photography: Colin Erricson
Food Styling: Kathryn Robertson
Prop Styling: Charlene Erricson

Cover image: Beef Bourguignon (page 212)

We acknowledge the financial support of the Government of Canada through the Book Publishing Industry Development Program (BPIDP) for our publishing activities.

Published by Robert Rose Inc.
120 Eglinton Avenue East, Suite 800, Toronto, Ontario, Canada M4P 1E2
Tel: (416) 322-6552 Fax: (416) 322-6936

Printed in China

1 2 3 4 5 6 7 8 RRD 15 14 13 12 11 10 09 08

CONTENTS

WHAT'S NEXT

A PARTNERSHIP OF 33 YEARS IS AN AMAZING ACHIEVEMENT - AND WE HAVE DELIGHTED IN THE EXPERIENCE EVERY STEP OF THE WAY!

NOW IT'S TIME TO ASSUME THE ROLE OF "WISE WOMEN." ROBERT ROSE INC. WILL BE OUR PUBLISHER AND DO ALL THE WORK, AND WE'LL BECOME ADVISORS AND OFFER THE BENEFIT OF OUR CONSIDERABLE ADVICE - CULINARY AND OTHERWISE!

WE ARE SO THANKFUL FOR THE LOVE AND SUPPORT OF OUR FAMILIES AND FRIENDS. OUR CUSTOMERS AND RETAILERS HAVE BECOME AN IMPORTANT PART OF THE BEST OF BRIDGE FAMILY, AND THEIR ENTHUSIASM IS ALWAYS APPRECIATED. THANK YOU ALL - IT'S BEEN A MAGICAL EXPERIENCE.

FOREWARNING

WHO ARE THOSE BEST OF BRIDGE WOMEN, AND WHERE DID THEY GET THAT GOOFY NAME?

IN 1975, AT A WEEKEND GETAWAY, EIGHT BRIDGE-PLAYING FRIENDS DECIDED TO WRITE A COOKBOOK AND CALL IT *THE BEST OF BRIDGE*, BECAUSE THE BEST PART OF BRIDGE IS THE FOOD. THESE YOUNG KITCHEN-COUNTER ENTREPRENEURS TURNED A GOOD IDEA INTO A GREAT BOOK AND SET THE STAGE FOR THE PHENOMENALLY SUCCESSFUL BEST OF BRIDGE COOKBOOK SERIES.

FROM THE OUTSET, "THE LADIES," AS THEIR CHILDREN NAMED THEM, HAD AN UNCONVENTIONAL BUSINESS SENSE AND AN UNCONVENTIONAL SENSE OF HUMOR. THEIRS WAS A PARTNERSHIP OF EQUALS AND A CELEBRATION OF FRIENDSHIP. THEY DID EVERYTHING (AND ANYTHING!) WITH ENTHUSIASM: RECIPE TESTING, WRITING, MARKETING, SHIPPING, PROMOTING AND EVEN PRODUCING A TV SERIES. THEY'VE SOLD OVER 3 MILLION COOKBOOKS, AND THEY'RE STILL BEST FRIENDS!

IN *THE COMPLETE BEST OF BRIDGE COOKBOOKS, VOLUME I,* ALL OF THE RECIPES FROM THE FIRST TWO BOOKS – *THE BEST OF BRIDGE* (THE RED BOOK) AND *ENJOY!* (THE YELLOW BOOK) – ARE COMPILED INTO ONE VOLUME SO THE NEXT GENERATION OF COOKS CAN ENJOY THE LADIES' FAMOUS COLLECTION OF RECIPES. THEY'RE EASY TO READ, EASY TO UNDERSTAND, WRITTEN WITH A SENSE OF HUMOR AND, BEST OF ALL, GUARANTEED TO WORK.

YOU'RE GOING TO LOVE THIS BOOK!

NEW ORLEANS STRIPS

PERFECT FOR A COFFEE PARTY!

2	EGGS	2
I TBSP	SUGAR	15 ML
PINCH	SALT	PINCH
3/4 CUP	MILK	175 ML
I TBSP	GRATED ORANGE ZEST	15 ML
12	THIN SLICES BREAD	12
	BUTTER	

ORANGE SUGAR

1/2 CUP	SUGAR	125 ML
1/4 CUP	GRATED ORANGE ZEST	50 ML

REMOVE CRUSTS FROM BREAD. BEAT EGGS, ADD SUGAR, SALT, MILK AND ORANGE ZEST. DIP BREAD SLICES QUICKLY IN MILK MIXTURE AND FRY IN BUTTER UNTIL GOLDEN. SPRINKLE WITH ORANGE SUGAR AND SERVE IMMEDIATELY. SERVES 6.

IF YOU WAIT TOO LONG TO MARRY YOUR DREAMBOAT, YOU MAY FIND, BY THE TIME YOU HAVE MADE UP YOUR MIND, HIS CARGO HAS SHIFTED.

HERB BREAD

1	LOAF FRENCH BREAD	1
½ CUP	SOFT BUTTER	125 ML
2 TSP	GARLIC POWDER	10 ML
½ TSP	SAVORY	2 ML
1 TSP	CELERY SALT	5 ML
½ TSP	ROSEMARY	2 ML
½ TSP	THYME	2 ML
½ TSP	CHERVIL	2 ML
½ TSP	BASIL	2 ML
1 TSP	SAGE	5 ML
1 TBSP	PARSLEY	15 ML
½ TSP	OREGANO	2 ML

COMBINE ALL INGREDIENTS. SPREAD ON SLICED BREAD.
WRAP IN FOIL. HEAT IN 350°F (180°C) OVEN FOR 30 MINUTES.
SERVES 8.

ALL I ASK IS THE CHANCE TO PROVE
MONEY CAN'T MAKE ME HAPPY.

IRISH PAN BUNS

2	PACKAGES RAPID-MIX YEAST	2
1/2 CUP	SUGAR	125 ML
2 TSP	SALT	10 ML
1/4 CUP	MARGARINE	50 ML
2 CUPS	WATER	500 ML
1	EGG, BEATEN	1
6 1/2 CUPS	FLOUR	1.625 L

MIX 1/4 AMOUNT OF FLOUR WITH OTHER DRY INGREDIENTS. HEAT LIQUIDS UNTIL HOT TO TOUCH. ADD LIQUIDS TO DRY MIXTURE AND BEAT 2 MINUTES ON MEDIUM SPEED.

ADD 1/2 CUP (125 ML) FLOUR, BEATEN EGG. MIX 1 MINUTE. ADD FLOUR GRADUALLY (MAY NOT NEED ALL FLOUR). FORM A BALL AND PUT IN GREASED BOWL. TURN OVER SO TOP IS GREASED. COVER WITH FOIL AND REFRIGERATE 2 HOURS.

TAKE 1/4 DOUGH AND SHAPE INTO BALLS 1-INCH (2.5 CM) DIAMETER. PUT IN LIGHTLY GREASED 8-INCH (20 CM) ROUND PAN. COVER AND LET RISE (35 MINUTES TO 45 MINUTES) COMBINE GARLIC SALT AND BUTTER AND MELT. BRUSH LIGHTLY ON TOP OF BALLS. SPRINKLE ON PARSLEY. COVER AND LET RISE ADDITIONAL 5 MINUTES. BAKE IN 400°F (200°C) OVEN FOR 15 MINUTES. REPEAT WITH REMAINING DOUGH.

DOUGH MAY BE REFRIGERATED FOR 2 DAYS. SERVES 16.

TWO PEOPLE CAN EAT AS CHEAPLY AS ONE WHAT?

FERGOSA

(AN ITALIAN BREAD) THIS IS A GREAT ACCOMPANIMENT WITH SALAD FOR A LADIES LUNCH OR GREAT WITH SALMON OR HOMEMADE SOUP. EVERYONE WILL LOVE IT – YOU'D BETTER MAKE TWO.

½ CUP	CHOPPED ONION	125 ML
1 TBSP	BUTTER	15 ML
1 CUP	DRY BISCUIT MIX	250 ML
½ CUP	GRATED CHEDDAR CHEESE	125 ML
⅓ CUP	MILK	75 ML
1 CUP	GRATED CHEDDAR CHEESE	250 ML
1	EGG, SLIGHTLY BEATEN	1
	POPPY SEEDS	

SAUTÉ ONION AND BUTTER UNTIL THE ONION IS TRANSPARENT. MEANWHILE, COMBINE THE BISCUIT MIX, ½ CUP (125 ML) GRATED CHEESE AND MILK AND BEAT UNTIL SMOOTH. THIS WILL BE STICKY. KNEAD 10 TIMES ON FLOURED BOARD WORKING IN SMALL AMOUNT OF FLOUR IF IT'S STICKING TOO MUCH. BUTTER 8-INCH (20 CM) OR 9-INCH (23 CM) PIE PLATE AND ALSO YOUR HANDS. SPREAD THIS MIXTURE ON THE BOTTOM OF THE PAN. COMBINE THE CUP OF GRATED CHEDDAR AND EGG.

SPREAD ON CRUST, SPRINKLE WITH ONION-BUTTER MIXTURE AND POPPY SEEDS. BAKE AT 425°F (220°C) FOR 20 MINUTES. TO SERVE, CUT IN WEDGES. SERVES 8.

A PENNY SAVED IS RIDICULOUS.

GARLIC-PARMESAN CHEESE BREAD

1 CUP	MILK	250 ML
1/4 CUP	BUTTER	50 ML
1 TBSP	PAPRIKA	15 ML
	GARLIC TO TASTE	

HEAT ALL INGREDIENTS TOGETHER. DIP FRENCH BREAD SLICES IN QUICKLY, COVERING BOTH SIDES. ROLL UNTIL COMPLETELY COVERED IN PARMESAN CHEESE. BAKE AT 400°F (200°C) FOR 5 MINUTES. WATCH THEM CAREFULLY SO THEY DON'T BURN. THE FRENCH BREAD SLICES MAY BE HALVED SO WHEN THEY ARE DIPPED THEY DON'T GET TOO SOGGY. USE A SHALLOW PAN FOR THE DIPPING.

PUMPKIN LOAF

3 CUPS	FLOUR	750 ML
1 TSP	SODA	5 ML
1 TSP	SALT	5 ML
1 TBSP	CINNAMON	15 ML
2 CUPS	PUMPKIN, CANNED	500 ML
2 CUPS	WHITE SUGAR	500 ML
4	EGGS	4
1 1/4 CUPS	OIL	300 ML

MIX DRY INGREDIENTS IN BOWL. MAKE A WELL IN CENTER. ADD THE REMAINING INGREDIENTS AND STIR JUST ENOUGH TO MIX. POUR INTO TWO 9- X 5-INCH (2 L) LOAF PANS. BAKE AT 350°F (180°C) FOR 1 HOUR. SERVES 10 TO 12.

JIFFY ORANGE BREAD

2 CUPS	FLOUR	500 ML
1 TSP	BAKING POWDER	5 ML
1 TSP	BAKING SODA	5 ML
1/2 TSP	SALT	2 ML
1/2 CUP	CHOPPED NUTS	125 ML
2 TBSP	BUTTER	25 ML
	GRATED ZEST OF 1 ORANGE	
1/3 CUP	ORANGE JUICE	75 ML
2 TSP	VANILLA	10 ML
1 CUP	WHITE SUGAR	250 ML
1	BEATEN EGG	1
1/2 CUP	BOILING WATER	125 ML

TOPPING

1 TBSP	SUGAR	15 ML
1 TBSP	ORANGE ZEST	15 ML
1 TBSP	CHOPPED NUTS	15 ML

SIFT FLOUR, BAKING POWDER, SODA AND SALT. CREAM TOGETHER BUTTER, ORANGE PEEL, JUICE, VANILLA, SUGAR, BEATEN EGG AND BOILING WATER. ADD DRY INGREDIENTS BEATING JUST UNTIL FLOUR DISAPPEARS. TURN INTO GREASED LOAF PAN AND SPRINKLE WITH LAST THREE INGREDIENTS. BAKE AT 350°F (180°C) FOR 30 TO 40 MINUTES, OR UNTIL IT TESTS DONE. SERVES 10 TO 12.

MOTHERS ARE THOSE WONDERFUL PEOPLE WHO CAN GET UP IN THE MORNING BEFORE THEY SMELL THE BACON FRYING.

ORANGE HONEY BREAD

2 TBSP	SHORTENING	25 ML
1 CUP	HONEY	250 ML
1	EGG, WELL BEATEN	1
1½ TSP	GRATED ORANGE ZEST	7 ML
2½ CUPS	FLOUR	625 ML
2½ TSP	BAKING POWDER	12 ML
½ TSP	BAKING POWDER	2 ML
½ TSP	BAKING SODA	2 ML
½ TSP	SALT	2 ML
3/4 CUP	JUICE	175 ML
3/4 CUP	CHOPPED NUTS	175 ML

CREAM SHORTENING AND HONEY. ADD EGG AND ZEST. SIFT FLOUR WITH BAKING POWDER, BAKING SODA AND SALT. ADD TO HONEY MIXTURE ALTERNATELY WITH JUICE. ADD NUTS. PUT IN GREASED 9- X 5-INCH (2 L) LOAF PAN AND BAKE 1 HOUR AND 10 MINUTES AT 325°F (160°C). SERVES 10 TO 12.

DENIAL IS A RIVER IN EGYPT.

L'IL RED'S APRICOT BREAD

VERY MOIST. EXCELLENT SERVED WITH MILD
WHITE CHEESE, AND IT FREEZES WELL.

I CUP	CHOPPED DRIED APRICOTS	250 ML
I CUP	WATER	250 ML
I	LARGE ORANGE, ZEST AND JUICE	I
2 TBSP	SHORTENING	25 ML
I CUP	WHITE SUGAR	250 ML
2	EGGS, BEATEN	2
I TSP	VANILLA	5 ML
2 CUPS	FLOUR	500 ML
2 TSP	BAKING POWDER	10 ML
I TSP	BAKING SODA	5 ML
1/2 TSP	SALT	2 ML
1/2 CUP	RAISINS	125 ML
I CUP	CHOPPED WALNUTS	250 ML

ADD WATER TO APRICOTS AND LET STAND OVERNIGHT.
DRAIN LIQUID AND RESERVE. ADD ORANGE JUICE TO
APRICOT LIQUID AND ENOUGH WATER TO MAKE I CUP
(250 ML) IN TOTAL. CREAM SHORTENING, GRATED ORANGE
ZEST AND SUGAR. ADD BEATEN EGGS AND VANILLA. SIFT
DRY INGREDIENTS AND ADD ALTERNATELY WITH THE I CUP
(250 ML) OF LIQUID. MIX IN APRICOTS, RAISINS AND WALNUTS.
POUR INTO 10- X 6-INCH (2.6 L) GREASED LOAF PAN. BAKE
AT 350°F (180°C) FOR 60 TO 70 MINUTES. SERVES 10 TO 12.

IT'S AMAZING HOW FAST LATER COMES
WHEN YOU BUY NOW.

LEMON LOAF

SUPERB FLAVOR. FREEZES WELL.

½ CUP	BUTTER	125 ML
I CUP	SUGAR	250 ML
2	EGGS, BEATEN	2
½ CUP	MILK	125 ML
I½ CUPS	FLOUR	375 ML
I TSP	BAKING POWDER	5 ML
I TSP	SALT	5 ML
	GRATED ZEST OF I LEMON	
½ CUP	CHOPPED WALNUTS (OPTIONAL)	125 ML

DRIZZLE

3 TBSP	LEMON JUICE	45 ML
¼ CUP	SUGAR	50 ML

PREHEAT OVEN TO 350°F (180°C). IN A LARGE BOWL, CREAM BUTTER AND SUGAR. ADD BEATEN EGGS AND MILK. ADD DRY INGREDIENTS, LEMON ZEST AND WALNUTS. MIX WELL. PLACE IN A 9- X 5-INCH (2 L) GREASED LOAF PAN AND BAKE FOR I HOUR. REMOVE FROM OVEN AND COOL ON A RACK FOR 5 MINUTES. PRICK CAKE WITH FORK AND POUR DRIZZLE OVER LOAF. LET STAND AT LEAST I HOUR BEFORE REMOVING FROM PAN. SERVES 10 TO 12.

WHAT CAN YOU EXPECT OF A DAY THAT STARTS WITH GETTING UP?

ZUCCHINI LOAVES

3	EGGS	3
I CUP	OIL	250 ML
2 CUPS	SUGAR	500 ML
I TSP	VANILLA	5 ML
2 CUPS	WASHED, FINELY SHREDDED, UNPARED ZUCCHINI, WELL PACKED	500 ML
I 1/2 CUPS	CAKE FLOUR	375 ML
I CUP	WHOLE WHEAT FLOUR	250 ML
1/2 CUP	WHEAT GERM	125 ML
I TSP	SALT	5 ML
2 TSP	NUTMEG	10 ML
I TSP	BAKING SODA	5 ML
1/2 TSP	BAKING POWDER	2 ML
1/2 CUP	CHOPPED NUTS	125 ML

IN A BOWL BEAT EGGS, OIL, SUGAR, VANILLA AND ZUCCHINI. TURN BEATERS ON LOW AND BEGIN ADDING ALL REMAINING INGREDIENTS AS YOU MEASURE THEM. STIR IN NUTS LAST. BATTER IS QUITE THIN. LINE TWO 9- X 5-INCH (2 L) GLASS LOAF PANS WITH BUTTERED DOUBLE WAX PAPER. POUR TWO-THIRDS FULL AND BAKE I HOUR AT 325°F (160°C). MAKES 2 LOAVES; EACH SERVES 10 TO 12.

THERE IS NO JUSTIFICATION FOR SPITTING IN A MAN'S FACE, UNLESS HIS MUSTACHE IS ON FIRE.

CHRISTMAS BRUNCH CARROT LOAF

SAVE YOUR 16 OZ (455 ML) AND 48 OZ (1.4 L) FRUIT JUICE CANS TO USE AS MOLDS.

3	BEATEN EGGS	3
1/2 CUP	COOKING OIL	125 ML
1/2 CUP	MILK	125 ML
2 1/2 CUPS	SIFTED FLOUR	625 ML
1 CUP	SUGAR	250 ML
1 TSP	BAKING POWDER	5 ML
1 TSP	BAKING SODA	5 ML
2 TSP	CINNAMON	10 ML
1 TSP	EACH NUTMEG AND GINGER (OPTIONAL)	5 ML
1/2 TSP	SALT	2 ML
2 CUPS	SHREDDED CARROT	500 ML
1 1/2 CUPS	COCONUT	375 ML
1/2 CUP	CHOPPED MARASCHINO CHERRIES (DRAINED)	125 ML
1/2 CUP	RAISINS	125 ML
1/2 CUP	CHOPPED PECANS	125 ML

IN LARGE BOWL, SIFT TOGETHER DRY INGREDIENTS. COMBINE EGGS, OIL AND MILK, AND ADD TO FIRST MIXTURE. WHEN WELL-COMBINED, ADD ADDITIONAL INGREDIENTS. TURN INTO FOUR 16-OZ (455 ML) CANS, LOAF PANS OR LARGE JUICE CANS. LINE GREASED CANS WITH WAXED PAPER. BAKE AT 350°F (150°C) FOR 50 TO 60 MINUTES. REMOVE FROM CANS AND COOL. THIS MAY BE KEPT IN REFRIGERATOR FOR SEVERAL WEEKS. SERVE BUTTERED SLICES AT BRUNCH INSTEAD OF TOAST.

MAKES 4 LOAVES; EACH SERVES 4 TO 6.

GOOD OLD-FASHIONED GINGERBREAD

FOUR GENERATIONS CAN'T BE WRONG - IT'S DELICIOUS.
SERVE WARM WITH WHIPPED CREAM OR WITH THE
FOLLOWING LEMON SAUCE.

1/4 CUP	BUTTER	50 ML
1/4 CUP	SUGAR	50 ML
1 TSP	CINNAMON	5 ML
1 TSP	GINGER	5 ML
1 TSP	CLOVES	5 ML
1 TSP	SALT	5 ML
1 TSP	BAKING POWDER	5 ML
1 1/4 CUPS	FLOUR	300 ML
1/2 TSP	BAKING SODA	2 ML
1/2 CUP	MOLASSES	125 ML
1/4 TSP	BAKING SODA	1 ML
3/4 CUP	BOILING WATER	175 ML
1	EGG, BEATEN	1

CREAM TOGETHER BUTTER AND SUGAR. IN A SEPARATE BOWL
MIX CINNAMON, GINGER, CLOVES, SALT, BAKING POWDER AND
FLOUR. BEAT BAKING SODA INTO MOLASSES UNTIL FOAMY.
ADD TO BUTTER MIXTURE. ADD THE 1/4 TSP (1 ML) OF BAKING
SODA TO THE BOILING WATER. ADD THIS ALTERNATELY
WITH THE DRY INGREDIENTS TO THE BUTTER-MOLASSES
MIXTURE. FOLD IN BEATEN EGG. (THE BATTER WILL BE
THIN). POUR INTO GREASED LOAF PAN AND BAKE 30 MINUTES
AT 400°F (200°C). SERVES 6 TO 8.

COFFEE CAN BREAD

THIS IS A SIMPLE NO-YEAST BREAD.

2 TBSP	HONEY OR SUGAR	25 ML
3 CUPS	FLOUR OR A MIXTURE OF 1 CUP (250 ML) EACH WHEAT GERM, WHOLE WHEAT FLOUR AND OATMEAL	750 ML
2 TBSP	BAKING POWDER	25 ML
$\frac{1}{2}$ TSP	BAKING SODA	2 ML
$\frac{1}{2}$ TSP	SALT	2 ML
1 $\frac{3}{4}$ CUPS	MILK	425 ML

MIX DRY INGREDIENTS IN LARGE BOWL. STIR IN MILK AND HONEY. PUT IN A WELL GREASED 1 LB (500 G) COFFEE CAN AND COVER WITH FOIL. LET STAND 5 MINUTES.

BAKE AT 350°F (180°C) FOR 1 $\frac{1}{2}$ HOURS. LET COOL 5 TO 10 MINUTES AND TURN OUT. SERVES 10 TO 12.

NOTE: IF YOU DON'T HAVE A COFFEE CAN, A LOAF PAN WILL DO – JUST REDUCE BAKING TIME BY ABOUT 20 MINUTES.

THE BEST TIME TO MAKE FRIENDS
IS BEFORE YOU NEED THEM.

SOUR CREAM COFFEE CAKE

6 TBSP	SOFT BUTTER	90 ML
I CUP	WHITE SUGAR	250 ML
2	EGGS (ROOM TEMPERATURE)	2
I 1/3 CUPS	FLOUR	325 ML
I 1/2 TSP	BAKING POWDER	7 ML
I TSP	BAKING SODA	5 ML
I TSP	CINNAMON	5 ML
I CUP	SOUR CREAM	250 ML
I	PACKAGE (6 OZ/170 G) SEMI-SWEET CHOCOLATE CHIPS	I
I TBSP	SUGAR	15 ML

BEAT BUTTER, SUGAR AND EGGS IN BOWL FOR IO MINUTES. SIFT DRY INGREDIENTS AND BLEND INTO SOUR CREAM. BLEND BOTH MIXTURES TOGETHER BY HAND. MIX WELL AND POUR BATTER INTO GREASED AND FLOURED 13- X 9-INCH (3 L) PAN. SCATTER CHOCOLATE CHIPS OVER TOP. SPRINKLE I TBSP (15 ML) SUGAR OVER TOP. BAKE AT 350°F (180°C) FOR 35 MINUTES OR UNTIL DONE. COOL IN PAN ON WIRE RACK AND KEEP AT ROOM TEMPERATURE. SERVES 12 TO 16.

THIRTY IS A NICE AGE FOR A WOMAN – ESPECIALLY IF SHE HAPPENS TO BE 40.

BLUEBERRY COFFEE CAKE

4	EGGS, SEPARATED	4
1 3/4 CUPS	SUGAR	425 ML
1 TBSP	VANILLA	15 ML
1 CUP	OIL	250 ML
	JUICE AND ZEST OF 2 LEMONS	
2 1/2 CUPS	FLOUR	625 ML
2 TSP	BAKING POWDER	10 ML
2 CUPS	FROZEN BLUEBERRIES (FLOURED)	500 ML

BEAT EGG WHITES UNTIL FROTHY, ADD SUGAR, EGG YOLKS, OIL, VANILLA, LEMON JUICE AND ZEST. FOLD IN DRY INGREDIENTS AND FLOURED BLUEBERRIES, RESERVING A HANDFUL FOR THE BOTTOM OF THE PAN. PLACE RESERVED BLUEBERRIES IN BOTTOM OF 10-INCH (3 L) BUNDT OR 10-INCH (4 L) TUBE PAN. POUR IN BATTER AND BAKE AT 350°F (180°C) FOR 1 HOUR. WHEN COOL, TURN OUT ON CAKE PLATE AND WAIT FOR THE RAVES! SERVES 10 TO 12.

MAYBE HARD WORK WON'T KILL A MAN, BUT ON THE OTHER HAND, WHO EVER HEARD OF ANYONE RESTING TO DEATH?

CHRISTMAS COFFEE CAKE

PRETTY AND DECORATIVE – MAKES A NICE LITTLE GIFT.

18 TO 20	PECAN HALVES	18 TO 20
12 TO 14	CHERRY HALVES	12 TO 14
1/3 CUP	BUTTER	75 ML
1/3 CUP	BROWN SUGAR	75 ML
1 1/2 CUPS	FLOUR	375 ML
1 1/2 TSP	BAKING POWDER	7 ML
1 TSP	BAKING SODA	5 ML
1 CUP	BROWN SUGAR	250 ML
1/4 CUP	BUTTER	50 ML
2	EGGS	2
1 TSP	VANILLA	5 ML
1 CUP	SOUR CREAM	250 ML

MELT 1/3 CUP (75 ML) BUTTER. ADD 1/3 CUP (75 ML) BROWN SUGAR AND STIR. PLACE IN THE BOTTOM OF A 10-INCH (4 L) TUBE PAN OR 10-INCH (3 L) BUNDT PAN. DECORATE THE BOTTOM WITH CHERRY AND PECAN HALVES. CREAM 1/4 CUP (50 ML) BUTTER AND 1 CUP (250 ML) BROWN SUGAR. ADD VANILLA AND EGGS. BEAT UNTIL FLUFFY. BLEND IN SOUR CREAM. MIX FLOUR, BAKING POWDER, BAKING SODA AND SIFT. MAKE A WELL IN CENTER OF DRY INGREDIENTS, ADD LIQUIDS AND STIR GENTLY. POUR IN GREASED PAN AND BAKE AT 350°F (180°C) FOR 30 MINUTES. SERVES 10 TO 12.

THERE ARE TWO THEORIES ABOUT ARGUING WITH WOMEN. NEITHER ONE WORKS.

OAT MUFFINS

1 CUP	OATMEAL	250 ML
1 CUP	BUTTERMILK	250 ML
1 CUP	FLOUR	250 ML
1 TSP	BAKING POWDER	5 ML
1/2 TSP	BAKING SODA	2 ML
1/2 TSP	SALT	2 ML
1	BEATEN EGG	1
4 TBSP	MELTED BUTTER	60 ML
1/2 CUP	RAISINS OR SNIPPED DATES	125 ML
1	ORANGE ZEST	1
1 CUP	BROWN SUGAR	250 ML

LET OATMEAL STAND FOR 10 MINUTES IN BUTTERMILK.
COMBINE FLOUR, BAKING POWDER, SODA, SALT AND
BROWN SUGAR. ADD EGG AND BUTTER, MIXING WELL. THEN
POURING IN BUTTERMILK MIXTURE, ADD RAISINS AND PEEL.
BAKE AT 400°F (200°C) FOR 20 MINUTES IN GREASED
MUFFIN TINS. MAKES 12 MUFFINS.

IF YOUR CHILDREN WANT TO LEARN TO DRIVE,
DON'T STAND IN THEIR WAY.

APPLE CINNAMON MUFFINS

*A PLEASANT CHANGE FOR YOUR FAMILY BREAKFAST
OR AN AFTER SCHOOL TREAT!*

2 CUPS	FLOUR	500 ML
1/2 CUP	WHITE SUGAR	125 ML
1 TBSP	BAKING POWDER	15 ML
1/2 TSP	CINNAMON	2 ML
1/2 TSP	SALT	2 ML
1/2 CUP	BUTTER	125 ML
1	LARGE APPLE, PEELED AND DICED	1
1/4 CUP	WALNUTS, FINELY CHOPPED	50 ML
1	EGG	1
2/3 CUP	MILK	150 ML
1 TSP	CINNAMON	5 ML
1 TBSP	BROWN SUGAR	15 ML

SIFT FLOUR, SUGAR, BAKING POWDER, 1/2 TSP (2 ML)
CINNAMON AND SALT INTO LARGE BOWL. CUT IN BUTTER
WITH PASTRY BLENDER. MEASURE OUT 1/4 CUP (50 ML) AND
RESERVE FOR TOPPING. ADD APPLE AND NUTS TO FLOUR
MIXTURE. BEAT EGG IN SMALL BOWL AND ADD MILK. OUR
INTO FLOUR MIXTURE AND STIR UNTIL JUST MIXED
(BATTER WILL BE LUMPY). SPOON INTO LIGHTLY GREASED
MUFFIN PANS 2/3 FULL. ADD 1 TSP (5 ML) CINNAMON AND
BROWN SUGAR TO RESERVED TOPPING MIXTURE. SPRINKLE
OVER EACH MUFFIN. BAKE AT 425°F (220°C) FOR 15 TO
20 MINUTES. MAKES 16 LARGE OR 32 SMALL MUFFINS.

SUPER BLUEBERRY LEMON MUFFINS

THESE WILL DISAPPEAR AS QUICKLY AS YOU MAKE THEM!

BLUEBERRY LEMON MUFFINS

2 CUPS	FLOUR	500 ML
1/2 CUP	SUGAR	125 ML
1 TBSP	BAKING POWDER	15 ML
1/2 TSP	SALT	2 ML
	ZEST OF 1 LEMON	
1	EGG	1
1 CUP	MILK	250 ML
1/2 CUP	BUTTER, MELTED	125 ML
1 CUP	FRESH OR FROZEN BLUEBERRIES	250 ML

LEMON BUTTER TOPPING

1/4 CUP	MELTED BUTTER	50 ML
2 TBSP	LEMON JUICE	25 ML
1/2 CUP	SUGAR	125 ML

TO MAKE MUFFINS: MIX FLOUR, SUGAR, BAKING POWDER, SALT AND LEMON ZEST IN LARGE BOWL. BEAT EGG IN MEDIUM BOWL; ADD MILK AND BUTTER. ADD EGG MIXTURE TO DRY INGREDIENTS. STIR UNTIL JUST MIXED (BATTER WILL BE LUMPY). STIR IN BLUEBERRIES. FILL MUFFIN PANS 2/3 FULL; BAKE AT 375°F (190°C) FOR 20 MINUTES.

TO MAKE TOPPING: COMBINE MELTED BUTTER AND LEMON JUICE. MEASURE SUGAR IN SEPARATE DISH. DUNK TOPS OF SLIGHTLY COOLED MUFFINS INTO LEMON BUTTER AND THEN SUGAR. MAKES 16 MEDIUM MUFFINS.

ASPARAGUS SANDWICH

DON'T FORGET THE SIMPLE PLEASURES OF FRESH BREAD AND COOL ASPARAGUS. A DELICIOUS DELIGHT AND A FAVORITE OF WOMEN AND MEN ALIKE – EASY ON THE HOSTESS TOO – A MAKE-AHEAD.

2	CANS GREEN ASPARAGUS	2
2	SANDWICH LOAVES	2
	MAYONNAISE	
	SALT	
	SEASONED PEPPER	
	BUTTER	

DRAIN ASPARAGUS IN CAN FOR A FEW MINUTES, THEN SPREAD OUT ON PAPER TOWELS, TO ALLOW IT TO BE COMPLETELY DRAINED AND DRY, 2 HOURS BEFORE MAKING SANDWICHES. TRIM CRUSTS FROM BREAD, BUTTER SLICES THEN SPREAD GENEROUSLY WITH MAYONNAISE. PLACE AN ASPARAGUS SPEAR AT ONE END OF PIECE OF BREAD, SPRINKLE WITH SALT AND PEPPER AND ROLL UP. PLACE ON SERVING PLATE. COVER WITH FOIL AND REFRIGERATE UNTIL $\frac{1}{2}$ HOUR BEFORE SERVING. MAKES ABOUT 40 SMALL SANDWICHES.

GIRLS WHO THINK THEY WILL HATE THEMSELVES IN THE MORNING SHOULD SLEEP TILL NOON.

RENÉ'S SANDWICH LOAF

PUTTIN' ON THE RITZ!

I	PACKAGE (8 OZ/250 G) CREAM CHEESE	I
I TBSP	MILK	15 ML
	UNSLICED SANDWICH LOAF, SLIGHTLY FROZEN	

HAM FILLING

I CUP	GROUND COOKED HAM	250 ML
2 TBSP	PICKLE RELISH, DRAINED	25 ML
$1/2$ TSP	HORSERADISH	2 ML
$1/3$ CUP	FINELY CHOPPED CELERY	75 ML
$1/4$ CUP	MAYONNAISE	50 ML

ASPARAGUS TIP FILLING

I	CAN ASPARAGUS TIPS, DRAINED	I
	CHEESE WHIZ	

EGG FILLING

4	HARD-BOILED EGGS, CHOPPED	4
2 TBSP	FINELY CHOPPED GREEN ONIONS	25 ML
$1/2$ TSP	PREPARED MUSTARD	2 ML
$1/4$ CUP	MAYONNAISE	50 ML
	SALT AND PEPPER TO TASTE	
	CHOPPED FRESH PARSLEY	
	PIMENTO-STUFFED OLIVES	

IN A SMALL BOWL, BEAT CREAM CHEESE WITH MILK UNTIL FLUFFY. SET ASIDE. TRIM CRUSTS FROM SANDWICH LOAF AND SLICE BREAD LENGTHWISE IN 4 EQUAL LAYERS. BUTTER EACH SLICE. SPREAD FIRST LAYER WITH HAM

CONTINUED ON NEXT PAGE...

FILLING, SECOND LAYER WITH CHEESE WHIZ; TOP WITH ASPARAGUS, AND THIRD LAYER WITH EGG FILLING. FROST TOP SLICE AND SIDES OF LOAF WITH CREAM CHEESE. SPRINKLE WITH PARSLEY AND GARNISH WITH OLIVES. SERVES 8 TO 10.

SUNDAY SANDWICHES

IF THE QUEEN SHOULD HAPPEN TO DROP IN, YOU CAN IMPRESS HER WITH MORE THAN JUST A GRILLED CHEESE! FOR ONE SERVING.

2	SLICES BUTTERED BREAD	2
1	PROCESSED CHEESE SLICE (NOT WHITE)	1
	MAYONNAISE	
	SLICED TOMATOES	
1	EGG, BEATEN WITH A LITTLE MILK (GOOD FOR 2 SANDWICHES)	1
	SALT AND PEPPER	
	BUTTER	

SPREAD MAYONNAISE ON EACH SLICE OF BUTTERED BREAD. ADD CHEESE SLICE, TOP WITH SLICED TOMATOES AND SPRINKLE LIBERALLY WITH SALT AND PEPPER. PUT TOP ON SANDWICH. BEAT EGG WITH MILK AND POUR ONTO LARGE PLATE. DIP BOTH SIDES OF SANDWICH INTO MIXTURE AND COOK BOTH SIDES ON BUTTERED GRILL UNTIL CHEESE MELTS. SERVE WITH KETCHUP OR YOUR FAVORITE RELISH. SERVES 1.

TOASTED TOMATO CHEESIES

8	SLICES BACON, CUT IN HALF	8
4	ENGLISH MUFFINS	4
1	PACKAGE (8 OZ/227 G) CHEESE SLICES	1
2 TBSP	ONION, FINELY CHOPPED	25 ML
1 TSP	WORCESTERSHIRE SAUCE	5 ML
2 TO 3	LARGE TOMATOES, SLICED	2 TO 3

COOK BACON CRISP. DRAIN AND KEEP WARM. HEAT BROILER. PRY MUFFINS APART WITH FORK AND LAY SIDE BY SIDE ON COOKIE SHEET. TOAST UNDERSIDES UNDER BROILER (LIGHTLY). REMOVE FROM OVEN, TURN UPRIGHT. TOP EACH WITH SLICE OF CHEESE. COMBINE ONION AND WORCESTERSHIRE AND PUT SMALL AMOUNT ON CHEESE. TOP WITH A TOMATO SLICE. BROIL UNTIL HOT AND BUBBLY. GARNISH WITH 2 PIECES OF BACON. SERVES 4.

GRILLED CHEESE ITALIANO

FOR EACH SANDWICH

2	SLICES RYE BREAD	2
1	SLICE MOZZARELLA CHEESE	1
1 OR 2	SLICES OF SALAMI	1 OR 2

GENEROUSLY BUTTER TOP AND BOTTOM OF SLICES OF RYE BREAD. GRILL ON BOTH SIDES UNTIL GOLDEN BROWN.

SERVE WITH DILL PICKLES AND ONION.

CRAB AND DEVILED EGG SANDWICH

1	CAN (6½ OZ/184 G) CRABMEAT	1
2	HARD-BOILED EGGS	2
½ TSP	MUSTARD (PREPARED)	2 ML
2 TBSP	MAYONNAISE	25 ML
1 TBSP	LEMON JUICE	15 ML
½ TSP	CURRY POWDER	2 ML

DRAIN CRABMEAT. MIX WITH OTHER INGREDIENTS. LOBSTER OR CHICKEN MAY BE USED. SERVE IN SMALL BUNS. SERVES 2 TO 4.

CRAB AND CHEESE TOASTIES

1	CAN (6½ OZ/184 G) CRABMEAT	1
2 TBSP	BUTTER OR MARGARINE	25 ML
1	PACKAGE (8 OZ/250 G) PROCESSED CHEESE	1
4	HAMBURGER BUNS	4

FLAKE CRABMEAT. MELT BUTTER AND CHEESE OVER LOW HEAT, STIRRING UNTIL SMOOTH. ADD CRABMEAT. CUT BUNS IN HALF AND SPREAD WITH CRAB MIXTURE. PLACE UNDER BROILER FOR 3 MINUTES UNTIL SLIGHTLY BROWN AND BUBBLY. SERVES 4.

WHEN A MAN BRINGS HOME FLOWERS FOR NO REASON, THERE'S A REASON.

CRAB AND CHEESE BUNS

2/3 LB	VELVEETA CHEESE	300 G
2/3 LB	BUTTER	300 G
2	CANS (EACH 6½ OZ/184 G) CRABMEAT	2
18	PARKER HOUSE ROLLS	18

HAVE CHEESE AND BUTTER AT ROOM TEMPERATURE AND THEN WHIP TOGETHER. ADD CRAB AND FILL BUNS REALLY FULL. PUT IN OVEN AT 325°F (160°C) UNTIL WARM AND CHEESE HAS MELTED. MAKES 18 SMALL SANDWICHES.

FAST SHRIMP ROLLS

1	PACKAGE (8 OZ/250 G) CREAM CHEESE	1
1 TBSP	MILK	15 ML
2 TSP	LEMON JUICE	10 ML
1 TBSP	CHOPPED GREEN ONION	15 ML
½ TSP	WORCESTERSHIRE SAUCE	2 ML
	SALT AND PEPPER	
3 TO 5	LONG CRUSTY ROLLS	3 TO 5
	CANNED OR COOKED SHRIMP	
	CHOPPED PARSLEY	

MIX CHEESE, MILK AND LEMON JUICE, BLEND UNTIL SMOOTH. ADD ONION, WORCESTERSHIRE SAUCE, SALT AND PEPPER; MIX WELL. CUT ROLLS LENGTHWISE. HEAT ROLLS IN FOIL IN OVEN. SPREAD WITH CHEESE MIXTURE. PLACE SHRIMP ON TOP AND SPRINKLE WITH PARSLEY. SERVES 3 TO 5.

Super Blueberry Lemon Muffins (page 26)

René's Sandwich Loaf (page 28)

Shrimp Sandwiches (page 33)

Senate Salad Bowl (page 49)

SHRIMP SANDWICHES

THESE ARE ALWAYS A HIT AND REALLY FILLING.
(HAVE YOU TRIED ALFALFA SPROUTS ON A
PEANUT BUTTER SANDWICH?)

2	SLICES, 7-GRAIN BREAD, BUTTERED	2
1/2 CUP	COOKED, FROZEN BABY SHRIMP THAWED AND RINSED	125 ML
1/4 CUP	ALFALFA SPROUTS	50 ML
1/2	AVOCADO, SLICED	1/2
	LEMON JUICE	
	MAYONNAISE	

PLACE SHRIMP ON ONE BUTTERED BREAD SLICE. TOP WITH SPROUTS AND PLACE AVOCADO SLICES OVER ALL. SPRINKLE LIBERALLY WITH FRESH SQUEEZED LEMON JUICE. SPREAD MAYONNAISE ON SECOND SLICE OF BREAD AND PLACE ON TOP OF AVOCADO. SLICE DIAGONALLY. SERVES 1.

SEAFOOD SALAD SANDWICHES

1	CAN (6 1/2 OZ/184 G) SMALL SHRIMP	1
1	CAN (6 1/2 OZ/184 G) CRABMEAT	1
1	PACKAGE (8 OZ/250 G) CREAM CHEESE	1

SOFTEN CHEESE AND ADD SEAFOOD. SPREAD ON WARM HOLLAND RUSKS. TOP WITH SLICE OF TOMATO AND CHEDDAR CHEESE. HEAT IN MODERATE OVEN UNTIL CHEESE IS MELTED (15 TO 20 MINUTES). SERVES 8.

COCKTAIL SANDWICHES

MAKE A TRAY OF INDIVIDUAL FANCY SANDWICHES -
GREAT AS YOU CAN DO THIS A DAY BEFORE.

SUGGESTIONS:

CHOPPED EGG AND ONION

MEAT: HAM, CHICKEN, BEEF

PEANUT BUTTER AND BANANA (ROLLED)

CHEESE AND PICKLE (ROLLED)

ASPARAGUS AND CREAM CHEESE (ROLLED)

CRAB, LOBSTER OR SHRIMP

HOT TUNA PIZZA BURGERS

1/3 CUP	MAYONNAISE	75 ML
1/2 TSP	SALT	2 ML
1/4 TSP	OREGANO	1 ML
1 TBSP	GRATED OR MINCED ONION	15 ML
1/4 CUP	TOMATO PASTE	50 ML
1/4 CUP	WATER	50 ML
	GRATED PARMESAN CHEESE	
1	CAN (6 1/2 OZ/184 G) SOLID TUNA (DRAINED AND BROKEN UP)	1
4	HAMBURGER BUNS, SPLIT	4

BLEND TOGETHER MAYONNAISE, SALT, TUNA, ONION,
OREGANO. SPREAD ON BUN HALVES. BLEND TOMATO PASTE
AND WATER. SPOON OVER TUNA MIXTURE. SPRINKLE WITH
GRATED PARMESAN CHEESE, USING 1 OR 2 TSP (5 OR 10 ML)
ON EACH. PLACE IN 400°F (200°C) OVEN. BAKE 10 MINUTES.
SERVE IMMEDIATELY. SERVES 4.

BRIDGE PIZZAS

	SLICED RYE BREAD (LIGHTLY TOASTED)	
1	SMALL CAN TOMATO PASTE	1
1/4 TSP	GARLIC SALT	1 ML
1/4 TSP	ONION SALT	1 ML
1	OREGANO LEAF, CRUSHED	1

MIX TOGETHER TOMATO PASTE, GARLIC SALT, ONION SALT AND OREGANO LEAF AND SPREAD ON RYE BREAD. PUT SLICE OF MOZZARELLA CHEESE AND PARMESAN ON PASTE. PUT ON ANY PIZZA INGREDIENTS YOU LIKE: MUSHROOMS, CHERRY TOMATO SLICES, ONION, PEPPERONI, SALAMI, GREEN PEPPER.

COVER WITH LARGE SLICE OF MOZZARELLA CHEESE AND BROIL TILL CHEESE MELTS AND IS BUBBLY HOT.

THEY SAY HARD WORK NEVER KILLED ANYONE, BUT WHY TAKE A CHANCE ON BEING THE FIRST CASUALTY.

TACOS

I	PACKAGE TACO SHELLS	I
I	PACKAGE TACO SEASONING	I
I LB	GROUND BEEF	500 G

BROWN GROUND BEEF, ADD SEASONING AND WATER.
SIMMER 15 TO 20 MINUTES.

PREPARE AND PUT INTO INDIVIDUAL BOWLS:

CHOPPED TOMATOES

SHREDDED LETTUCE

SHREDDED CHEDDAR CHEESE

CHOPPED OLIVES

CHOPPED GREEN ONIONS

SOUR CREAM (HELPS HOLD TOGETHER)

MAYONNAISE

AVOCADO

FILL TACO SHELLS WITH MEAT MIXTURE AND ADD ANY
OR ALL OF THE ABOVE. SERVES 4.

*EVER NOTICE THAT THE JOLLY GREEN GIANT STANDS
AROUND LAUGHING HIS HEAD OFF WHILE THE LITTLE
PEOPLE DO ALL THE WORK CANNING VEGETABLES.*

HAM BUNS

MINCE 1 LB (500 G) OF HAM. (FREEZE YOUR LEFTOVER READY-TO-EAT HAM TO USE FOR ENTERTAINING EMERGENCIES.)

TO MINCED HAM, ADD THE FOLLOWING:

3 TO 4	STALKS FINELY CHOPPED CELERY	3 TO 4
1	SMALL ONION, CHOPPED FINE	1
1/2 CUP	MAYONNAISE	125 ML
2 TSP	MUSTARD	10 ML
1/2 TSP	WORCESTERSHIRE SAUCE	2 ML

SPRINKLE WITH SEASONED SALT. MIX ALL INGREDIENTS WELL, TO MOISTEN THOROUGHLY. SPLIT PARKER HOUSE ROLLS, BUTTER, AND PILE IN FILLING. THESE CAN BE PREPARED DAYS BEFORE, WRAPPED IN FOIL AND FROZEN UNTIL NEEDED. TO SERVE, HEAT IN 350°F (180°C) OVEN, COVERED IN FOIL UNTIL WARMED THROUGH, ABOUT 1/2 HOUR. MAKES ABOUT 24 SMALL SANDWICHES.

PEOPLE GO ON VACATIONS TO FORGET THINGS AND WHEN THEY OPEN THEIR BAGS, THEY FIND OUT THEY DID.

HAM-FILLED BUNS

½ LB	CUBED HAM	250 G
½ LB	CUBED CHEDDAR CHEESE	250 G
I TBSP	SLICED GREEN OLIVES	I5 ML
½ CUP	CHILI SAUCE	I25 ML
½ CUP	MAYONNAISE	I25 ML

MIX INGREDIENTS AND FILL BUNS. BAKE AT 400 °F (200°C) FOR I5 MINUTES. SERVES 4. CHILI SAUCE RECIPE BELOW:

CHILI SAUCE

I	CAN (28 OZ/796 ML) TOMATOES	I
I CUP	BROWN SUGAR	250 ML
I CUP	VINEGAR	250 ML
I	LARGE CHOPPED ONION	I
I TSP	CINNAMON	5 ML
I TSP	ALLSPICE	5 ML
I	SPRINKLE OF GINGER	I
	CHILI PEPPERS	

THESE INGREDIENTS ARE COOKED TOGETHER UNTIL THE MIXTURE THICKENS AND BECOMES A DARK RED. THIS WILL TAKE PRETTY WELL THE WHOLE DAY AT LOW HEAT. STIR OCCASIONALLY. THE TOMATOES SHOULD BE CUT UP. USE YOUR DISCRETION WITH THE CHILI PEPPERS. USE THE BOTTLED CRUSHED CHILIES FROM THE SPICE SECTION. I KEEP TASTING IT THROUGH THE DAY AND ADD MORE UNTIL IT IS AS HOT AS I WANT IT. THIS IS A NICE CONDIMENT WITH BEEF OR MACARONI DISH. MAKES ABOUT 2 CUPS (500 ML).

OPEN-FACE HAM BUNS

½ LB	VELVEETA CHEESE (CUBED)	250 G
½ LB	COOKED HAM (CUBED)	250 G
2	HARD BOILED EGGS (CHOPPED)	2
½ CUP	GREEN OLIVES (SLICED)	125 ML
⅓ CUP	CHOPPED ONIONS	75 ML
2 TBSP	MAYONNAISE	25 ML
½ CUP	CHILI SAUCE	125 ML
12	HAMBURGER BUNS	12

COMBINE ALL INGREDIENTS. SPREAD ON BUN HALVES. PLACE UNDER BROILER 5 TO 8 MINUTES OR UNTIL MIXTURE IS BUBBLY AND CHEESE IS MELTED. SERVE HOT. MAKES ENOUGH FOR 24 BUN HALVES.

DOCTORS WILL TELL YOU THAT IF YOU EAT SLOWLY, YOU WILL EAT LESS. THAT IS PARTICULARLY TRUE IF YOU ARE A MEMBER OF A LARGE FAMILY.

GOURMET TOAST

A GOOD LATE-NIGHT SNACK. COMBINE ALL
INGREDIENTS EXCEPT FOR WINE – REFRIGERATE
UNTIL READY TO BAKE.

1	SLICE FRENCH BREAD	1
4	VERY THIN SLICES DILL PICKLE	4
4	VERY THIN SLICES TOMATO	4
1	SLICE HAM	1
1	SLICE SWISS CHEESE	1
1 OZ	DRY WHITE WINE	30 ML
	FRESHLY GROUND BLACK PEPPER	
2 TBSP	BUTTER	25 ML

PAN-FRY BOTH SIDES OF BREAD IN THE BUTTER TO A
GOLDEN BROWN. PLACE IN A BAKING DISH OR PAN. COVER
FIRST WITH PICKLES, THEN TOMATOES, HAM AND FINALLY
CHEESE. POUR WINE OVER THE WHOLE THING, AND BAKE
OR BROIL UNTIL THE CHEESE MELTS EVENLY. GRIND BLACK
PEPPER OVER THE TOP TO TASTE. SERVES 1.

AN AFTER-DINNER MINT IS WHAT YOU NEED
TO PAY THE RESTAURANT CHECK.

HAM AND CHEESE TOWERS

RAISIN BREAD

SHAVED HAM

MILD CHEESE SLICES

TRIM EACH SLICE OF BREAD TO REMOVE CRUSTS.
(SCISSORS ARE OFTEN FASTEST METHOD, IF BREAD
IS REALLY FRESH, AND THE WASTE IS NOT EXCESSIVE.)
EACH SANDWICH REQUIRES THREE SLICES OF BREAD.
BUTTER EACH SLICE AND PILE A GENEROUS PORTION
OF HAM ON TWO SLICES OF BREAD TOPPING WITH
THIRD SLICE. TOP WITH A SLICE OF CHEESE. THESE
MAY BE MADE AHEAD AND FROZEN ON COOKIE SHEET.
REMOVE FROM FREEZER SEVERAL HOURS AHEAD OF
SERVING TIME. ONE HALF HOUR BEFORE SERVING,
PLACE IN 250°F (120°C) OVEN, COVERED, REMOVING FOIL
DURING LAST 3 MINUTES, AND TURNING OVEN TO BROIL.
WATCH CAREFULLY NOT TO BURN. SERVE WITH PICKLES.
THESE ARE FILLING AND DELICIOUS.

*IF YOU WANT TO GET SOMETHING FOR
YOUR MONEY, BUY A PURSE.*

HAM 'N' CHEESE PARTY SANDWICH

RAISIN BREAD

HAM SLICES

CREAM CHEESE

SOFTEN CHEESE WITH MILK AND A SMALL AMOUNT OF MAYONNAISE SO THAT IT'S EASY TO SPREAD.

FOR EACH INDIVIDUAL SANDWICH YOU NEED TWO SLICES OF BREAD. ON THE OUTSIDE OF EACH SLICE SPREAD CHEESE MIXTURE. BUTTER INSIDE AND FILL WITH TWO SLICES OF HAM. TOP EACH SANDWICH WITH A CURLED CARROT ON A TOOTH PICK.

YOU MAY SERVE THESE SANDWICHES COLD OR STICK UNDER BROILER UNTIL CHEESE BUBBLES. SERVE WITH A PICKLE TRAY AND BEVERAGE.

TALK ABOUT CYNICAL. MY WIFE NOT ONLY DOESN'T BELIEVE THE STORIES IN THE NEWSPAPERS, SHE DOUBTS THE PHOTOGRAPHS.

STUFFED HAM LOAF

1	LOAF UNSLICED ITALIAN BREAD	1
1/4 CUP	MAYONNAISE OR SALAD DRESSING	50 ML
1/3 CUP	CHOPPED PARSLEY	75 ML
1	PACKAGE (8 OZ/250 G) CREAM CHEESE	1
3/4 CUP	CELERY, FINELY CHOPPED	175 ML
1/2 CUP	SHREDDED CHEDDAR CHEESE	125 ML
2 TBSP	ONION, FINELY CHOPPED	25 ML
1/4 TSP	SALT	1 ML
2	PACKAGES (EACH 4 OZ/125 G) HAM (8 SLICES)	2
1	LARGE DILL PICKLE	1

CUT BREAD LENGTHWISE; HOLLOW OUT EACH HALF WITH FORK LEAVING 1/2-INCH (1 CM) THICK SHELL (SAVE INSIDES FOR BREAD CRUMBS). SPREAD MAYONNAISE OVER HOLLOWS; SPRINKLE PARSLEY OVER MAYONNAISE. BLEND CREAM CHEESE, CELERY, CHEDDAR CHEESE, ONION AND SALT AND SPOON INTO BREAD HALVES, PACKING DOWN WELL WITH BACK OF SPOON. LEAVE A SMALL HOLLOW DOWN THE CENTER. QUARTER PICKLE LENGTHWISE. ROLL EACH QUARTER INSIDE A DOUBLE THICK SLICE OF HAM. PLACE ROLLS, END TO END, IN CENTER OF HALF OF BREAD AND TOP WITH OTHER HALF. WRAP LOAF TIGHTLY IN TRANSPARENT WRAP. CHILL SEVERAL HOURS. TO SERVE, CUT INTO 16 SLICES. SERVES 8.

THERE IS ONE ADVANTAGE IN BEING MARRIED. YOU CAN'T MAKE A FOOL OF YOURSELF WITHOUT KNOWING IT.

REUBEN SANDWICHES

PREPARE THESE AHEAD OF TIME – EITHER FREEZE OR REFRIGERATE UNTIL TIME TO GRILL.

	THIN SLICED RYE BREAD (2 PER SANDWICH)	
	THOUSAND ISLAND DRESSING	
	SWISS CHEESE SLICES	
I TBSP	DRAINED SAUERKRAUT (PER SANDWICH)	15 ML
12	PAPER-THIN SLICES CORNED BEEF (PER SANDWICH)	12

SPREAD THOUSAND ISLAND DRESSING ON BOTTOM SLICES OF RYE BREAD, TOP WITH I TO 2 SLICES OF CHEESE, I TBSP (15 ML) SAUERKRAUT; MOUND CORNED BEEF AND TOP WITH SECOND SLICE OF BREAD. BUTTER OUTSIDE, TOP AND BOTTOM. COVER AND REFRIGERATE UNTIL READY TO GRILL. MELT BUTTER IN HEAVY SKILLET THEN GRILL UNTIL BROWNED AND CHEESE IS MELTED.

FRUIT COCKTAIL SALAD

I	PACKAGE (3 OZ/85 G) LEMON JELL-O	I
I	ENVELOPE DREAM WHIP, PREPARED	I
I CUP	CANNED FRUIT COCKTAIL, DRAINED	250 ML
I CUP	MINIATURE MARSHMALLOWS	250 ML
¼ CUP	MAYONNAISE	50 ML

PREPARE JELL-O AS DIRECTED. LET SET UNTIL LIGHTLY JELLED. FOLD IN REMAINING INGREDIENTS. SERVE WITH HOT CHEESE ROLLS. *SERVES 4 TO 8.*

COTTAGE CHEESE SALAD

1	PACKAGE (3 OZ/85 G) LIME JELL-O	1
1 CUP	HOT WATER	250 ML
1 TBSP	VINEGAR OR LEMON JUICE	15 ML
1 TBSP	GRATED CARROT	15 ML
1 TBSP	CHOPPED CELERY	15 ML
1 TBSP	CHOPPED GREEN ONION	15 ML
1 TBSP	CHOPPED GREEN OLIVES	15 ML
1/2 CUP	MAYONNAISE	125 ML
1/2 CUP	MILK	125 ML
12 OZ	COTTAGE CHEESE	375 G

COMBINE JELL-O, HOT WATER AND VINEGAR OR LEMON JUICE. REFRIGERATE UNTIL PARTIALLY SET. MEANWHILE, PREPARE CARROT, CELERY, GREEN ONIONS AND OLIVES. COMBINE MAYONNAISE AND MILK AND ADD VEGETABLES, AND COTTAGE CHEESE. FOLD MIXTURE INTO PARTIALLY SET JELL-O AND POUR INTO LIGHTLY GREASED MOLD, REFRIGERATING UNTIL COMPLETELY SET.

THIS IS A GOOD SALAD BY ITSELF WITH HOT ROLLS, OR AS A COMPLEMENT TO TURKEY OR CHICKEN. SERVES 4 TO 6.

A MODERN WOMAN IS ONE WHO DRESSES FIT TO KILL, AND COOKS THE SAME WAY.

CURRIED CHICKEN BOATS

THIS SOUNDS COMPLICATED, BUT IS
WELL WORTH THE EFFORT.

4	CHICKEN BREASTS (3 LBS/1.5 KG TOTAL)	4
1	MEDIUM ONION, SLICED	1
1	STALK CELERY, CUT IN 1-INCH (2.5 CM) PIECES	1
2½ TSP	SALT	12 ML
6	WHOLE BLACK PEPPER CORNS	6
1	BAY LEAF	1
1 CUP	MAYONNAISE	250 ML
½ CUP	HEAVY CREAM	125 ML
¼ CUP	CHUTNEY	50 ML
1½ TSP	CURRY POWDER	7 ML
1 CUP	THINLY SLICED CELERY	250 ML
¼ CUP	FINELY CHOPPED GREEN ONION	50 ML
1	SMALL PACKAGE TOASTED SLIVERED ALMONDS	1
1	SMALL FRESH PINEAPPLE (OR ONE CAN DRAINED TIDBITS)	1
4	LARGE, RIPE AVOCADOS	4
2 TBSP	ITALIAN DRESSING	25 ML

IN LARGE SAUCEPAN COMBINE CHICKEN, ONION, CELERY, SALT, PEPPER CORNS, BAY LEAF AND 4 CUPS (1 L) OF WATER. BRING TO A BOIL, REDUCE HEAT, SIMMER 30 MINUTES OR UNTIL CHICKEN IS TENDER. REMOVE FROM HEAT, LET CHICKEN COOL IN BROTH ONE HOUR. REMOVE SKIN AND DEBONE CHICKEN, THEN REFRIGERATE, COVERED, TWO HOURS OR OVERNIGHT. IN LARGE BOWL, COMBINE MAYONNAISE, HEAVY CREAM, CHUTNEY, CURRY AND

CONTINUED ON NEXT PAGE...

½ TSP (2 ML) SALT. CUT CHICKEN IN CUBES, FOLD INTO DRESSING WITH SLICED CELERY, GREEN ONION AND ALMONDS. COVER, REFRIGERATE 2 HOURS OR OVERNIGHT.

BEFORE SERVING, PARE AND CORE PINEAPPLE. CUT INTO SMALL CUBES, AND FOLD INTO CHICKEN MIXTURE. (OR ADD CANNED PINEAPPLE TIDBITS.) CUT AVOCADOS IN HALF LENGTHWISE, TWIST AND REMOVE PITS AND PEEL. BRUSH WITH ITALIAN DRESSING. FILL WITH CHICKEN SALAD AND PLACE ON LETTUCE LINED PLATES. SERVES 8.

SHRIMP SALAD

1 CUP	COOKED RICE (AMOUNT MAY BE VARIED)	250 ML
1 CUP	MEDIUM COOKED SHRIMP, CLEANED AND PEELED	250 ML
¾ TSP	SALT	4 ML
1 TBSP	LEMON JUICE	15 ML
1 CUP	DICED RAW CAULIFLOWER	250 ML
1 TBSP	GREEN ONION	15 ML
1 TBSP	CHOPPED GREEN OLIVES	15 ML
½ CUP	GREEN PEPPER	125 ML
2 TBSP	FRENCH DRESSING	25 ML
¾ CUP	MAYONNAISE	175 ML

MIX ALL INGREDIENTS. SERVE ON LETTUCE LINED INDIVIDUAL SERVING PLATES GARNISHED WITH GREEN OLIVES AND TWO OR THREE EXTRA SHRIMP. SERVES 2 TO 4.

CHICKEN GUMBO SALAD

2	CANS (EACH 10 OZ/284 ML) CHICKEN GUMBO SOUP	500 ML
2	CANS (EACH 6½ OZ/184 G) SOLID TUNA OR 2 TO 3 CUPS (500 ML TO 750 ML) CUBED CHICKEN	2
1 CUP	CHOPPED CELERY	250 ML
½ CUP	CHOPPED GREEN ONION	125 ML
2	PACKAGES (EACH 3 OZ/85 G) LEMON JELL-O	2
1 CUP	BOILING WATER	250 ML
1 CUP	WHIPPING CREAM, WHIPPED	250 ML
1 CUP	MAYONNAISE	250 ML

DISSOLVE JELL-O IN BOILING WATER. ADD ALL INGREDIENTS EXCEPT CREAM AND MAYONNAISE. MIX WHIPPED CREAM AND MAYONNAISE AND ADD TO SALAD MIXTURE. POUR INTO INDIVIDUAL MOLDS AND REFRIGERATE UNTIL SET. SERVES 8.

MAN HAS GREAT NEED FOR WOMAN. NAPOLEON HAD HIS JOSEPHINE; ANTONY HAD HIS CLEOPATRA, AND EVEN HEINZ HAD HIS TOMATO.

SENATE SALAD BOWL

1 CUP	TORN ICEBERG LETTUCE LEAVES	250 ML
1 CUP	TORN ROMAINE LETTUCE	250 ML
1/2 CUP	WATERCRESS, STEMS REMOVED	125 ML
1 CUP	DICED CELERY	250 ML
1/4 CUP	CHOPPED GREEN ONION	50 ML
1 1/2 CUPS	CUBED, COOKED LOBSTER OR SHRIMP	375 ML
2	MEDIUM TOMATOES, DICED	2
1	AVOCADO, PEELED AND SLICED	1
1/2	MEDIUM GRAPEFRUIT, SECTIONED	1/2
5	LARGE PITTED RIPE OLIVES, SLICED	5
1/4 CUP	LEMON JUICE, FRESH, FROZEN OR CANNED	50 ML

CREAM DRESSING

1 CUP	CREAMED COTTAGE CHEESE	250 ML
1/4 TSP	SALT	1 ML
1/4 CUP	SOUR CREAM	50 ML
PINCH	PEPPER	PINCH

TOSS TOGETHER FIRST 5 INGREDIENTS IN LARGE SALAD BOWL. COMBINE NEXT 5 INGREDIENTS, SPRINKLE ALL WITH LEMON JUICE AND ADD TO GREENS. GARNISH WITH ADDITIONAL TOMATO SLICES AND RIPE OLIVES. REFRIGERATE UNTIL WELL CHILLED. MEANWHILE MAKE DRESSING, COMBINE ALL INGREDIENTS IN BLENDER OR MIXING BOWL AND BEAT UNTIL CREAMY SMOOTH. POUR OVER SALAD JUST BEFORE SERVING. SERVES 4.

GIVE ME AMBIGUITY - OR GIVE ME SOMETHING ELSE.

MEXICAN CHEF SALAD

1 LB	GROUND BEEF	500 G
1	CAN (15 OZ/426 ML) RED KIDNEY BEANS (DRAINED)	1
1	SMALL BUNCH GREEN ONIONS	1
1	HEAD OF LETTUCE	1
4	TOMATOES	4
1/4 LB	GRATED CHEDDAR CHEESE	125 G
1 CUP	THOUSAND ISLAND DRESSING OR FRENCH DRESSING	250 ML
1	MEDIUM BAG TORTILLA CHIPS, CRUSHED	1
1	LARGE AVOCADO, DICED	1

BROWN GROUND BEEF, DRAIN, AND ADD KIDNEY BEANS, COOKING FOR 5 MINUTES. ALLOW TO COOL. CHOP LETTUCE, ONION, TOMATOES AND SALAD DRESSING. MIX BEEF AND BEANS INTO COLD SALAD INGREDIENTS AND ADD CRUSHED CHIPS. GARNISH WITH AVOCADO AND TOMATO WEDGES. SERVE IMMEDIATELY. IF MAKING AHEAD, RESERVE TORTILLA CHIPS AND ADD JUST BEFORE SERVING. SERVES 4 TO 8.

LIVE YOUR LIFE SO THAT YOU WON'T BE AFRAID TO BE THE FIRST WOMAN TO LEAVE A LADIES' BRIDGE PARTY.

CHEESE FONDUE

2 CUPS	DRY WHITE WINE	500 ML
1/2 LB	SWISS EMMENTAL CHEESE, GRATED	250 G
1/2 LB	NATURAL GRUYÈRE, GRATED	250 G
2 TBSP	FLOUR	25 ML
1	CLOVE GARLIC, HALVED	1
3 TBSP	BRANDY (OR MORE)	45 ML
	FRENCH BREAD CUT IN CUBES	
PINCH	PAPRIKA	PINCH

TOSS CHEESE WITH FLOUR IN LARGE BOWL. RUB CUT
ENDS OF GARLIC AROUND "CROCKERY FONDUE" DISH. POUR
WINE IN FONDUE DISH AND HEAT SLOWLY OVER BURNER
UNTIL BUBBLES RISE. STIR IN CHEESE MIXTURE (A SMALL
AMOUNT AT A TIME) WITH WOODEN SPOON. LET EACH
ADDITION MELT BEFORE ADDING MORE. STIR IN BRANDY
AND SPRINKLE WITH PAPRIKA.

USE AS DIP FOR FRENCH BREAD. SERVES 6.

IF YOU HAVE HALF A MIND TO GET MARRIED, DO IT!
THAT'S ALL IT TAKES.

CHEESE SOUFFLÉ

1/4 CUP	QUICK COOKING TAPIOCA	50 ML
1 TSP	SALT	5 ML
1 1/3 CUPS	MILK	325 ML
1 CUP	GRATED CHEDDAR CHEESE	250 ML
4	EGG WHITES	4
4	EGG YOLKS	4

COMBINE TAPIOCA, SALT AND MILK IN SAUCEPAN. COOK AND STIR OVER MEDIUM HEAT UNTIL MIXTURE COMES TO A BOIL. REMOVE FROM HEAT. ADD CHEESE, STIRRING UNTIL MELTED. COOL SLIGHTLY WHILE BEATING EGG WHITES UNTIL STIFF. BEAT EGG YOLKS UNTIL THICK AND LEMON-COLORED. ADD TAPIOCA MIXTURE TO YOLKS AND MIX WELL. FOLD INTO EGG WHITES. POUR INTO 6-CUP (1.5 L) CASSEROLE. SET IN PAN OF HOT WATER AND BAKE AT 350°F (180°C) FOR 40 MINUTES OR UNTIL FIRM. SERVE AT ONCE. SERVES 4 TO 6.

THE BEST WAY TO REMEMBER YOUR WIFE'S BIRTHDAY
IS TO FORGET IT ONCE.

BAKED EGGS

NICE LUNCHEON DISH OR A DAY WHEN YOU WANT
TO SKIP MEAT AT DINNER. SERVE WITH A SALAD.

18	EGGS	18
1/4 CUP	MILK OR CREAM	50 ML
1 TSP	SALT	5 ML
1	CAN (10 OZ/284 ML) MUSHROOM SOUP	1
2	CANS (EACH 10 OZ/284 ML) MUSHROOMS	2
1/4 LB	CHEDDAR CHEESE	125 G

ADD MILK AND SALT TO EGGS. BEAT AND SCRAMBLE UNTIL
SOFT. DON'T OVERCOOK! MIX SOUP AND MUSHROOMS
TOGETHER. SPRAY A 13- X 9-INCH (3 L) CASSEROLE DISH
WITH PAM OR GREASE WITH BUTTER. PUT EGGS IN PAN
AND POUR SOUP MIXTURE OVER. SPRINKLE GRATED
CHEESE OR LAY SLICES ON TOP. BAKE AT 350°F (180°C)
FOR 30 MINUTES. CUT INTO SQUARES AND SERVE HOT.
SERVES 8 TO 10.

GOLF IS LIKE SEX: WHEN IT'S GOOD, IT'S TERRIFIC,
AND WHEN IT'S BAD, IT'S STILL PRETTY GOOD.

CHRISTMAS MORNING WIFE SAVER

A CANADIAN TRADITION - DON'T WAIT FOR CHRISTMAS!
MAKE BREAKFAST THE NIGHT BEFORE
AND ENJOY YOUR MORNING.

16	SLICES WHITE BREAD, CRUSTS REMOVED	16
	SLICES OF CANADIAN BACK BACON OR HAM	
	SLICES OF SHARP (OLD) CHEDDAR CHEESE	
6	EGGS	6
1/2 TSP	PEPPER	2 ML
1/2 TO 1 TSP	DRY MUSTARD	2 TO 5 ML
1/4 CUP	MINCED ONION	50 ML
1/4 CUP	FINELY CHOPPED GREEN PEPPER	50 ML
1 TO 2 TSP	WORCESTERSHIRE SAUCE	5-10 ML
3 CUPS	MILK	750 ML
	DASH TABASCO	
1/2 CUP	BUTTER	125 ML
	SPECIAL "K" OR CRUSHED CORNFLAKES	

PUT 8 PIECES OF BREAD IN A 13- X 9-INCH (3 L) BUTTERED
GLASS BAKING DISH. ADD PIECES TO COVER DISH ENTIRELY.
COVER BREAD WITH THINLY SLICED BACON. TOP WITH
SLICES OF CHEDDAR CHEESE. COVER WITH SLICES OF
BREAD. IN A BOWL, BEAT EGGS AND PEPPER. ADD MUSTARD,
ONION, GREEN PEPPER, WORCESTERSHIRE, MILK AND

CONTINUED ON NEXT PAGE...

TABASCO. POUR OVER BREAD, COVER AND REFRIGERATE
OVERNIGHT. IN THE MORNING, MELT BUTTER AND POUR OVER
TOP. COVER WITH CRUSHED SPECIAL "K" OR CORNFLAKES.
BAKE AT 350°F (180°C) UNCOVERED, 1 HOUR. LET SIT
10 MINUTES BEFORE SERVING. SERVE WITH FRESH FRUIT.
SERVES 8.

THE MODERN WOMAN WEARS JUST AS MANY CLOTHES
AS HER GRANDMOTHER, BUT NOT ALL AT THE SAME TIME.

POPEYE'S SOUFFLÉ

2	PACKAGES (10 OZ/300 G) CHOPPED SPINACH, COOKED AND DRAINED	2
1	EGG	1
1 1/2 CUPS	SOUR CREAM	375 ML
1/2	PACKAGE ONION SOUP MIX	1/2
1 CUP	GRATED CHEDDAR CHEESE	250 ML
1/4 CUP	BREAD CRUMBS	50 ML

ADD EGG TO SPINACH, THEN MIX IN SOUR CREAM AND SOUP
MIX. POUR INTO CASSEROLE DISH. COVER WITH BREAD CRUMBS
AND CHEDDAR CHEESE. BAKE 40 MINUTES AT 350°F (180°C).
SERVES 6 TO 8.

THE BEACH IS A PLACE WHERE A GIRL GOES
IN HER BAITING SUIT.

HUEVOS RANCHEROS

POACHED EGGS – SOUTHWESTERN STYLE

CHILI SAUCE

2 TBSP	VEGETABLE OIL	25 ML
I CUP	FINELY CHOPPED ONION	250 ML
I CUP	FINELY CHOPPED RED OR ANAHEIM PEPPER	250 ML
2	GARLIC CLOVES, MINCED	2
I	CAN (28 OZ/796 ML) CHOPPED TOMATOES	I
I TSP	SUGAR	5 ML
	SALT AND PEPPER TO TASTE	
1/4 TSP	CRUSHED HOT PEPPER FLAKES (OPTIONAL)	I ML
I CUP	GRATED CHEDDAR CHEESE	250 ML
4	8-INCH (20 CM) FLOUR OR CORN TORTILLAS	4
8	EGGS (FOR POACHING)	8

GARNISH

SALSA, SOUR CREAM, GRATED CHEDDAR, GUACAMOLE, CANNED BLACK BEANS, RINSED AND DRAINED

TO PREPARE SAUCE: IN A DEEP FRYING PAN, HEAT OIL; SAUTÉ ONION, PEPPER AND GARLIC UNTIL SOFT. ADD TOMATOES AND SEASONINGS; SIMMER 20 MINUTES. ADD CHEESE; HEAT AND STIR UNTIL MELTED AND WELL BLENDED.

WRAP TORTILLAS IN FOIL AND HEAT IN OVEN. HEAT BEANS.

TO POACH EGGS: BREAK EGGS INTO BUBBLING SAUCE AND POACH 3-5 MINUTES TO DESIRED DONENESS. PLACE EGGS AND CHILI SAUCE ON TORTILLAS AND PASS THE GARNISHES. SERVES 4.

CHICKEN SCRAMBLE

1/2 CUP	ONION, CHOPPED	125 ML
1/2 CUP	GREEN PEPPER, CHOPPED	125 ML
1/3 CUP	SLIVERED ALMONDS	75 ML
1/4 CUP	BUTTER	50 ML
2 1/2 CUPS	COOKED CHICKEN	625 ML
3/4 TSP	SALT	4 ML
PINCH	PEPPER	PINCH
6	SLIGHTLY BEATEN EGGS	6
1/2 CUP	GRATED PARMESAN CHEESE	125 ML

IN MEDIUM FRYING PAN COOK ONION, GREEN PEPPER AND ALMONDS IN BUTTER UNTIL VEGETABLES ARE TENDER BUT NOT BROWN. ADD CHICKEN, SALT AND PEPPER. MIX WELL. COVER AND COOK UNTIL CHICKEN IS HEATED THROUGH (2 TO 3 MINUTES). COMBINE EGGS AND CHEESE; POUR OVER CHICKEN. COOK AND STIR GENTLY OVER LOW HEAT UNTIL DONE (7 TO 10 MINUTES). SERVES 6.

*I HAVE THE MOST FRUSTRATED PET IN THE WORLD –
A TURTLE THAT CHASES CARS!*

CRAB OR CHICKEN CRÊPES

CRÊPES MAY BE MADE AHEAD OF TIME AND STORED
FROZEN BETWEEN LAYERS OF WAXED PAPER.

CRÊPE BATTER

1 CUP	COLD WATER	250 ML
1 CUP	COLD MILK	250 ML
4	EGGS	4
1/2 TSP	SALT	2 ML
2 CUPS	FLOUR	500 ML
2 TBSP	BUTTER	25 ML

WHIRL CRÊPE INGREDIENTS IN BLENDER FOR 2 MINUTES.
REFRIGERATE 2 HOURS. USING 6-INCH (15 CM) CRÊPE PAN
OR SMALL NONSTICK FRYING PAN, MELT A LITTLE BUTTER
AND POUR ABOUT 1/4 CUP (50 ML) BATTER INTO PAN,
TIPPING UNTIL BATTER COVERS THE BOTTOM. COOK
AND TURN UNTIL CRÊPE IS GOLDEN ON BOTH SIDES.
TRANSFER TO PLATE. REPEAT METHOD UNTIL ALL BATTER
IS USED.

FILLING

1/4 CUP	CHOPPED GREEN ONION	50 ML
1 TBSP	BUTTER	15 ML
1/2 CUP	SHERRY	125 ML
3 CUPS	CRAB OR COOKED DICED CHICKEN	750 ML
	SALT AND FRESHLY GROUND PEPPER TO TASTE	

CONTINUED ON NEXT PAGE...

SWISS CHEESE SAUCE

1/4 CUP	BUTTER	50 ML
1/3 CUP	FLOUR	75 ML
2 CUPS	MILK, HEATED	500 ML
	SALT AND FRESHLY GROUND PEPPER TO TASTE	
2	EGG YOLKS	2
1/2 CUP	WHIPPING CREAM	125 ML
3/4 CUP	GRATED SWISS CHEESE	175 ML

TO MAKE FILLING: SAUTÉ ONION IN BUTTER; ADD SHERRY AND MIX IN CRAB, SALT AND PEPPER. SET ASIDE.

TO MAKE SAUCE: IN A SAUCEPAN, MELT BUTTER AND ADD FLOUR. BLEND. GRADUALLY ADD MILK, SALT AND PEPPER, STIRRING CONSTANTLY. BOIL FOR 1 MINUTE THEN REMOVE FROM HEAT. BEAT YOLKS AND CREAM TOGETHER. ADD EGG MIXTURE TO SAUCEPAN, STIRRING CONSTANTLY. FOLD IN CHEESE (SAUCE SHOULD BE THICK). SET 1/3 OF THE SAUCE ASIDE. POUR REMAINING SAUCE INTO THE FILLING. FILL AND ROLL CRÊPES AND PLACE IN A SHALLOW 13- X 9-INCH (3 L) BAKING DISH. DRIZZLE WITH RESERVED SAUCE. HEAT IN WARM OVEN UNTIL SERVING TIME. SERVES 6 TO 8.

NOTE: THIN SAUCE WITH CREAM IF NECESSARY.

*MARRIED LIFE IS LIKE SITTING IN THE BATHTUB...
AFTER A WHILE, IT'S NOT SO HOT.*

CRABMEAT QUICHE

9-INCH (23 CM) PASTRY SHELL

2 TBSP	GREEN ONIONS	25 ML
3 TBSP	BUTTER	45 ML
I CUP	CRABMEAT (OR SHRIMP)	250 ML
2 TBSP	MADEIRA OR DRY WHITE VERMOUTH	25 ML
3	EGGS	3
I CUP	WHIPPING CREAM	250 ML
I TBSP	TOMATO PASTE	15 ML
	SALT AND PEPPER TO TASTE	
1/4 CUP	GRATED CHEDDAR CHEESE	50 ML

PREHEAT OVEN TO 375°F (190°C). SAUTÉ ONIONS IN BUTTER. BEAT EGGS AND CREAM CHEESE, ADD TOMATO PASTE, SALT AND PEPPER ADD CRABMEAT AND MADEIRA TO ONIONS. BOIL FOR A MINUTE SO WINE EVAPORATES. PUT FISH MIXTURE INTO EGGS AND CREAM MIXTURE. BAKE PASTRY SHELL AND PARTIALLY COOK IT. COOL. ADD FILLING. SPRINKLE WITH 1/4 CUP (50 ML) GRATED CHEDDAR CHEESE. BAKE 30 MINUTES UNTIL FIRM. SERVES 6 TO 8.

SUMMER IS THAT TIME OF YEAR WHEN CHILDREN SLAM THE DOORS THEY LEFT OPEN ALL WINTER.

CRAB CASSEROLE

I CUP	UNCOOKED RICE	250 ML
2	PACKAGES (EACH 6 OZ/175 G) FROZEN KING CRABMEAT (THAWED)	2
2 TBSP	BUTTER	25 ML
1/2 CUP	SLICES CELERY	125 ML
I	CAN (10 OZ/284 ML) CONDENSED CREAM OF MUSHROOM SOUP	I
I CUP	SHREDDED CHEDDAR CHEESE	250 ML
I CUP	PLAIN YOGURT	250 ML
1/2 CUP	CHOPPED GREEN PEPPER	125 ML
1/4 CUP	CHOPPED ONION	50 ML
1/4 CUP	CHOPPED PIMENTO	50 ML
1/8 TSP	WORCESTERSHIRE SAUCE	0.5 ML
1/2 TSP	SALT	2 ML

PREHEAT OVEN TO 350°F (180°C). COOK RICE ACCORDING TO PACKAGE DIRECTIONS. DRAIN AND FLAKE CRABMEAT. MELT BUTTER IN LARGE SKILLET. SAUTÉ CELERY, GREEN PEPPER AND ONION. REMOVE FROM HEAT; STIR IN SOUP, CHEESE, YOGURT, PIMENTO, SALT AND WORCESTERSHIRE SAUCE. LAYER RICE AND CRAB IN BAKING DISH AND POUR SAUCE OVER ALL. BAKE FOR 30 MINUTES. SERVES 6 TO 8.

WHEN YOU'RE RIGHT, NO ONE REMEMBERS.
WHEN YOU'RE WRONG, NO ONE FORGETS.

BAKED CRAB CASSEROLE

1/2 CUP	CURRANTS	125 ML
1/2 CUP	CHOPPED APPLE PEELED (ONE APPLE)	125 ML
1 LB	CRABMEAT	500 G
2 TBSP	FLOUR	25 ML
1 CUP	MILK	250 ML
1 CUP	CELERY (CHOPPED FINE)	250 ML
3 CUPS	HOT COOKED RICE	750 ML
1/3 CUP	BUTTER	75 ML
	CURRY POWDER (ADD AS DESIRED)	
	SALT AND PEPPER TO TASTE	
1/2 CUP	CRUSHED CANNED ONION RINGS (FRIED)	125 ML

COOK CURRANTS, CELERY AND APPLE IN SMALL AMOUNT OF WATER UNTIL SOFT. MAKE SAUCE WITH FLOUR, BUTTER AND CURRY POWDER, MELTING BUTTER AND ADDING FLOUR AND THE AMOUNT OF CURRY POWDER DESIRED. ADD MILK STIRRING CONSTANTLY. WHEN THICKENED ADD CURRANTS, CELERY AND APPLE. SALT AND PEPPER TO TASTE. PLACE COOKED RICE IN BUTTERED CASSEROLE. MIX CRABMEAT WITH SAUCE MIXTURE. POUR OVER RICE. TOP WITH CRUSHED ONIONS. PLACE IN 375°F (190°C) OVEN AND COOK 25 MINUTES. SERVES 6.

A WOMAN HAS THE LAST WORD IN ANY ARGUMENT.
ANYTHING A MAN SAYS AFTER THAT IS
THE BEGINNING OF A NEW ARGUMENT.

AVOCADO CRAB QUICKIE

THIS IS A FAST AND REFRESHING LUNCHEON MEAL.

4	RIPE AVOCADOS	4
2	LARGE CANS CRABMEAT	2
	LETTUCE	
1/2 CUP	MAYONNAISE (OR TO TASTE)	125 ML

SLICE AVOCADOS IN HALF, LENGTHWISE. (CUT AROUND AVOCADO THEN HOLD IN BOTH HANDS AND TWIST IN OPPOSITE DIRECTIONS TO SEPARATE.) REMOVE PIT. FLAKE CRABMEAT, MIX IN MAYONNAISE. PLACE MIXTURE IN AVOCADO HALVES AND SERVE ON A BED OF LETTUCE. SERVE WITH HOT ROLLS. SERVES 8.

EVERY MAN SHOULD SERVE A HITCH IN THE SERVICE. HE LEARNS TO MAKE BEDS, TO TAKE ORDERS, NOT TO VOLUNTEER AND MANY OTHER SKILLS HE'LL NEED WHEN HE'S MARRIED.

SHRIMP AND CRAB QUICHE

THIS IS GREAT FOR AN AFTER FOOTBALL GATHERING SERVED WITH A SALAD.

2 TBSP	CHOPPED GREEN ONION	25 ML
2 TBSP	BUTTER	25 ML
1	LARGE CAN CRABMEAT	1
1	PACKAGE (6 OZ/175 G) FROZEN COOKED SHRIMP	1
1/4 TSP	SALT	1 ML
1/4 TSP	PEPPER	1 ML
3	EGGS	3
1 CUP	WHIPPING CREAM	250 ML
1 TO 2 TBSP	KETCHUP	15 TO 25 ML
1/4 TSP	SALT	1 ML
1	9-INCH (23 CM) PARTIALLY COOKED PASTRY SHELL	1
1/4 CUP	GRATED SWISS CHEESE	50 ML

PREHEAT OVEN TO 375°F (190°C). COOK ONIONS IN BUTTER. ADD SHRIMP AND CRAB; STIR 2 MINUTES. SPRINKLE WITH SALT AND PEPPER. ALLOW TO COOL. BEAT EGGS WITH CREAM, KETCHUP AND SALT. SLOWLY ADD SHRIMP AND CRAB. POUR INTO PASTRY SHELL AND SPRINKLE WITH CHEESE. BAKE IN UPPER PART OF OVEN FOR 25 TO 35 MINUTES UNTIL QUICHE IS PUFFED AND BROWNED. SERVES 6 TO 8.

WHAT DO YOU GET IF YOU CROSS AN ELEPHANT WITH A KANGEROO? BIG HOLES ALL OVER AUSTRALIA.

SHRIMP BOATS

1/4 CUP	VINEGAR	50 ML
1 TBSP	KETCHUP	15 ML
2 TBSP	HORSERADISH MUSTARD	25 ML
1/2 TSP	TARRAGON	2 ML
1 1/2 TSP	PAPRIKA	7 ML
1/2 TSP	SALT	2 ML
1/4 TSP	CAYENNE	1 ML
1/2 CUP	SALAD OIL	125 ML
1/4 CUP	FINELY CHOPPED CELERY	50 ML
1/4 CUP	FINELY CHOPPED GREEN ONION	50 ML
2 LBS	MEDIUM OR LARGE CLEANED, COOKED SHRIMP	1 KG
4	RIPE AVOCADOS	4

COMBINE FIRST SEVEN INGREDIENTS, ADDING OIL SLOWLY AND BEATING CONSTANTLY. ADD CELERY AND ONIONS. POUR OVER THE SHRIMP AND REFRIGERATE 4 HOURS OR OVERNIGHT. HALVE AND PEEL AVOCADO AND ARRANGE SHRIMP ON EACH HALF. SERVE ON LETTUCE LEAVES WITH CHILLED ASPARAGUS, CARROT CURLS, SLICED BOILED EGGS, ALONG WITH MARINADE OR FRENCH DRESSING. SERVES 8 TO 12.

A MAN'S HOME IS HIS HASSLE.

LOBSTER MOUSSE

THIS SALAD LOOKS PARTICULARLY ATTRACTIVE WHEN SERVED IN A FISH-SHAPED MOLD. THE CONTOURS OF THE FISH LEND THEMSELVES BEAUTIFULLY TO DECORATION. (PIMENTO AND GREEN PEPPER STRIPS FOR FINS AND GILLS AND SLICED STUFFED OLIVE FOR THE EYE.)

2	PACKAGES (EACH 3 OZ/85 G) LEMON JELL-O	2
I CUP	COLD WATER	250 ML
I CUP	MIRACLE WHIP	250 ML
2	CANS (EACH 5 OZ/142 G) LOBSTER	2
1/2 CUP	SLICED STUFFED OLIVES	125 ML
3 TBSP	CHOPPED PIMENTOS	45 ML
I TSP	GRATED ONION	5 ML
2 CUPS	HOT WATER	500 ML
1/2 TSP	SALT	2 ML
1 1/2 CUPS	DICED CELERY	375 ML
4 TBSP	LEMON JUICE	60 ML

DISSOLVE JELL-O IN HOT WATER, ADD COLD WATER, LEMON JUICE, MIRACLE WHIP, SALT AND ONION. BLEND WITH ROTARY BEATER. POUR INTO BOWL AND REFRIGERATE UNTIL PARTIALLY JELLED (ABOUT 1/2 HOUR). OIL SALAD MOLD. DECORATE BOTTOM OF MOLD WHILE WAITING, USING PIMENTO STRIPS, GREEN PEPPER STRIPS, SLICED STUFFED OLIVES. REMOVE GELATIN MIXTURE FROM FRIDGE AND WHIP UNTIL FLUFFY. FOLD IN REMAINING INGREDIENTS. POUR INTO DECORATED MOLD AND CHILL.

DECORATE WITH ENDIVE AND CHERRY TOMATOES. SERVES 8 TO 10.

SEAFOOD SCALLOP SHELLS

A PERFECT MAKE AHEAD. ALL INGREDIENTS CAN BE
COMBINED, PLACED IN SHELLS AND FROZEN WITHOUT
COOKING. JUST THAW AND BAKE TO SERVE.

1	CAN (10 OZ/284 ML) CREAM OF CELERY SOUP	1
1/4 CUP	MILK	50 ML
1	BEATEN EGG	1
1/4 CUP	PARMESAN CHEESE	50 ML
1	CAN (5 OZ/142 G) CRABMEAT, FLAKED	1
1	CAN (4 1/4 OZ/120 G) SHRIMP, RINSED AND DRAINED	1
1	CAN (10 OZ/284 ML) SLICED MUSHROOMS, DRAINED	1
1/4 CUP	FINE BREAD CRUMBS	50 ML
1 TBSP	MELTED BUTTER	15 ML

COMBINE SOUP, MILK, BEATEN EGG AND 2 TBSP (25 ML)
CHEESE IN SAUCEPAN. STIR OVER LOW HEAT TILL HOT.
ADD SEAFOOD AND MUSHROOMS. SPOON INTO ONE
LARGE CASSEROLE OR FOUR LARGE SHELLS. MELT BUTTER.
ADD LAST 2 TBSP (25 ML) CHEESE AND BREAD CRUMBS.
SPRINKLE OVER SEAFOOD MIXTURE. BAKE AT 375°F (190°C)
FOR 30 MINUTES. SERVES 4.

THIS RECIPE MAY BE DOUBLED.

A BATH IS SOMETHING YOU TAKE WHEN
YOU FIND YOURSELF IN HOT WATER.

HELLO SUNSHINE!

GOODBYE BRAIN!

3 OZ	SPARKLING WHITE WINE	90 ML
3 OZ	ORANGE JUICE	90 ML
	ICE (OPTIONAL)	

COMBINE ALL INGREDIENTS AND DRINK! SERVES 1.

GERRY'S MORNING FLIP

6	ICE CUBES	6
1	CAN (6¼ OZ/177 ML) FROZEN LEMONADE	1
1	CANS' WORTH GIN	1
2	CANS' WORTH COLD WATER	2
2	DROPS ALMOND FLAVORING	2
1	EGG	1
1 TO 2 TBSP	LEMON JUICE	15 TO 25 ML

COMBINE ALL INGREDIENTS IN BLENDER. BLEND WELL AND SERVE IN STEM GLASSES. SERVES 4.

BLUEBERRY TEA

SOME BLUEBERRIES! ONE SERVING.

½ OZ	GRAND MARNIER LIQUEUR	15 ML
½ OZ	AMARETTO LIQUEUR	15 ML
	TEA, HOT	

IN A CUP, PLACE EACH OF THE LIQUEURS. ADD TEA. THIS IS A SUPER END TO DINNER! SERVES 1.

BLENDER BREAKFAST

A FAST AND NUTRITIOUS BREAKFAST FOR THOSE WHO NEVER HAVE TIME.

I	EGG	I
I TBSP	LIQUID HONEY	15 ML
3/4 CUP	APRICOT NECTAR	175 ML
1/4 CUP	PINEAPPLE JUICE	50 ML

COMBINE ALL INGREDIENTS IN BLENDER AND WHIRL UNTIL SMOOTH. SERVES I.

BLENDER LEMONADE

2 TO 3	LEMONS	2 TO 3
I TO 2 CUPS	WHITE SUGAR	125 TO 250 ML

CUT LEMONS INTO FOUR PIECES EACH AND PUT IN BLENDER CONTAINER, ADDING ABOUT 4 ICE CUBES. FILL BLENDER WITH COLD WATER, BLEND AND STRAIN.

YOU MAY VARY THE AMOUNT OF SUGAR ACCORDING TO YOUR OWN TASTE BUDS. SERVES 8.

A MINOR OPERATION IS ONE PERFORMED ON SOMEBODY ELSE.

SKIP AND GO NAKED

WHAT ELSE CAN YOU DO WHEN IT'S HOT?

1	CAN (6¼ OZ/177 ML) FROZEN LEMONADE	1
1	CAN (6¼ OZ/177 ML) WATER	1
1	CAN (6¼ OZ/177 ML) GIN	1
4	ICE CUBES	4
1	BOTTLE (12 OZ/341 ML) BEER, COLD	1

PLACE LEMONADE, WATER, GIN AND ICE CUBES IN BLENDER. BLEND UNTIL ICE IS CRUSHED. POUR INTO 4 MEDIUM GLASSES AND TOP WITH BEER. SERVES 8.

LEMONADE CONCENTRATE

A CONVENIENT SUMMER REFRESHER.

2 OZ	CITRIC ACID	60 G
1 OZ	TARTARIC ACID (BUY THEM AT A DRUG STORE)	30 G
5 LBS	WHITE SUGAR	2.5 KG
6 CUPS	WATER	1.5 L
6	LEMONS, WITH ZEST OF 3	6

BRING WATER TO A BOIL, THROW IN ALL INGREDIENTS AND BOIL FOR 5 MINUTES. STRAIN INTO STERILIZED JARS. MAKES ABOUT 8 CUPS (2 L). TO SERVE, ADD AMOUNT OF SYRUP DESIRED IN GLASS OR JUG WITH COLD WATER AND ICE CUBES, TO TASTE.

SPICED TEA

THIS MIXTURE CAN BE STORED IN A PLASTIC CONTAINER INDEFINITELY. GREAT WITH LATE SNACKS, ON THE SKI TRAIL, AT MEETINGS, ANY TIME!

1/2 CUP	INSTANT TEA	125 ML
1 1/2 CUPS	SUGAR	375 ML
2	PACKAGES (3 1/2 OZ/100 G) ORANGE TANG	2
1 TSP	CINNAMON	5 ML
1/2 TSP	CLOVES	2 ML

USE 2 TO 3 TSP (10 TO 15 ML) PER CUP, ADD BOILING WATER.

COFFEE BRANDY FREEZE

A SIMPLY DELICIOUS WAY TO END AN ELEGANT MEAL. YOU DESERVE IT!

4 CUPS	COFFEE ICE CREAM	1 L
1/2 CUP	BRANDY	125 ML
	SHAVED CHOCOLATE (SEMI-SWEET)	

SET ICE CREAM OUT WHILE YOU CLEAR THE TABLE SO IT IS SOFT. COMBINE ICE CREAM AND BRANDY IN A BLENDER. BLEND UNTIL ALL LUMPS DISAPPEAR. SERVE IN YOUR PRETTIEST LONG-STEMMED GLASSES. SHAVE CHOCOLATE ON TOP AND SERVE. (I SUGGEST YOU HAVE EXTRA INGREDIENTS ON HAND.) SO SIMPLE AND SOOOO GOOD. SERVES 4 TO 6.

BRANDY MINT CREAM

THIS IS A TERRIFIC DRINK TO SERVE AS A DESSERT.

2 QUARTS	FRENCH VANILLA ICE CREAM	2 L
1/2 CUP	CRÈME DE MENTHE	125 ML
1 CUP	BRANDY	250 ML

LET ICE CREAM SIT AT ROOM TEMPERATURE TO SOFTEN. WHIRL ALL INGREDIENTS TOGETHER IN A BLENDER. POUR INTO STEM GLASSES. SERVES 6.

MONGOLIAN DINGBATS

THESE TURN YOU INTO ONE. DO NOT LIGHT A MATCH!

1 OZ	VODKA	30 ML
1 OZ	KAHLÚA	30 ML
1 OZ	TIA MARIA LIQUEUR	30 ML
1/2 CUP	CREAM	125 ML
	ICE	

COMBINE ALL INGREDIENTS IN GLASS. SERVES 1.

THEY CALL OUR LANGUAGE THE MOTHER TONGUE BECAUSE FATHER SELDOM GETS A CHANCE TO USE IT.

DICKERY DAIQUIRI DOCKS

1	CAN (6¼ OZ/177 ML) FROZEN LEMONADE	1
1	CAN (6¼ OZ/177 ML) FROZEN LIMEADE	1
1	CAN (6¼ OZ/177 ML) UNSWEETENED LEMON JUICE	1
3	CANS' WORTH WHITE RUM	3
3	CANS' WORTH WATER	3

MIX ALL INGREDIENTS IN PLASTIC CONTAINER. PLACE IN FREEZER OVERNIGHT. REMOVE 10 MINUTES BEFORE SERVING. SERVES 8.

HOT RUM CANADIENNE

MARVELOUS AFTER SKIING, AFTER FOOTBALL GAMES, AFTER TOBOGGANING, AFTER ANYTHING!

2 OZ	DARK RUM	60 ML
2 TBSP	MAPLE SYRUP	25 ML
	SQUIRT OF LEMON JUICE	
	NUTMEG	
	CINNAMON (A CINNAMON STICK IS BEST)	
	BOILING WATER	
	DAB OF BUTTER	

COMBINE FIRST FIVE INGREDIENTS, TOP OFF WITH BOILING WATER AND A SMALL DAB OF BUTTER. MAKES 1 STEAMING MUG.

WINTER PUNCH

FUN TO SERVE THE GALS WHEN THEY ARRIVE FOR BRIDGE ON THOSE COLD WINTER NIGHTS. YOU MAY WANT TO DOUBLE THIS RECIPE BECAUSE THEY'LL WANT MORE.

6 CUPS	APPLE JUICE	1.5 L
2 CUPS	CRANBERRY COCKTAIL	500 ML
1 TSP	BITTERS	5 ML
4 OZ	CINNAMON RED HOTS	125 G
1 CUP	RUM (LIGHT)	250 ML
2	CINNAMON STICKS	2
16	CLOVES	16

THE CINNAMON STICKS AND CLOVES IN A CHEESE CLOTH BAG. MIX REST OF INGREDIENTS, EXCEPT RUM, TOGETHER AND PLACE CHEESE CLOTH BAG IN MIXTURE. SIMMER IN A LARGE POT FOR 45 MINUTES. ADD 1 CUP (250 ML) RUM OR MORE. SERVES 8.

A HOBBY IS GETTING EXHAUSTED ON YOUR OWN TIME.

EGGNOG SUPREME

THIS IS A BEST OF BRIDGE CHRISTMAS TRADITION.

12	EGG YOLKS	12
1 CUP	SUGAR	250 ML
7/8 CUP	BRANDY (OKAY! USE THE WHOLE CUP)	210 ML
1 1/3 CUPS	RYE OR RUM	325 ML
2 CUPS	HALF-AND-HALF CREAM	500 ML
12	EGG WHITES	12
3 CUPS	WHIPPING CREAM	750 ML
	NUTMEG FOR GARNISH	

IN A LARGE BOWL, BEAT EGG YOLKS AND SUGAR TOGETHER UNTIL LEMON COLORED AND THICK. ADD BRANDY, RYE OR RUM AND CREAM. BLEND WELL. CHILL FOR SEVERAL HOURS. BEAT EGG WHITES UNTIL STIFF. BEAT WHIPPING CREAM IN LARGE BOWL AND FOLD IN EGG WHITES. FOLD INTO EGG YOLK MIXTURE. POUR INTO A LARGE PUNCH BOWL. SPRINKLE WITH GRATED NUTMEG. ENJOY! SERVES 24.

SUBURBIA: WHERE THEY TEAR OUT THE TREES
AND NAME THE STREETS AFTER THEM.

PART II
BUFFETS

SUPPER CASSEROLES

CONTINUED ON NEXT PAGE...

ANTIPASTO

A DELICIOUS APPETIZER TO SERVE DURING THE
FESTIVE SEASON. IT'S A LOT OF CHOPPING,
BUT DON'T USE A FOOD PROCESSOR!

I CUP	OLIVE OIL	250 ML
I	LARGE CAULIFLOWER, CUT INTO BITE-SIZED PIECES	I
2	LARGE GREEN PEPPERS, CHOPPED	2
2	CANS (EACH IO½ OZ/294 ML) SLICED RIPE OLIVES, CHOPPED	2
I	JAR (I6 OZ/454 ML) GREEN OLIVES WITH PIMIENTO, CHOPPED	I
2	JARS (EACH I3 OZ/370 ML) PICKLED ONIONS, CHOPPED	2
2	CANS (EACH IO OZ/284 ML) MUSHROOM STEMS AND PIECES	2
I	JAR (48 OZ/I.4 L) MIXED PICKLES, CHOPPED	I
2	BOTTLES (EACH 48 OZ/I.4 L) KETCHUP	2
I	BOTTLE (I5 OZ/426 ML) HOT KETCHUP	I
2	CANS (EACH 2 OZ/56 G) ANCHOVIES, CHOPPED (OPTIONAL)	2
3	CANS (EACH 4½ OZ/I28 G) SOLID TUNA, CHOPPED	3
3	CANS (EACH 4 OZ/II4 G) SMALL SHRIMP	3

DRAIN ALL JARS AND CANS. PUT ALL INGREDIENTS, EXCEPT
THE FISH, INTO A LARGE DUTCH OVEN. BRING TO A BOIL,
THEN SIMMER FOR 20 MINUTES, STIRRING OFTEN. POUR
BOILING WATER OVER ALL THE FISH TO RINSE. DRAIN AND
ADD TO MIXTURE. GENTLY STIR AND SIMMER FOR
ANOTHER IO MINUTES.

CONTINUED ON NEXT PAGE...

POUR INTO CLEAN AIRTIGHT CONTAINERS, LEAVING 1 INCH (2.5 CM) HEADSPACE. LET COOL COMPLETELY. COVER AND FREEZE FOR UP TO 6 MONTHS. THAW OVERNIGHT IN THE REFRIGERATOR. SERVE WITH CRACKERS. MAKES 8 TO 9 CUPS (2 TO 2.25 L).

HE WAS BORN WITH A SILVER SPOON IN HIS MOUTH, AND EVERY TIME HE GOES TO A RESTAURANT, HE TRIES TO COMPLETE THE SET.

ARTICHOKE NIBBLERS

2	JARS (EACH 6 OZ/170 ML) MARINATED ARTICHOKE HEARTS	2
1	SMALL ONION, FINELY CHOPPED	1
1	GARLIC CLOVE, MINCED	1
4	EGGS, BEATEN	4
1/4 CUP	FINE DRY BREAD CRUMBS	50 ML
1/4 TSP	SALT	1 ML
1/4 TSP	EACH PEPPER, OREGANO AND TABASCO SAUCE	1 ML
2 CUPS	GRATED SHARP (OLD) CHEDDAR CHEESE	500 ML
4 OZ	JAR PIMENTOS	113 ML
2 TBSP	SNIPPED PARSLEY	25 ML

DRAIN LIQUID FROM 1 JAR OF ARTICHOKE HEARTS AND DISCARD. DRAIN LIQUID FROM THE OTHER JAR INTO FRYING PAN. ADD ONION AND GARLIC AND SAUTÉ. CHOP ARTICHOKES INTO QUARTERS. COMBINE EGGS, CRUMBS, SALT, PEPPER, OREGANO AND TABASCO. STIR IN CHEESE, PIMIENTO AND ARTICHOKES. ADD ONION MIXTURE. POUR INTO 9-INCH (2.5 L) SQUARE BUTTERED BAKING DISH. SPRINKLE WITH PARSLEY AND BAKE AT 325°F (160°C) FOR 30 MINUTES, OR UNTIL LIGHTLY SET. CUT INTO 1-INCH (2.5 CM) SQUARES. MAKES 81 PIECES.

ALL THINGS BEING EQUAL, YOU'RE BOUND TO LOSE.

RUTH'S CHOKES

QUICK AND EASY.

1	CAN (14 OZ/398 ML) ARTICHOKE HEARTS	1
½ CUP	MAYONNAISE	125 ML
½ CUP	GRATED PARMESAN CHEESE	125 ML

PLACE ARTICHOKE HEARTS ON COOKIE SHEET. YOU MAY HAVE TO TRIM THEM SO THEY WILL STAND UP. MIX PARMESAN CHEESE IN MAYONNAISE AND TOP EACH ARTICHOKE WITH 1 TSP (5 ML) OF MIXTURE. PUT UNDER BROILER FOR ABOUT 2 MINUTES, OR UNTIL TOP IS BROWNED. WATCH CONSTANTLY. SERVES 4 TO 6.

NOTE: IF LARGE ARTICHOKES ARE USED, CUT IN HALF AND REST ON SIDES TO BROIL.

COUPLE ON THEIR FIFTIETH WEDDING ANNIVERSARY ...
SHE: "WHY DON'T YOU BITE ME ON THE NECK LIKE YOU USED TO DO?" HE: "OKAY, GO GET MY TEETH."

STUFFED MUSHROOM CAPS

18	LARGE WHOLE FRESH MUSHROOMS	18
2 TBSP	VEGETABLE OIL	25 ML
1	SMALL ONION FINELY CHOPPED	1
1/4 LB	GROUND BEEF	125 G
2	SLICES HAM, COARSELY CHOPPED	2
1/3 CUP	DRY SHERRY	75 ML
1/4 CUP	FINE BREAD CRUMBS	50 ML
1 TSP	GARLIC POWDER	5 ML
1 TSP	SALT	5 ML
1/2 TSP	PEPPER	2 ML
1/4 CUP	GRATED PARMESAN CHEESE	50 ML

CAREFULLY REMOVE STEMS FROM THE MUSHROOMS.
CHOP STEMS FINELY AND RESERVE. PLACE MUSHROOM
CAPS ON A COOKIE SHEET. HEAT OIL IN A LARGE SKILLET
OVER MODERATE HEAT, COOK ONION AND BEEF UNTIL
LIGHTLY BROWNED, STIRRING FREQUENTLY. ADD THE
CHOPPED STEMS, HAM AND SHERRY TO ONION-BEEF
MIXTURE AND COOK FIVE MINUTES. ADD BREAD CRUMBS,
GARLIC POWDER, SALT AND PEPPER AND MIX WELL. STUFF
MIXTURE INTO CAPS. SPRINKLE WITH CHEESE. BROIL
MUSHROOMS IN PREHEATED BROILER, 3 INCHES (7.5 CM)
FROM SOURCE OF HEAT 2 TO 5 MINUTES. SERVE HOT.
MAKES 18.

WHAT THIS COUNTRY REALLY NEEDS IS A SHOPPING CART
WITH WHEELS THAT ALL GO IN THE SAME DIRECTION.

HA' PENNIES – GOD BLESS YOU

*THIS IS A COCKTAIL COOKIE AND DOUBLES VERY WELL.
A SPECIAL FAVORITE WITH THE LADIES.*

1/2 CUP	BUTTER	125 ML
1 CUP	FLOUR	250 ML
8 OZ	GRATED CHEDDAR CHEESE	250 G
3 TBSP	ONION "SOUP IN A MUG" OR ONION SOUP MIX	45 ML

MIX ALL TOGETHER AND KNEAD UNTIL THOROUGHLY MIXED.
ROLL INTO A LOG, WRAP IN WAX PAPER. CHILL. WHEN READY
TO BAKE, SLICE IN 1/4-INCH (0.5 CM) THICKNESS AND PLACE
ON AN UNGREASED COOKIE SHEET. BAKE AT 350°F (180°C)
FOR 20 TO 25 MINUTES. THESE FREEZE WELL FOR UP TO
8 MONTHS, COOKED OR UNCOOKED. MAKES 12 TO 18.

BLUE CHEESE APPETIZERS

FAST AND EASY FOR UNEXPECTED GUESTS.

2 TBSP	BUTTER	25 ML
2 TBSP	CRUMBLED BLUE CHEESE	25 ML
1	PACKAGE REFRIGERATED BISCUITS	1

PREHEAT OVEN TO 450°F (230°C). MELT BUTTER AND
ADD CHEESE STIRRING UNTIL SMOOTH. CUT UNCOOKED
BISCUITS INTO QUARTERS AND PLACE IN PAN TOUCHING
TOGETHER. POUR CHEESE MIXTURE OVER TOP AND
BAKE APPROXIMATELY 10 MINUTES OR UNTIL BROWNED.
SERVES 8.

CHEESE STICKS

1 1/2 TO 2 CUPS	SHARP (OLD) CHEDDAR CHEESE (GRATED)	375 ML TO 500 ML
2 TSP	DRY MUSTARD	10 ML
1/4 TSP	CAYENNE PEPPER	1 ML
1 CUP	FLOUR	250 ML
1/2 CUP	BUTTER OR MARGARINE	125 ML
1/4 CUP	WATER	50 ML

BLEND ABOVE INGREDIENTS INTO SOFT MIXTURE. PUT INTO COOKIE PRESS OR ROLL OUT AND CUT INTO STRIPS. BAKE AT 300°F (150°C) UNTIL LIGHTLY BROWNED. MAKES ABOUT 24.

OLIVE CHEESE PUFFS

24	STUFFED GREEN OLIVES (MAY ALSO USE GHERKINS OR COCKTAIL ONIONS)	24
1/4 CUP	SOFT BUTTER	50 ML
1 CUP	SHARP (OLD) CHEDDAR CHEESE, GRATED	250 ML
1/4 TSP	SALT	1 ML
1/2 CUP	FLOUR	125 ML
1/2 TSP	PAPRIKA	2 ML

BLEND CHEESE, BUTTER AND STIR IN FLOUR, SALT, PAPRIKA, MIXING WELL. MOLD DOUGH AROUND OLIVE. BAKE AT 400°F (200°C) FOR 10 MINUTES OR UNTIL GOLDEN. THESE MAY BE FROZEN AND REHEATED IN FOIL FOR 5 MINUTES AT 325°F (160°C). MAKES 24.

MAD MADELEINE'S CHEESE PUFFS

2	THIN SLICED SANDWICH LOAVES, DAY OLD (SKYLARK BREAD IF POSSIBLE)	2
I LB	VELVEETA CHEESE	500 G
3/4 LB	BUTTER	375 G

WHIP SOFTENED CHEESE AND BUTTER UNTIL FLUFFY.
TAKE 3 SLICES OF BREAD. SPREAD CHEESE MIXTURE ON
EACH AND STACK. REMOVE CRUSTS. CUT INTO QUARTERS.
ICE EACH PIECE ON SIDES AND TOP. YOU CAN USE A FORK
THROUGH THE BOTTOM TO DO THIS. PLACE ON A COOKIE
SHEET, COVER WITH FOIL AND FREEZE. WHEN READY
TO USE, PREHEAT OVEN TO 350°F (180°C). BAKE 10 TO
15 MINUTES UNTIL CHEESE MELTS. WATCH THEM CAREFULLY
SO THEY DON'T BURN. MAKE SURE THE SQUARES ARE
FROZEN BEFORE HEATING. THESE ARE REALLY DELICIOUS
BUT QUITE FIDDLY TO MAKE. HOWEVER, BECAUSE THEY
MUST BE FROZEN IN ADVANCE, THEY CAN BE MADE WELL
AHEAD AND WILL KEEP IF CAREFULLY COVERED. MAKES
4 DOZEN.

I ALWAYS DO MY BEST THINKING OVER A GLASS OF BEER.
TWO HEADS ARE BETTER THAN ONE.

QUICHE LORRAINE TARTS

*THIS MAY BE FROZEN! LINE 34 MUFFIN CUPS
WITH PASTRY. IF YOU'RE IN A HURRY, USE
PIE CRUST MIX – IT <u>NEVER</u> FAILS.*

FILLING

6	SLICES CRISP BACON, CRUMBLED	6
2 OZ	NATURAL SWISS CHEESE	60 G
2	EGGS	2
I CUP	WHIPPING CREAM	250 ML
1/2 TSP	SALT	2 ML
PINCH	NUTMEG	PINCH
I TSP	SUGAR	5 ML
PINCH	PEPPER	PINCH

HEAT OVEN TO 400°F (200°C). SHRED CHEESE. COMBINE
EGGS, CREAM, SALT, NUTMEG, SUGAR AND PEPPER. BEAT
TO BLEND WELL. SPRINKLE BOTTOM OF EACH TART WITH
BACON, THEN CHEESE. FILL EACH CUP 3/4 FULL WITH EGG
MIXTURE. SPRINKLE WITH NUTMEG ON TOP. BAKE 10 MINUTES
AT 400°F (200°C) THEN 10 MINUTES LONGER AT 350°F
(180°C). MAKES 34 TARTS.

NOTE: IF FROZEN, REHEAT AT 325°F (160°C).

*WEDDINGS? FOR THE BRIDE A WEDDING MEANS
A SHOWER; FOR THE GROOM, IT'S CURTAINS!*

DRUMSTICK CANAPÉS

THESE HAVE BEEN A PERENNIAL FAVORITE, ESPECIALLY WITH THE MEN. BE SURE TO MAKE LOTS - A GUARANTEED SELL-OUT!

3 LBS	SMALL CHICKEN WINGS (ABOUT 15)	1.5 KG
1/2 CUP	SUGAR	125 ML
3 TBSP	CORNSTARCH	45 ML
1/2 TSP	SALT	2 ML
1/2 TSP	GROUND GINGER	2 ML
1/4 TSP	PEPPER	1 ML
2/3 CUP	WATER	150 ML
1/3 CUP	LEMON JUICE	75 ML
1/4 CUP	SOYA SAUCE	50 ML

CUT WINGS IN HALF AT JOINT. DISCARD TIPS. PLACE ON BROILER RACK AND BAKE AT 400°F (200°C) FOR 15 MINUTES, TURN AND BAKE ADDITIONAL 15 MINUTES. MIX THE SUGAR, CORNSTARCH, SALT, GINGER AND PEPPER. ADD LIQUIDS. COOK, STIRRING CONSTANTLY, OVER MEDIUM HEAT UNTIL MIXTURE THICKENS. BOIL ABOUT 2 MINUTES. BRUSH OVER WINGS. CONTINUE BAKING AT 400°F (200°C) FOR ABOUT 35 MINUTES. DURING BAKING BRUSH SOY MIXTURE ON WINGS FREQUENTLY. SERVE IN CHAFING DISH. SERVES 4.

BEAUTY IS ONLY SKIN!

RUMAKI

*A TRADITIONAL HORS D'OEUVRE THAT'S ALWAYS
A HIT - EVEN IF YOU'RE NOT A LIVER LOVER.*

4 OZ	CHICKEN LIVERS	125 G
I	CAN (5 OZ/I42 ML) WATER CHESTNUTS, CUT IN HALF	I
1/2 LB	BACON STRIPS, CUT IN HALF	250 G
1/2 CUP	SOY SAUCE	125 ML

CUT CHICKEN LIVERS INTO BITE-SIZE PIECES AND MARINATE IN 1/4 CUP (50 ML) SOY SAUCE FOR TWO HOURS. IN ANOTHER BOWL, DO THE SAME WITH THE WATER CHESTNUTS. WRAP A PIECE OF EACH IN A STRIP OF BACON (MESSY, BUT PERSIST) AND SECURE WITH WOODEN TOOTHPICK. SET ON BROILER PAN AND BROIL SLOWLY, TURNING ONCE, UNTIL BACON IS CRISP. SERVES 6 TO 8.

SMOKED SALMON HORS D'OEUVRE

I	PACKAGE (8 OZ/250 G) CREAM CHEESE	I
I TSP	CAPERS	5 ML
I TSP	CAPER JUICE	5 ML
I TSP	FINELY CHOPPED GREEN ONION	5 ML
I TSP	MAYONNAISE	5 ML
1/2 LB	SMOKED SALMON OR LOX CUT INTO I-INCH (2.5 CM) STRIPS	250 G

CREAM FIRST FIVE INGREDIENTS. SPOON SMALL AMOUNT ONTO SALMON STRIP AND ROLL. FASTEN WITH COCKTAIL TOOTHPICKS. SERVES 6.

CURRIED SCALLOPS

1 LB	SCALLOPS (FRESH OR FROZEN)	500 G
1/3 CUP	VERY FINE BREAD CRUMBS	75 ML
1 TSP	SALT	5 ML
3 TBSP	BUTTER	45 ML
1 TSP	CURRY POWDER	5 ML
2 TSP	LEMON JUICE	10 ML

BUTTER A LARGE BAKING DISH AND PREHEAT OVEN TO 450°F (230°C). RINSE SCALLOPS UNDER COLD WATER AND DRY WELL ON PAPER TOWELING. CUT EACH SCALLOP IN HALF AND ROLL IN BREAD CRUMBS. PLACE ON LAYER IN BAKING DISH AND SPRINKLE LIGHTLY WITH SALT. MELT BUTTER IN SMALL SAUCEPAN, ADD CURRY AND COOK GENTLY FOR 2 MINUTES. STIR IN LEMON JUICE AND DRIZZLE THIS MIXTURE OVER SCALLOPS. BAKE 15 TO 20 MINUTES, UNTIL SCALLOPS ARE TENDER. SERVE IMMEDIATELY WITH COCKTAIL PICKS. SERVES 4.

CRUNCHY SHRIMP

LARGE FROZEN SHRIMP

MELTED BUTTER

SEASONED BREAD CRUMBS

THAW PEELED, CLEANED AND DEVEINED SHRIMP. DIP IN BUTTER AND ROLL IN BREAD CRUMBS. BAKE ON A COOKIE SHEET AT 500°F (260°C) FOR ABOUT 10 MINUTES.

PICKLED SHRIMP

A SPECIAL OCCASION APPETIZER TO SERVE WITH CRACKERS AND CHEESE TRAY, FOR EYE-APPEAL, SERVE IN CLEAR GLASS BOWL WITH TOOTHPICKS.

2 LBS	FROZEN JUMBO SHRIMP, PEELED AND DEVEINED	1 KG
1/2 CUP	CELERY LEAVES	125 ML
3 TBSP	MIXED PICKLING SPICES	45 ML
1 TSP	SALT	5 ML
2 CUPS	SLICED ONIONS	500 ML
	SEVERAL BAY LEAVES	
1 CUP	SALAD OIL	250 ML
3/4 CUP	WHITE VINEGAR	175 ML
3 TBSP	CAPERS WITH JUICE	45 ML
2 1/2 TSP	CELERY SEED	12 ML
1 1/2 TSP	SALT	7 ML
6	DROPS TABASCO SAUCE	6
	JUICE OF 2 LEMONS	

IN LARGE POT COVER SHRIMP WITH BOILING WATER. ADD CELERY, PICKLING SPICES AND SALT. COVER AND SIMMER 5 MINUTES. DRAIN AND RINSE EACH SHRIMP UNDER COLD RUNNING WATER. LAYER SHRIMP, ONION AND BAY LEAVES IN SHALLOW DISH.

COMBINE REMAINING INGREDIENTS. POUR OVER SHRIMP COVER AND CHILL AT LEAST 24 HOURS SPOONING THE MARINADE OVER OCCASIONALLY. SERVES 8 TO 12.

THEY SAY CHILDREN BRIGHTEN UP THE HOME.
THAT'S RIGHT - THEY NEVER TURN OFF THE LIGHTS.

CURRIED SEAFOOD COCKTAIL PUFFS

THESE ELEGANT PUFFS CAN BE MADE AHEAD, FROZEN THEN FILLED AT SERVING TIME.

PUFFS (CHOUX PASTRY)

I CUP	WATER	250 ML
1/2 CUP	BUTTER	125 ML
I CUP	FLOUR	250 ML
1/2 TSP	SALT	2 ML
4	EGGS	4

SEAFOOD FILLING

7 OZ	CRAB OR SHRIMP	200 G
1/3 CUP	MAYONNAISE	75 ML
I TSP	CURRY POWDER	5 ML
2 TBSP	CHOPPED GREEN ONION	25 ML

PREHEAT OVEN TO 400°F (200°C).

TO MAKE PUFFS: IN A MEDIUM SAUCEPAN, BOIL WATER. ADD BUTTER AND STIR UNTIL MELTED. TURN HEAT TO LOW, ADD FLOUR AND SALT, STIRRING VIGOROUSLY UNTIL MIXTURE FORMS A SMOOTH BALL. REMOVE FROM HEAT. ADD EGGS I AT A TIME, BEATING WELL WITH A SPOON AFTER EACH ADDITION. DROP BY TEASPOONFULS ONTO LIGHTLY GREASED COOKIE SHEET; BAKE 20-25 MINUTES, UNTIL GOLDEN. COOL, CUT IN HALF.

TO MAKE FILLING: MIX FILLING INGREDIENTS TOGETHER. FILL PUFFS, REPLACING TOPS. HEAT BEFORE SERVING. MAKES ABOUT 24.

IS THERE LIFE AFTER BIRTH?

SOYA ALMONDS

SOMETHING SPECIAL FOR CHRISTMAS GIFTING.

1¼ LBS	BLANCHED WHOLE ALMONDS	625 G
¼ CUP	BUTTER	50 ML
¼ CUP	SOY SAUCE	50 ML

SPREAD ALMONDS IN A 13- X 9-INCH (3 L) BAKING PAN. TOAST AT 400°F (200°C) FOR 15 MINUTES. STIR OFTEN. BE CAREFUL NOT TO BURN. ADD BUTTER AND SOY SAUCE AND STIR. TOAST 12 TO 15 MINUTES LONGER, OR UNTIL NUTS ARE COATED AND FAIRLY DRY. COOL AND STORE IN A JAR. MAKES ABOUT 3 CUPS (750 ML).

SPICED PECANS

A GREAT GIFTABLE.

2 CUPS	PECAN HALVES	500 ML
1½ TBSP	BUTTER	22 ML
1 TSP	SALT	5 ML
2 TSP	SOY SAUCE	10 ML
¼ TSP	TABASCO SAUCE	1 ML

PREHEAT OVEN TO 300°F (150°C). PLACE PECANS ON A BAKING SHEET. MELT BUTTER AND ADD REMAINING INGREDIENTS. POUR OVER PECANS. BAKE 15 MINUTES. STIR AND TOSS DURING COOKING TIME. COOL AND DIG IN – YUMMY! MAKES 2 CUPS (500 ML).

MOST FAMILIES USE CREDIT CARDS FOR EVERYTHING – THE ONLY ONE WHO STILL PAYS CASH IS THE TOOTH FAIRY.

CARAMELIZED WALNUTS

1 LB	SHELLED WHOLE WALNUTS	500 G
1	EGG WHITE	1
1 TSP	COLD WATER	5 ML
1 CUP	BROWN SUGAR	250 ML
1/4 TSP	SALT	1 ML

BEAT EGG WHITE AND WATER UNTIL FROTHY. ADD WALNUTS AND STIR UNTIL WELL COATED. COMBINE SUGAR AND SALT AND COVER WALNUTS. BAKE 1 HOUR AT 225°F (110°C) ON A GREASED COOKIE SHEET. STIR EVERY 15 MINUTES. MAKES ABOUT 2 1/2 CUPS (625 ML).

CRAZY CRUNCH

PUT THIS IN FANCY JARS AND GIVE IT AS A LITTLE EXTRA AT CHRISTMAS TIME.

2 QUARTS	POPPED POPCORN	2 L
1 1/3 CUPS	PECANS	325 ML
2/3 CUP	ALMONDS	150 ML
1 1/3 CUPS	SUGAR	325 ML
1 CUP	MARGARINE	250 ML
1 TSP	VANILLA	5 ML
1/2 CUP	CORN SYRUP	125 ML

MIX POPCORN, PECANS AND ALMONDS ON A COOKIE SHEET. COMBINE SUGAR, VANILLA, MARGARINE AND SYRUP IN A PAN. BOIL 10 TO 15 MINUTES OR TO A LIGHT CARAMEL COLOR. POUR OVER CORN, PECANS AND ALMONDS. MIX WELL. SPREAD TO DRY. MAKES ABOUT 10 CUPS (2.5 L).

NOVEL NUTS

I LB	LARGE PECAN HALVES	500 G
I	EGG WHITE	I
I TSP	COLD WATER	5 ML
1/2 CUP	SUGAR	125 ML
1/4 TSP	SALT	I ML
1/2 TSP	CINNAMON	2 ML
SPRINKLE	FRESHLY GROUND NUTMEG	SPRINKLE

BEAT EGG WHITE AND WATER UNTIL FROTHY. ADD PECANS AND MIX UNTIL WELL COATED. COMBINE SUGAR, SALT, CINNAMON AND NUTMEG. ADD TO PECAN MIXTURE. BAKE I HOUR AT 225°F (110°C) ON BUTTERED COOKIE SHEET, STIRRING EVERY 15 MINUTES. THESE KEEP WELL IN A COVERED CONTAINER AND MAKE A LOVELY HOSTESS GIFT. MAKES ABOUT 2 1/2 CUPS (625 ML).

TOM'S (TRAIL) MIX

2 CUPS	RAISINS	500 ML
I CUP	SHELLED SUNFLOWER SEEDS	250 ML
2 CUPS	CASHEW NUTS	500 ML

MIX TOGETHER. ANY PROPORTION OF THESE INGREDIENTS MAY BE USED. MAKES ABOUT 5 CUPS (1.25 L).

HEADLINE IN NEWSPAPER FOLLOWING ALFRED WONG'S UNSUCCESSFUL FLIGHT IN HOMEMADE AIRPLANE: ONE WONG BANGED UP IN BID TO COPY TWO WRIGHTS.

Christmas Morning Wife Saver (page 54)

Crazy Crunch (page 95)

Zippy Avocado Dip (page 98)

Crab and Corn Chowder (page 117)

PURK'S POO-POO'S

MY KIND OF APPETIZER – A 24-HOUR MAKE AHEAD!

1 CUP	MINCED RED ONION	250 ML
3 CUPS	GRATED SWISS CHEESE	750 ML
3/4 CUP	MAYONNAISE	175 ML
	SALT AND PEPPER TO TASTE	

COMBINE ALL INGREDIENTS. ADD MORE MAYONNAISE TO MAKE A NICE SMOOTH SPREADING CONSISTENCY, IF NECESSARY. SERVE WITH TRISCUITS OR YOUR FAVORITE CRACKER. CHILL 24 HOURS BEFORE SERVING. MAKES ABOUT 3 CUPS (750 ML).

AVOCADO DIP

1/2 CUP	SOUR CREAM	125 ML
3	RIPE AVOCADOS	3
1/2	PACKAGE GARLIC-FLAVORED SALAD DRESSING	1/2
1 TBSP	VINEGAR OR LEMON JUICE	15 ML
1 TSP	CHOPPED CHIVES OR GREEN ONION	5 ML
3	SLICES BACON	3

BLEND FIRST FIVE INGREDIENTS. COOK AND CRUMBLE BACON FOR TOP. SERVE WITH VEGETABLE PLATTER OR CORN CHIPS. MAKES ABOUT 3 CUPS (750 ML).

THIS DOES NOT KEEP WELL AS THE AVOCADO WILL DISCOLOR.

ZIPPY AVOCADO DIP

I	LARGE AVOCADO	I
2 TBSP	SLICED GREEN ONION	25 ML
I TBSP	LEMON JUICE	15 ML
I CUP	MAYONNAISE	250 ML
2 TBSP	DAIRY SOUR CREAM	25 ML
I TSP	SUGAR	5 ML
2 TSP	WORCESTERSHIRE SAUCE	10 ML
2 TSP	SOY SAUCE	10 ML
1/4 TSP	EACH HOT PEPPER SAUCE, CELERY SEED AND DRY MUSTARD	I ML
1/8 TSP	WHITE PEPPER	0.5 ML

PEEL AVOCADO AND DICE INTO BLENDER CONTAINER.
ADD GREEN ONION AND LEMON JUICE AND BLEND UNTIL
SMOOTH. ADD ALL REMAINING INGREDIENTS AND MIX
WELL; CHILL. SERVE WITH POTATO OR CORN CHIPS.
MAKES 2 TO 2½ CUPS (500 TO 625 ML).

AS EVERY INTELLIGENT HUSBAND KNOWS,
THE BEST TIME TO WASH THE DISHES IS
RIGHT AFTER HIS WIFE TELLS HIM TO.

CHILI CON QUESO

THIS IS A DELICIOUS HOT DIP - A REAL HIT
FOR MID-WINTER GET-TOGETHERS

I	SMALL ONION, FINELY CHOPPED	I
2 TBSP	BUTTER	25 ML
I CUP	CANNED TOMATOES, CHOPPED AND DRAINED	250 ML
I	CAN PICKLED GREEN CHILIES, CHOPPED	I
I TSP	BASIL	5 ML
	SALT AND FRESHLY GROUND PEPPER, TO TASTE	
1/2 LB	MONTEREY JACK CHEESE, CUBED	250 G
I CUP	CREAM	250 ML

SAUTÉ ONIONS IN BUTTER UNTIL TRANSPARENT. ADD TOMATOES, CHILIES, BASIL, SALT, AND PEPPER. SIMMER 15 MINUTES. ADD CUBED CHEESE AND AS IT MELTS, STIR IN CREAM. COOK UNTIL BLENDED AND VERY SMOOTH.

SERVE HOT FROM CHAFING DISH OR AS A HOT DIP WITH STRIPS OF RAW VEGETABLES SUCH AS CARROTS, CELERY, GREEN PEPPER, ZUCCHINI, OR CAULIFLOWER CHUNKS AND ARTICHOKE HEARTS, AS WELL AS TACO CHIPS. MAKES ABOUT 3 CUPS (750 ML).

MOST KIDS ONLY EAT SPINACH SO THEY'LL GROW UP AND BE BIG AND STRONG ENOUGH TO TELL MOM WHAT SHE CAN DO WITH HER SPINACH.

HOT SEAFOOD DIP

1	PACKAGE (8 OZ/250 G) CREAM CHEESE (AT ROOM TEMPERATURE)	1
1	CAN (6½ OZ/184 G) CRABMEAT, TUNA OR LOBSTER	1
2 TBSP	CHOPPED GREEN ONION	25 ML
½ TSP	HORSERADISH	2 ML
⅓ CUP	SLIVERED ALMONDS	75 ML
1 TBSP	MILK	15 ML
¼ TSP	SALT	1 ML
1 TBSP	LEMON JUICE	15 ML
	CHOPPED GREEN PEPPER (OPTIONAL)	
PINCH	PEPPER	PINCH

COMBINE ALL INGREDIENTS EXCEPT ALMONDS. MIX WELL. GARNISH WITH ALMONDS.

WARM IN OVEN AT 350°F (180°C) FOR 20 MINUTES.

SERVE AS A DIP WITH CRACKERS AND CHIPS. MAKES ABOUT 2 CUPS (500 ML).

WHEN AN EIGHTY-FOUR YEAR OLD MAN MARRIES AN EIGHTY-FOUR YEAR OLD WOMAN, DON'T THROW RICE. THROW VITAMINS.

LOBSTER DIP

THIS DIP IS SERVED WARM IN A CHAFING DISH WITH A VARIETY OF CRACKERS.

2 TBSP	CHOPPED GREEN ONION	25 ML
2 TBSP	CHOPPED GREEN PEPPER	25 ML
2 TBSP	BUTTER	25 ML
1	CAN (10 OZ/284 ML) MUSHROOM SOUP	1
1/2 CUP	CREAM	125 ML
1 TBSP	CORNSTARCH	15 ML
2 TBSP	SHERRY	25 ML
2	EGG YOLKS	2
1/8 TSP	NUTMEG	0.5 ML
2	CANS (EACH 5 1/2 OZ/156 G) LOBSTER	2
1 CUP	GRATED CHEDDAR CHEESE	250 ML

SAUTÉ ONION AND GREEN PEPPER IN BUTTER FOR 5 MINUTES. IN SEPARATE SAUCEPAN, MIX SOUP, CREAM, CORNSTARCH, SHERRY, YOLKS AND NUTMEG. HEAT SLOWLY UNTIL IT STARTS TO THICKEN, ADD ONION AND GREEN PEPPER; CONTINUE COOKING UNTIL THICK. ADD CHEESE AND LOBSTER CHUNKS, STIRRING WELL UNTIL CHEESE MELTS. TRANSFER TO CHAFING DISH AND KEEP WARM OVER LOW FLAME, UNCOVERED. MAKES 3 1/2 CUPS (875 ML).

THE RESORT WAS SO DULL, ONE DAY THE TIDE WENT OUT AND NEVER CAME BACK.

SHRIMP DIP

I	PACKAGE (8 OZ/250 G) CREAM CHEESE, SOFTENED	I
1/3 CUP	MAYONNAISE	75 ML
2 TBSP	KETCHUP	25 ML
2 TSP	CHOPPED GREEN ONION	10 ML
1/4 TSP	TABASCO	I ML
1/2 TO 3/4 LB	FRESH COOKED BABY SHRIMP	250 TO 375 G

MIX FIRST FIVE INGREDIENTS TOGETHER AND FOLD IN SHRIMP. SERVE WITH CELERY OR CRACKERS. MAKES ABOUT 3 CUPS (750 ML).

CRABMEAT DIP

I	CAN (6 1/2 OZ/184 G) DRAINED CRABMEAT	I
1/2 CUP	MAYONNAISE	125 ML
2 TBSP	KETCHUP OR CHILI SAUCE	25 ML
2 TO 3 TBSP	LEMON JUICE	25 TO 45 ML
	SEASONED PEPPER TO TASTE	
	GARLIC SALT OR POWDER TO TASTE	
1/2 TSP	HORSERADISH	2 ML

COMBINE ALL INGREDIENTS, MIXING WELL. SERVE AS AN APPETIZER WITH COLD, FRESH VEGETABLE TRAY, INCLUDING ZUCCHINI STICKS, CAULIFLOWER CHUNKS, CARROT AND CELERY STICKS, CHERRY TOMATOES. MAKES ABOUT 1 1/2 CUPS (375 ML).

CRAB MOUSSE

AN ELEGANT HORS D'OEUVRE MADE IN A 4-CUP (1 L) MOLD.

1	CAN (10 OZ/284 ML) CREAM OF MUSHROOM SOUP	1
6 OZ	CREAM CHEESE	175 G
1 TBSP	UNFLAVORED GELATIN	15 ML
1/4 CUP	COLD WATER	50 ML
1/2 CUP	FINELY CHOPPED CELERY	125 ML
1/2 CUP	FINELY CHOPPED GREEN ONIONS	125 ML
1 CUP	MAYONNAISE	250 ML
1	CAN (5 OZ/142 G) CRABMEAT	1
1/4 TSP	CURRY POWDER	1 ML

HEAT MUSHROOM SOUP AND CREAM CHEESE, STIRRING UNTIL SMOOTH. ADD GELATIN TO COLD WATER AND SOFTEN 5 MINUTES. ADD GELATIN MIXTURE TO SOUP MIXTURE. ADD CELERY, ONION, MAYONNAISE, CRABMEAT AND CURRY POWDER, MIXING WELL. POUR INTO 4-CUP (1 L) COLD MOLD (OIL OR SPRAY MOLD WITH PAM BEFOREHAND). CHILL OVERNIGHT. UNMOLD ONTO SERVING PLATE AND DECORATE WITH SPRIGS OF FRESH PARSLEY. SERVE WITH CRACKERS. MAKES ABOUT 4 CUPS (1 L).

*MAY YOUR LIFE BE LIKE A ROLL OF TOILET PAPER -
LONG AND USEFUL.*

CURRY DIP FOR VEGETABLE PLATTER

I CUP	MAYONNAISE	250 ML
1/2 CUP	KETCHUP	125 ML
I TBSP	CURRY POWDER (MORE OR LESS, TO YOUR TASTE)	15 ML
I TBSP	WORCESTERSHIRE SAUCE	15 ML
I TSP	SALT	5 ML
I TSP	PEPPER	5 ML

MIX ALL TOGETHER AND CHILL FOR A COUPLE OF HOURS. THIS WILL KEEP IN COVERED CONTAINER FOR A FEW DAYS. MAKES 1 1/2 CUPS (375 ML).

LIVER PÂTÉ

I LB	CHICKEN LIVERS	500 G
I	ONION, SLICED	I
4 TBSP	GRATED ONION	60 ML
I TSP	DRY MUSTARD	5 ML
2 TBSP	DRY SHERRY	25 ML
1/2 TO 3/4 CUP	SOFT BUTTER	125 TO 175 ML
PINCH	MACE	PINCH
	SALT AND PEPPER	

SIMMER CHICKEN LIVERS IN WATER WITH ONION, FOR ABOUT 20 MINUTES. DRAIN LIVERS AND REMOVE ONION. GRIND LIVERS VERY FINE. ADD REMAINING INGREDIENTS AND MIX WELL. SERVE AS AN HORS D'OEUVRE WITH THINLY SLICED BROWN BREAD OR MELBA TOAST. MAKES 2 TO 3 CUPS (500 TO 750 ML).

COUNTRY PÂTÉ

I LB	GROUND VEAL	500 G
2 OZ	PORK LIVER	60 G
1/2 LB	GROUND PORK	250 G
3	SLICES OF BACON	3
1/2 CUP	CHOPPED ONION	125 ML
I TBSP	CHOPPED PARSLEY	15 ML
1 1/2 TSP	SALT	7 ML
I TSP	PEPPER	5 ML
1/3 TSP	GINGER	1.5 ML
1/8 TSP	EACH CLOVES AND CINNAMON	0.5 ML
I TSP	WORCESTERSHIRE SAUCE	5 ML
2	DROPS TABASCO	2
I TBSP	EACH BRANDY AND MADEIRA (OR SHERRY)	15 ML

COMBINE ALL INGREDIENTS EXCEPT BACON. BUTTER A LOAF PAN. PRESS MIXTURE AND TOP WITH BACON. COVER WITH OILED FOIL AND COOK AT 350°F (180°C) FOR I HOUR.

SERVE ONE OR TWO DAYS AFTER COOKING. MAY BE FROZEN. THIS IS GREAT WITH RYE BREAD, AS A BEFORE DINNER APPETIZER. MAKES I LOAF.

LOVE IS LIKE A MUSHROOM. YOU NEVER KNOW IF IT'S THE REAL THING UNTIL IT'S TOO LATE.

JOHNNY'S MOMMY'S PÂTÉ

1½ TSP	UNFLAVORED GELATIN	7 ML
1 CUP	CONDENSED CONSOMMÉ SOUP	250 ML
1½ CUPS	CHICKEN FAT OR BUTTER	375 ML
6 TBSP	FINELY MINCED ONION	90 ML
2 TSP	SALT	10 ML
½ TSP	NUTMEG	2 ML
¼ TSP	GROUND CLOVES	1 ML
¼ TSP	CAYENNE PEPPER	1 ML
2 TSP	DRY MUSTARD	10 ML
1½ LBS	CHICKEN LIVERS	750 G

PUT ½ ENVELOPE OF GELATIN IN CONSOMMÉ. LET STAND 5 MINUTES, THEN STIR AND HEAT UNTIL GELATIN IS DISSOLVED. POUR INTO GLASS MEAT LOAF MOLD WHICH HAS BEEN SPRAYED WITH A "NO-STICK" PRODUCT. CHILL UNTIL SET. MEANWHILE, MIX BUTTER, ONION, SALT, NUTMEG, CLOVES, CAYENNE AND DRY MUSTARD IN A BLENDER OR FOOD PROCESSOR. CUT AWAY EXCESS FAT FROM CHICKEN LIVERS AND SIMMER IN A ¼ CUP (50 ML) WATER FOR 15 TO 20 MINUTES (COVERED). DRAIN AND ADD TO MIXTURE IN BLENDER ONE OR TWO AT A TIME WHILE STILL HOT. WHEN EVERYTHING IS BLENDED, AND HAS A VERY SMOOTH TEXTURE, PLACE GENTLY ON ASPIC WHICH HAS SET. CHILL. TO UNMOLD, PLACE BRIEFLY IN HOT WATER. THIS AMOUNT WILL SERVE A COCKTAIL PARTY OF 50. ANY LEFTOVERS MAY BE FROZEN. TO FREEZE, SCRAPE OFF ASPIC. WHEN READY TO USE AGAIN, PUT THAWED PÂTÉ IN BLENDER. REMOLD AND CHILL.

HOT CHEESE SPREAD

3 CUPS	GRATED SHARP CHEESE	750 ML
1/2 CUP	CHOPPED RIPE OLIVES	125 ML
1	MEDIUM ONION, CHOPPED	1
1 CUP	MAYONNAISE	250 ML
1/2 TSP	CURRY POWDER	2 ML
1	SMALL GARLIC CLOVE, MINCED	1
	DASH OF PAPRIKA	

MIX CHEESE, OLIVES AND ONION TOGETHER. ADD MAYONNAISE, CURRY POWDER, GARLIC AND PAPRIKA. SPOON INTO A JAR AND STORE IN REFRIGERATOR. MAKES ABOUT 3 CUPS (750 ML). TO SERVE, SPREAD ON SMALL RYE BREAD OR CRACKERS. HEAT UNDER BROILER UNTIL CHEESE MELTS.

SESAME CHEESE

THE FASTEST HORS D'OEUVRE YOU EVER MADE AND DELICIOUS!

1	PACKAGE (8 OZ/250 G) CREAM CHEESE	1
1 TBSP	SESAME SEEDS, TOASTED	15 ML
1 TBSP	SOY SAUCE	15 ML

UNWRAP CREAM CHEESE AND SET IN SHALLOW, SMALL SERVING DISH. PRICK ALL OVER WITH TOOTHPICK. SPRINKLE SESAME SEEDS OVER CHEESE. POUR SOY SAUCE OVER ALL. SPREAD ON MELBA TOAST, TRISCUITS OR BACON DIPPERS. SERVES 8.

HAM AND CHEESE BALL

YUMMY HORS D'OEUVRE OR CASUAL AFTERNOON SNACK. SERVE WITH CRACKERS.

1	PACKAGE (8 OZ/250 G) CREAM CHEESE	1
¼ CUP	MAYONNAISE	50 ML
2	CANS (EACH 8 OZ/227 G) FLAKED HAM	2
2 TBSP	CHOPPED PARSLEY	25 ML
1 TSP	MINCED ONION	5 ML
¼ TSP	DRY MUSTARD	1 ML
¼ TSP	TABASCO	1 ML
½ CUP	CHOPPED WALNUTS	125 ML

BEAT CHEESE AND MAYONNAISE UNTIL SMOOTH. STIR IN NEXT 5 INGREDIENTS. COVER AND CHILL SEVERAL HOURS. FORM INTO TWO MEDIUM-SIZED BALLS. ROLL IN NUTS TO COAT. FREEZES WELL. SERVES 16.

SUCCESS IS RELATIVE. THE MORE SUCCESS, THE MORE RELATIVES.

COLD CUCUMBER SOUP

A DELICIOUS COLD SOUP. MAKE THE DAY BEFORE.
(YOU'LL NEED A BLENDER.)

2	8-INCH (20 CM) ENGLISH CUCUMBERS	2
2 TBSP	BUTTER	25 ML
1/4 CUP	CHOPPED GREEN ONIONS	50 ML
4 CUPS	CHICKEN BROTH	1 L
1 TBSP	WHITE WINE VINEGAR	15 ML
1/2 TSP	DRIED TARRAGON (OR MORE)	2 ML
3 TBSP	CREAM OF WHEAT (QUICK COOKING)	45 ML
	SALT AND WHITE PEPPER	
1 CUP	FAT-FREE SOUR CREAM	250 ML

CUT 12 PAPER-THIN SLICES OF CUCUMBER (SKIN ON) TO
BE USED FOR GARNISH AND RESERVE. PEEL REMAINING
CUCUMBERS AND CHOP INTO CHUNKS. IN A LARGE POT,
MELT BUTTER; STIR IN ONIONS AND COOK 1 MINUTE OVER
MODERATE HEAT. ADD CUCUMBER CHUNKS, CHICKEN BROTH,
VINEGAR AND TARRAGON. BRING TO A BOIL. STIR IN
CREAM OF WHEAT. SIMMER, UNCOVERED, FOR 20 MINUTES.
BLENDERIZE (IF TOO THICK, ADD SMALL AMOUNT OF
CHICKEN BROTH OR MILK). SEASON TO TASTE WITH SALT
AND WHITE PEPPER. LET COOL AND ADD SOUR CREAM TO
SOUP IN BLENDER. CHILL UNTIL READY TO SERVE. SERVE
WITH 2 THIN SLICES OF RESERVED CUCUMBER ON TOP.
SERVES 6.

A JOURNEY OF 1,000 MILES BEGINS
WITH A LARGE CASH ADVANCE.

HABITANT PEA SOUP

1½ LBS	DRIED YELLOW PEAS	750 G
½ LB	SALT PORK OR HAM BONE (USE ANY SIZE BONE)	250 G
½ CUP	DICED RAW POTATOES	125 ML
1	DICED ONION	1
½ CUP	CELERY, FINELY CHOPPED	125 ML
PINCH	THYME	PINCH
PINCH	BASIL	PINCH
PINCH	OREGANO	PINCH
	SALT AND PEPPER TO TASTE	
SPRINKLE	PARSLEY	SPRINKLE

SOAK PEAS IN COLD WATER AT LEAST 12 HOURS. RINSE WELL AND PLACE IN LARGE SOUP POT. ADD 14 CUPS (3.5 L) COLD WATER AND HAM BONE. BRING TO A BOIL, SKIM OFF FOAM AND ADD REMAINING INGREDIENTS. SIMMER OVER LOW HEAT, COVERED, FOR 3 HOURS. ADD SALT AND PEPPER TO TASTE. SPRINKLE WITH PARSLEY. REMOVE BONE AND TAKE OFF MEAT. RETURN MEAT TO SOUP. SERVES 12.

*I ASKED HER IF I COULD SEE HER HOME,
SO SHE GAVE ME A PICTURE OF IT.*

GAZPACHO

A CHILLED TOMATO SOUP - PERFECT ON A HOT DAY!

3 LBS	FRESH TOMATOES, PEELED AND CUT UP (6 CUPS/1.5 L)	1.5 KG
1	ONION, CUT IN CHUNKS	1
1/2 CUP	GREEN PEPPER CHUNKS	125 ML
1/2 CUP	CUCUMBER CHUNKS	125 ML
2 CUPS	TOMATO JUICE	500 ML
1	GARLIC CLOVE, MINCED	1
1/2 TSP	CUMIN	2 ML
1 TSP	SALT	5 ML
1 TSP	PEPPER	5 ML
1/4 CUP	OLIVE OIL	50 ML
1/4 CUP	WHITE WINE VINEGAR	50 ML

GARNISH

1/2 CUP	FINELY CHOPPED GREEN ONION	125 ML
1/2 CUP	FINELY CHOPPED GREEN PEPPER	125 ML
1/2 CUP	CROUTONS	125 ML

IMMERSE TOMATOES IN BOILING WATER FOR 2 MINUTES. DRAIN AND SKIN. IN BLENDER OR FOOD PROCESSOR COMBINE TOMATOES, ONION, GREEN PEPPER AND CUCUMBER. WHIRL BUT LEAVE A LITTLE BIT CHUNKY. TRANSFER TO LARGE TUREEN. ADD JUICE, GARLIC, CUMIN, SALT AND PEPPER. COVER AND CHILL WELL. BEFORE SERVING, STIR IN OIL AND VINEGAR. GARNISH AND SERVE COLD. SERVES 8.

IT'S NOT HARD TO MEET EXPENSES - THEY'RE EVERYWHERE.

MINESTRONE SOUP

A MEAL IN ITSELF! (NOT UNLIKE TURKEY SOUP.)

1 1/2 LBS	GROUND ROUND	750 G
1 CUP	DICED ONIONS	250 ML
1 CUP	DICED ZUCCHINI	250 ML
1/2 CUP	DICED OKRA	125 ML
1 CUP	CUBED POTATOES	250 ML
1 CUP	SLICED CARROTS	250 ML
1/2 CUP	DICED CELERY	125 ML
1 CUP	SHREDDED CABBAGE	250 ML
1	CAN (15 OZ/426 ML) TOMATOES	1
1/4 CUP	RICE (OR 1/2 CUP/125 ML MACARONI ELBOW NOODLES)	50 ML
6 CUPS	WATER	1.5 L
1	BAY LEAF	1
1/2 TSP	THYME	2 ML
	SALT AND PEPPER TO TASTE	
1 TSP	WORCESTERSHIRE SAUCE	5 ML
1/2 CUP	GRATED PARMESAN CHEESE	125 ML

BROWN GROUND ROUND IN LARGE KETTLE. ADD VEGETABLES, WATER AND SPICES AND BRING TO A BOIL. SPRINKLE RICE (OR NOODLES) INTO MIXTURE. COVER AND SIMMER AT LEAST ONE HOUR. SPRINKLE WITH GRATED CHEESE. SERVES 8 TO 10.

LET NOT THE SANDS OF TIME GET IN YOUR LUNCH.

HAMBURGER SOUP

DON'T BE DECEIVED BY THE NAME, THIS IS A
FAMILY FAVORITE. FREEZES VERY WELL.

1½ LBS	LEAN GROUND BEEF	750 G
1	MEDIUM ONION, FINELY CHOPPED	1
1	CAN (28 OZ/796 ML) TOMATOES	1
2 CUPS	WATER	500 ML
3	CANS (EACH 10 OZ/284 ML) CONSOMMÉ	3
1	CAN (10 OZ/284 ML) TOMATO SOUP	1
4	CARROTS, FINELY CHOPPED	4
1	BAY LEAF	1
3	CELERY STALKS, FINELY CHOPPED	3
	PARSLEY	
½ TSP	THYME	2 ML
	PEPPER TO TASTE	
½ CUP	BARLEY	125 ML

BROWN MEAT AND ONIONS. DRAIN WELL. COMBINE ALL
INGREDIENTS IN LARGE POT. SIMMER, COVERED, A
MINIMUM OF 2 HOURS. SERVES 10.

IF AT FIRST YOU DON'T SUCCEED...
WELL SO MUCH FOR SKY DIVING.

ELEPHANT SOUP

THIS HAS BEEN A BIG FAVORITE WITH OUR FAMILY.
GREAT FOR LARGE "GRAY" CUP PARTIES,
DEMOCRATIC CONVENTIONS.

I	MEDIUM ELEPHANT (AFRICAN IS BEST)	I
500 GALLONS	HOT WATER	2000 L
2 PECKS	ONIONS, FINELY CHOPPED	16 L
I BUSHEL	POTATOES, PEELED AND SLICED	32 L
5	SHOVELS SALT	5
3	SHOVELS PEPPER	3
1½	CASES WORCESTERSHIRE SAUCE	1½
10	BOTTLES RUM (OR MORE IF COOKING TIME IS LONGER OR YOU'RE EXPECTING MORE THAN 8 GUESTS)	10
	COKE TO TASTE	
5 QUARTS	PEANUT OIL (OPTIONAL)*	5 L

MIX 1½ OZ (45 ML) OF RUM WITH COKE; DRINK. WASH AND DRY ELEPHANT (DON'T USE SOAP AS THIS WILL SPOIL FLAVOR.) CHOP INTO BITE-SIZE CHUNKS. IN BACK OF ½-TON TRUCK (OR RENTED U-HAUL) POUR HOT WATER. HAVE ANOTHER RUM AND COKE AND ADD ELEPHANT, SPUDS AND OTHER INGREDIENTS. ALLOW TO SIMMER. MEANWHILE, FINISH FIRST BOTTLE OF RUM. STIR MIXTURE USING CANOE PADDLE OR SMALL OUTBOARD MOTOR. WHEN GUESTS ARRIVE, START THEM OFF WITH REMAINING RUM. SERVES 50 SCORE.

*THE PEANUT OIL WON'T REALLY ADD TO THE SOUP, BUT IT'S THE WAY THE ELEPHANT WOULD HAVE WANTED IT!

TURKEY SOUP

AHHH – THE AROMA OF SOUP BUBBLING ON
THE BACK BURNER – LIFE IS GOOD!

	LEFTOVER TURKEY CARCASS (BONES, SKIN, EVERYTHING!)	
8 CUPS	WATER	2 L
3	CHICKEN BOUILLON CUBES	3
1 TSP	SALT	5 ML
1/4 TSP	POULTRY SEASONING OR SAGE	1 ML
1	BAY LEAF	1
1/2 CUP	BARLEY	125 ML
2 CUPS	CHOPPED CARROTS	500 ML
1 CUP	CHOPPED ONION	250 ML
1 CUP	CHOPPED CELERY	250 ML
1	CAN (28 OZ/796 ML) TOMATOES	1
3 CUPS	CHOPPED TURKEY	750 ML
1 CUP	MACARONI OR NOODLES, UNCOOKED (OPTIONAL)	250 ML
1/4 CUP	CHOPPED FRESH PARSLEY	50 ML

IN A LARGE DUTCH OVEN, COMBINE TURKEY CARCASS, WATER, BOUILLON CUBES, SALT, POULTRY SEASONING AND BAY LEAF. BRING TO A BOIL. REDUCE HEAT, COVER AND SIMMER FOR 2 HOURS. STRAIN AND DISCARD BONES. PLACE BROTH IN REFRIGERATOR OVERNIGHT. SKIM FAT OFF SOLIDIFIED BROTH. SIMMER IN DUTCH OVEN WITH REMAINING INGREDIENTS FOR 2-3 HOURS. SERVE WITH FRESH BREAD AND A GREEN SALAD. *SERVES 6 TO 8.*

AN ALLOWANCE IS WHAT YOU PAY YOUR
CHILDREN TO LIVE WITH YOU.

CRAB BISQUE

1/4 LB	CRABMEAT		125 G
3 TBSP	SHERRY		45 ML
1	CAN (10 OZ/284 ML) TOMATO SOUP		1
1 CUP	LIGHT CREAM		250 ML
	SALT AND WHITE PEPPER TO TASTE		

FLAKE CRAB AND SOAK IN SHERRY 10 MINUTES. BLEND UNDILUTED SOUPS AND SIMMER UNTIL HOT. ADD CREAM AND BLEND THOROUGHLY. ADD CRABMEAT AND SEASONINGS. HEAT BUT DO NOT BOIL. SERVES 4.

CRAB CREAM SOUP

1	CAN (10 OZ/284 ML) MUSHROOM SOUP		1
1	CAN (10 OZ/284 ML) ASPARAGUS SOUP		1
1 CUP	MILK		250 ML
1	CAN (6 1/2 OZ/184 G) CRABMEAT		1
1 TSP	WORCESTERSHIRE SAUCE		5 ML
3 TBSP	SHERRY		45 ML
1/2 CUP	WHIPPING CREAM		125 ML

HEAT SOUPS AND MILK TOGETHER. ADD CRABMEAT AND WORCESTERSHIRE SAUCE. STIR IN SHERRY AND FLUFF. STIR IN WHIPPING CREAM. SERVES 4.

ON THE OTHER HAND, YOU HAVE DIFFERENT FINGERS.

CRAB AND CORN CHOWDER

WHAT COULD BE BETTER THAN CHOWDER, FRENCH BREAD AND WINE AFTER A DAY'S SKIING – OR A DAY OF ANYTHING!

4	SLICES BACON	4
1/4 CUP	BUTTER	50 ML
1	SMALL ONION, CHOPPED	1
1/3 CUP	FLOUR	75 ML
3 CUPS	MILK	750 ML
2	MEDIUM POTATOES, PEELED AND DICED AND SET IN COLD WATER	2
1	SMALL GREEN PEPPER, SEEDED AND CHOPPED	1
1	STALK CELERY, DICED	1
1	BAY LEAF	1
1 CUP	HALF-AND-HALF CREAM	250 ML
10 OZ	CRABMEAT	300 G
1	CAN (12 OZ/341 ML) WHOLE KERNEL CORN	1
	SALT AND PEPPER TO TASTE	
1 TBSP	CHOPPED PARSLEY	15 ML

FRY BACON UNTIL CRISP. COOL AND CRUMBLE. SET ASIDE. IN A LARGE SAUCEPAN, MELT BUTTER AND SAUTÉ ONION UNTIL SOFT. ADD FLOUR, STIR AND COOK GENTLY FOR 1 MINUTE. GRADUALLY ADD MILK, STIRRING CONSTANTLY UNTIL THICKENED. DRAIN POTATOES AND ADD TO SAUCE WITH PEPPER, CELERY, BAY LEAF AND CREAM. SIMMER 35 TO 40 MINUTES. ADD CRAB, CORN AND BACON; HEAT THROUGH. SEASON WITH SALT AND PEPPER. GARNISH EACH BOWL WITH PARSLEY. SERVES 6.

CLAM CHOWDER

4	STRIPS BACON, DICED	4
1	SMALL ONION, CHOPPED	1
2	STALKS CELERY, CHOPPED	2
1/2	GREEN PEPPER, CHOPPED	1/2
1	CLOVE GARLIC, MINCED	1
1	BAY LEAF	1
2	CANS (EACH 10 OZ/284 ML) CLAMS AND LIQUID	2
1/2 CUP	WATER	125 ML
2 CUPS	RAW POTATOES, DICED	500 ML
1 TSP	WORCESTERSHIRE SAUCE	5 ML
1/4 TSP	SALT	1 ML
1/8 TSP	PEPPER	0.5 ML
2 CUPS	MILK	500 ML

SAUTÉ BACON, ONION, CELERY, GREEN PEPPER AND GARLIC 5 MINUTES. ADD BAY LEAF, LIQUID FROM CANNED CLAMS, WATER, DICED POTATOES, SALT AND PEPPER. SIMMER UNTIL POTATOES ARE BARELY TENDER. ADD CLAMS, MILK AND WORCESTERSHIRE SAUCE. REMOVE BAY LEAF. SERVES 4.

SHE'S SO NEAT, SHE EVEN CHANGES THE PAPER UNDER THE CUCKOO CLOCK!

GRAMPA MAC'S OYSTER STEW

THIS VERY RICH SOUP RECIPE COMES FROM A GRANDFATHER FROM P.E.I. SERVES FOUR HUNGRY PEOPLE - A MEAL BY ITSELF SERVED WITH TOAST AND CHEESE.

2	CANS (EACH 5 OZ/142 G) OYSTERS, WITH LIQUID	2
1/3 CUP	BUTTER	75 ML
3/4 TSP	SALT	4 ML
1/8 TSP	WORCESTERSHIRE SAUCE	0.5 ML
	PEPPER TO TASTE	
1	CAN (16 OZ/454 ML) EVAPORATED MILK	1
2/3 CUP	REGULAR MILK	150 ML
12	SINGLE SODA CRACKERS	12

HEAT EVERYTHING EXCEPT MILK AND CRACKERS OVER MEDIUM HEAT TO A NEAR BOIL. ADD EVAPORATED MILK AND CONTINUE STIRRING OVER HEAT. BREAK SODA CRACKERS ON TOP AND STIR. ADD REMAINING MILK BEING CAREFUL NOT TO BOIL. SERVES 4.

MARRIAGE IS LIKE A CAFETERIA; YOU TAKE WHAT LOOKS GOOD TO YOU, AND PAY FOR IT LATER.

PICKLED COLESLAW

I	LARGE CABBAGE, FINELY CHOPPED	I
2	LARGE ONIONS, THINLY SLICED	2
3/4 CUP	SUGAR	175 ML
I TSP	SALT	5 ML
I CUP	WHITE VINEGAR	250 ML
2 TSP	PREPARED MUSTARD	10 ML
1/4 CUP	SUGAR	50 ML
I TBSP	CELERY SEED	15 ML
3/4 CUP	SALAD OIL	175 ML

TOSS CABBAGE, ONION 3/4 CUP (175 ML) SUGAR AND SALT. LET STAND WHILE MAKING THE DRESSING.

MIX VINEGAR, MUSTARD, 1/4 CUP (50 ML) SUGAR AND CELERY SEED IN SAUCEPAN. BRING TO A BOIL. ADD OIL. WHILE BUBBLING, POUR OVER CABBAGE MIXTURE. STIR. CHILL OVERNIGHT. THIS WILL KEEP SEVERAL WEEKS IN THE REFRIGERATOR. SERVES 20.

THE BEST WAY TO REMOVE COFFEE STAINS FROM
A SILK BLOUSE IS WITH A PAIR OF SCISSORS.

PINEAPPLE COLESLAW

1	MEDIUM CABBAGE	1
2	CANS (EACH 14 OZ/398 ML) PINEAPPLE TIDBITS	2
1 TBSP	LEMON JUICE	15 ML
3	RED APPLES	3
3/4 CUP	SLICED ALMONDS	175 ML

FINELY SHRED CABBAGE. DICE APPLES AND SPRINKLE WITH LEMON JUICE TO AVOID DISCOLORING. ADD PINEAPPLE AND ALMONDS.

DRESSING

1/2 CUP	MAYONNAISE	125 ML
1/2 CUP	HEAVY CREAM, WHIPPED	125 ML
1/2 CUP	LEMONADE CONCENTRATE	125 ML

COMBINE MAYONNAISE AND LEMONADE. ADD TO CREAM AND MIX THOROUGHLY WITH SALAD INGREDIENTS. SERVES 12 TO 16.

THE TROUBLE WITH THE WORLD TODAY IS THAT EVERY DAY BEGINS WITH THE FIRST HALF-HOUR.

MARINATED TOMATOES

1	CAN (10 OZ/284 ML) MUSHROOMS (OR FRESH)	1
3 TBSP	GREEN ONIONS	45 ML
5	LARGE TOMATOES, SLICED	5

MARINADE

1 TSP	CURRY	5 ML
1 TSP	SUGAR	5 ML
1/2 CUP	SALAD OIL	125 ML
1/4 CUP	VINEGAR	50 ML
1	CRUSHED GARLIC CLOVE	1
1 TBSP	PARSLEY	15 ML
	SALT AND PEPPER	

COMBINE ALL MARINADE INGREDIENTS IN JAR AND SHAKE WELL. MARINATE VEGETABLES FOR SEVERAL HOURS BEFORE SERVING. ARRANGE ON BED OF LETTUCE IN LARGE OR INDIVIDUAL BOWLS. SERVES 6 TO 8.

THE HAPPIEST FAMILIES ARE THOSE IN WHICH THE CHILDREN ARE PROPERLY SPACED. ABOUT TEN FEET APART.

LEE HONG'S CUCUMBERS

3 TBSP	SALT (APPROXIMATELY)	45 ML
1	CUCUMBER, SLICED VERY THIN	1
3 TBSP	SUGAR	45 ML
2 TBSP	VEGETABLE OIL	25 ML
1	THINLY SLICED SPANISH ONION	1
4 TBSP	WHITE VINEGAR	60 ML
4 TBSP	WATER	60 ML

ARRANGE CUCUMBER SLICES IN BOWL IN LAYERS, SALTING BETWEEN LAYERS. LET STAND 2 HOURS. STAND BOWL UNDER FAUCET AND LET COOL WATER RUN THROUGH GENTLY UNTIL NO SALT REMAINS. DRAIN WELL. ADD SUGAR AND OIL. MIX AND ADD ONION, VINEGAR AND WATER. ADD MORE SUGAR OR VINEGAR IF NOT SWEET OR SOUR ENOUGH. RELISH SHOULD STAND A FEW HOURS BEFORE SERVING. GREAT WITH STEAK OR CHICKEN, HOT OR COLD MEAT. EXCELLENT! SERVES 6 TO 8.

AN ALARM CLOCK IS A SMALL MECHANICAL DEVICE TO WAKE UP PEOPLE WHO HAVE NO CHILDREN.

CUCUMBER CREAM SALAD

I	PACKAGE (3 OZ/85 G) LIME JELL-O	I
I TSP	SALT	5 ML
I CUP	BOILING WATER	250 ML
2 TBSP	VINEGAR	25 ML
I TSP	GRATED ONION	5 ML
I CUP	SOUR CREAM	250 ML
½ CUP	MAYONNAISE	125 ML
2 CUPS	DICED CUCUMBER	500 ML

DISSOLVE JELL-O AND SALT IN BOILING WATER. ADD VINEGAR AND ONION. CHILL UNTIL PARTIALLY SET. BLEND IN SOUR CREAM AND MAYONNAISE. FOLD IN DICED CUCUMBERS AND CHILL UNTIL FIRM. A LIGHT AND REFRESHING TREAT. SERVES 6 TO 8.

HORSERADISH SALAD

I	PACKAGE (3 OZ/85 G) LEMON JELL-O	I
I CUP	BOILING WATER	250 ML
I TSP	SALT	5 ML
2 TBSP	VINEGAR	25 ML
I	SMALL BOTTLE HORSERADISH, DRAINED	I
I CUP	WHIPPING CREAM, WHIPPED	250 ML

MIX ALL BUT WHIPPED CREAM AND LET COOL UNTIL JELL-O IS PARTIALLY SET. FOLD IN WHIPPED CREAM. SERVES 6 TO 8. THIS IS DELICIOUS WITH ROAST OR BAR-B-QUED BEEF.

GREEN GODDESS SALAD

THE NAME SAYS IT ALL!

DRESSING

1	CLOVE MINCED GARLIC	1
1/2 TSP	SALT	2 ML
1/2 TSP	DRY MUSTARD	2 ML
1 TSP	WORCESTERSHIRE SAUCE	5 ML
1 TBSP	GREEN ONION, CHOPPED	15 ML
1 CUP	MAYONNAISE	250 ML
1/2 CUP	SOUR CREAM	125 ML
PINCH	PEPPER	PINCH

SALAD

1	HEAD LETTUCE	1
2 TSP	ANCHOVIES, CHOPPED	10 ML
1 TBSP	CHOPPED PARSLEY	15 ML
1 CUP	SHRIMP OR CRAB, COOKED	250 ML
2	TOMATOES, QUARTERED	2

MIX INGREDIENTS FOR DRESSING TOGETHER AND CHILL.
PREPARE SALAD AND TOSS GENTLY. POUR DRESSING OVER
SALAD AND TOSS AGAIN, COATING WELL. DELICIOUS SERVED
WITH A BUFFET OR LUNCHEON ALONG WITH WARM ROLLS.
SERVES 4 TO 6.

*SHE WENT ON A 14-DAY DIET, BUT ALL
SHE LOST WAS TWO WEEKS.*

FRESH SPINACH SALAD

DRESSING

1	GARLIC CLOVE, MINCED	1
2 TBSP	CIDER OR RED WINE VINEGAR	25 ML
1 TSP	SUGAR	5 ML
½ TSP	SALT	2 ML
1 TSP	DRY MUSTARD	5 ML
½ TSP	FRESHLY GROUND PEPPER	2 ML
¼ CUP	SALAD OIL	50 ML

SALAD

8 CUPS	CRISP YOUNG SPINACH, STEMS REMOVED	2 L
3	HARD-COOKED EGGS, GRATED	3
8	SLICES BACON, COOKED AND CRUMBLED	8
4	GREEN ONIONS, FINELY CHOPPED	4
	FRESH MUSHROOMS, SLICED	
	FRESH CAULIFLOWER, SLICED	

TO MAKE DRESSING: BEAT ALL INGREDIENTS TOGETHER AND REFRIGERATE.

TO MAKE SALAD: PREPARE SALAD INGREDIENTS, TOSS WITH DRESSING JUST BEFORE SERVING. SERVES 4 TO 6.

THE GOOD THING ABOUT SPOILED CHILDREN IS THAT YOU NEVER HAVE ANY IN YOUR OWN FAMILY.

WILTED SPINACH SALAD

8	SLICES BACON	8
2 TBSP	BACON DRIPPINGS	25 ML
8 CUPS	SPINACH, HARD STEMS REMOVED	2 L
3	HARD-COOKED EGGS, GRATED	3
2	CHOPPED GREEN ONIONS	2

COOK BACON, DRAIN AND CRUMBLE. HEAT DRIPPINGS AND ADD DRESSING AS PER FRESH SPINACH SALAD RECIPE (SEE PAGE 126), ALONG WITH BACON. POUR DRESSING WHILE HOT OVER SALAD GREENS AND SERVE AT ONCE ON INDIVIDUAL SERVING PLATES. SERVES 4 TO 8.

ARMENIAN SPINACH SALAD

1	CUCUMBER, THINLY SLICED	1
2	BUNCHES FRESH SPINACH	2
1	RED ONION, THINLY SLICED	1
1/2 CUP	GREEK OLIVES	125 ML
1 CUP	FETA CHEESE	250 ML
	COARSELY GROUND PEPPER	

DRESSING

2/3 CUP	GRAPE SEED OIL, OR OLIVE OIL	150 ML
1/3 CUP	LEMON JUICE	75 ML

WASH, DRY AND TEAR SPINACH. COMBINE ALL SALAD INGREDIENTS IN SALAD BOWL. COMBINE OIL AND LEMON JUICE IN JAR AND SHAKE WELL. POUR OVER SALAD AND TOSS. SERVES 4 TO 6.

LAYERED SALAD

AN AMAZINGLY FRESH, CRISP SALAD.
A DIFFERENT ACCOMPANIMENT TO ANY MEAL.

I	HEAD ICEBERG LETTUCE, CUT INTO BITE-SIZE PIECES	I
I	BUNCH FRESH SPINACH, CUT INTO BITE-SIZE PIECES	I
I	PACKAGE (10 OZ/300 G) FROZEN PEAS (UNCOOKED)	I
I	BUNCH GREEN ONION, SLICED	I
5	HARD-BOILED EGGS	5
I LB	CRISP BACON, CRUMBLED	500 G
1½ CUPS	MAYONNAISE	375 ML

IN A 13- X 9-INCH (3 L) GLASS DISH, LAYER LETTUCE, SPINACH, PEAS, ONIONS, SLICED EGGS AND SOME BACON. SEAL COMPLETELY WITH MAYONNAISE. REFRIGERATE FOR 24 HOURS. SPRINKLE REMAINING BACON ON TOP BEFORE SERVING. SERVES 8 TO 10.

SOCIAL TACT IS MAKING YOUR COMPANY FEEL AT HOME,
EVEN THOUGH YOU WISH THEY WERE.

SUPER SALAD

THIS MAKES A HUGE SALAD. IT'S GREAT FOR BUFFETS OR BAR-B-QUES.

1	HEAD ROMAINE LETTUCE	1
1	HEAD BUTTER LETTUCE	1
1	HEAD ICEBERG LETTUCE	1
1/2 CUP	PARMESAN CHEESE	125 ML
2 OZ	BLUE CHEESE, CRUMBLED	60 G
3	AVOCADOS	3
1	LARGE CUCUMBER, PEELED AND DICED	1
1 1/2 CUPS	CHERRY TOMATOES, HALVED	375 ML
6	SLICES OF BACON, DRAINED AND CRUMBLED	6
	SLICED RED AND GREEN PEPPERS (OPTIONAL)	
1/2 CUP	SLICED RIPE OLIVES	125 ML
1	BOTTLE (8 OZ/227 ML) ITALIAN DRESSING	1
SPRINKLE	PARSLEY	SPRINKLE

TEAR SALAD GREENS INTO LARGE BOWL, SPRINKLE WITH CHEESE. ARRANGE REMAINING INGREDIENTS ON TOP AND TOSS WITH DRESSING. SERVES 12 TO 14.

AN APPLE A DAY KEEPS THE DOCTOR AWAY;
AN ONION A DAY KEEPS EVERYONE AWAY.

VEGETABLE SALAD PLATTER

THIS SALAD IS A REAL DELIGHT AND MAY BE SERVED
WITH CRAB FILLED BUNS OR AS A BUFFET SALAD. THE
LADIES WILL LOVE YOU FOR THIS LOW CALORIE DISH.

I TO 2	HEADS CAULIFLOWER	I TO 2
I TO 2	BASKETS CHERRY TOMATOES	I TO 2
I	BUNCH BROCCOLI, WITH STEMS	I
3 TO 4	CARROTS, CUT IN SMALL STRIPS	3 TO 4
I	BUNCH CHOPPED GREEN ONIONS	I
2 TO 3	STALKS OF CELERY	2 TO 3
2	CANS (10 OZ/284 ML) BUTTON MUSHROOMS	2
I	BOTTLE (8 OZ/227 ML) ITALIAN DRESSING	I
	PITTED BLACK OLIVES, DRAINED	

PREPARE ALL VEGETABLES, CUTTING INTO BITE-SIZE
PIECES. CHERRY TOMATOES SHOULD BE LEFT WHOLE. PUT
ALL INGREDIENTS IN SEALED PLASTIC BOWL OR DOUBLE
PLASTIC BAG. POUR DRESSING OVER TO COVER ALL
VEGETABLES. MARINATE AND REFRIGERATE FOR 24 HOURS
TURNING FREQUENTLY.

DRAIN THOROUGHLY BEFORE SERVING ON A PLATTER.
SERVES 16 TO 20.

WHAT IS REALLY APPALLING IS THAT IN TWENTY YEARS,
THESE WILL BE THE GOOD OLD DAYS.

FROSTED WALDORF SALAD

2 CUPS	MINIATURE MARSHMALLOWS	500 ML
3 TO 4 CUPS	GREEN GRAPES, SEEDLESS IF AVAILABLE, IF NOT, REMOVE SEEDS	750 ML TO 1 L
2 TO 3	UNPEELED CHOPPED RED APPLES	2 TO 3
1	PEELED ORANGE, OR 1 CAN (10 OZ/284 ML) MANDARIN ORANGES, DRAINED (RESERVE JUICE TO COAT APPLES)	1
1 TBSP	ORANGE JUICE	15 ML

TOSS TOGETHER TO PREVENT APPLES FROM DISCOLORING, THEN ADD:

1/2 CUP	CHOPPED CELERY	125 ML
1/2 CUP	CHOPPED WALNUTS OR PECANS	125 ML
1/2 CUP	SEEDLESS RAISINS, OR SNIPPED DATES (OPTIONAL)	125 ML

IN A BOWL COMBINE:

1 CUP	WHIPPING CREAM, WHIPPED (OR WHIPPED TOPPING)	250 ML
1/2 CUP	MAYONNAISE	125 ML
1 TBSP	SUGAR	15 ML

COMBINE ALL INGREDIENTS. SERVE IN LETTUCE LINED GLASS BOWL OR ON INDIVIDUAL SERVING PLATES, ALONG WITH WARM BUTTERED ROLLS. GARNISH WITH ADDITIONAL GREEN GRAPE CLUSTERS, WASHED AND WHILE DAMP, DIP IN GRANULATED SUGAR. SERVES 8 TO 10.

LIFE IS TOO COMPLICATED IN THE MORNING.

SUNOMONO SALAD PLATTER

COLORFUL, MAKE AHEAD AND DIFFERENT YEAR-ROUND.

MARINATED CARROTS

8	MEDIUM CARROTS, PEELED AND GRATED	8
	JUICE OF 2 LEMONS	
I TBSP	SUGAR	15 ML
I TSP	SALT	5 ML

SUNOMONO

2	LARGE CUCUMBERS, SLICED PAPER THIN	2
1/3 CUP	VINEGAR	75 ML
I TSP	SALT	5 ML
4 TSP	SUGAR	20 ML
I TBSP	WATER	15 ML
2	SLICES FRESH GINGER ROOT, FINELY CHOPPED, OR I TSP (5 ML) GROUND GINGER	2
	LEAFY LETTUCE	
2	CANS GREEN ASPARAGUS	2
2	CANS WHITE ASPARAGUS	2
	1/4-INCH (0.5 CM) WIDE PIMENTO STRIPS	
	BOTTLED ITALIAN DRESSING	
	BLACK PITTED OLIVES	

MARINATED CARROTS: COMBINE LEMON JUICE, SUGAR AND SALT. POUR OVER GRATED CARROTS AND MARINATE. COVER AND CHILL FOR AT LEAST ONE HOUR.

CONTINUED ON NEXT PAGE...

SUNOMONO: COMBINE VINEGAR, SALT, SUGAR, WATER AND GINGER. POUR OVER CUCUMBER SLICES AND MARINATE. COVER AND CHILL AT LEAST ONE HOUR.

TO ASSEMBLE SALAD PLATTER: LINE A LARGE PLATTER WITH LEAFY LETTUCE. DRAIN AND PLACE CUCUMBERS IN SMALL BOWL AND PLACE IN CENTER OF THE PLATTER. DRAIN ASPARAGUS AND PLACE FOUR OF EACH COLOR ON A LETTUCE LEAF AT 3-INCH (7.5 CM) INTERVALS. SLICE PIMENTO IN $\frac{1}{4}$-INCH (0.5 CM) WIDE STRIPS AND PLACE 2 OR 3 OVER ASPARAGUS. DRAIN CARROTS AND SPOON BETWEEN ASPARAGUS CLUMPS. PLACE BLACK OLIVES AT RANDOM AROUND THE EDGE OF THE PLATTER. CAREFULLY POUR A SMALL AMOUNT OF ITALIAN DRESSING ON EACH BUNCH OF ASPARAGUS. THIS CAN BE MADE WELL AHEAD. SERVES 12 TO 16.

LET HIM WHO IS WITHOUT AIM THROW THE FIRST STONE.

FOO YUNG TOSSED SALAD

1	HEAD ROMAINE LETTUCE (TORN INTO BITE-SIZE PIECES)	1
1	CAN (16 OZ/454 ML) BEAN SPROUTS, DRAINED (OR USE FRESH BEAN SPROUTS)	1
1	CAN (5 OZ/142 ML) WATER CHESTNUTS, SLICED	1
6	SLICES BACON, COOKED CRISP AND CRUMBLED	6
2	HARD-COOKED EGGS, SLICED	2
	SALT AND PEPPER TO TASTE	
1	CAN (6½ OZ/184 G) SHRIMP (OPTIONAL)	1

COMBINE ALL INGREDIENTS AND TOSS. ONCE YOU HAVE MADE AND TASTED THIS SALAD, YOU MAY USE YOUR IMAGINATION AND ADD DIFFERENT INGREDIENTS OR TRY CREAMY ITALIAN DRESSING. SERVES 6 TO 8.

DRESSING

½ CUP	SALAD OIL	125 ML
⅓ CUP	VINEGAR	75 ML
2 TBSP	SUGAR	25 ML
1 TBSP	SOY SAUCE	15 ML
¼ TSP	GROUND GINGER	1 ML

IN SCREW TOP JAR COMBINE OIL, VINEGAR, SUGAR, SOY SAUCE AND GINGER. SHAKE VIGOROUSLY, CHILL. JUST BEFORE SERVING, POUR OVER SALAD AND TOSS.

FIGHT TOOTH DECAY – EAT THROUGH YOUR NOSE.

CAESAR SALAD

YOU'LL DESERVE THE "HAILS" WHEN YOU
SERVE THIS CLASSIC.

I	LARGE HEAD ROMAINE LETTUCE	I
I	GARLIC CLOVE, MINCED	I
1/3 CUP	OIL	75 ML
	SALT AND FRESH GROUND BLACK PEPPER TO TASTE	
1/4 TSP	DRY MUSTARD	I ML
1 1/2 TSP	WORCESTERSHIRE SAUCE	7 ML
3 (OR MORE)	ANCHOVY FILLETS, DRAINED	3 (OR MORE)
I	EGG	I
I TO 2 TBSP	FRESH LEMON JUICE	15 TO 25 ML
2 TBSP	FRESHLY GRATED PARMESAN CHEESE	25 ML
	CROUTONS	

WASH AND TEAR ROMAINE INTO BITE-SIZED PIECES.
BLENDERIZE REMAINING INGREDIENTS, EXCEPT PARMESAN
AND CROUTONS. TOSS LETTUCE AND DRESSING. SPRINKLE
ON PARMESAN AND CROUTONS. TOSS AGAIN. SERVES 6.

IF YOU THINK ENGLISH IS AN EASY LANGUAGE TO LEARN,
THEN HOW COME "FAT CHANCE" MEANS THE SAME
AS "SLIM CHANCE."

CANLIS' SPECIAL SALAD

ORIGINATED BY CANLIS' RESTAURANT IN HONOLULU.

SALAD

2	HEADS ROMAINE LETTUCE	2
2	PEELED TOMATOES	2
1	CLOVE GARLIC	1
	SALT	
2 TBSP	OLIVE OIL	25 ML

CONDIMENTS

1/4 CUP	GREEN ONION, CHOPPED	50 ML
1/2 CUP	ROMANO CHEESE, GRATED	125 ML
1 LB	COOKED BACON, FINELY CHOPPED	500 G

DRESSING

6 TBSP	OLIVE OIL	90 ML
	JUICE OF 2 LEMONS	
1/2 TSP	FRESH GROUND PEPPER	2 ML
1/2 TSP	FRESH MINT, CHOPPED	2 ML
1/4 TSP	OREGANO	1 ML
1	CODDLED EGG	1
1 CUP	CROUTONS	250 ML

INTO A LARGE BOWL (WOODEN) POUR APPROXIMATELY
2 TBSP (25 ML) OF GOOD OLIVE OIL, SPRINKLE WITH SALT
AND RUB WITH A LARGE CLOVE OF GARLIC. (THE OIL WILL
ACT AS A LUBRICANT AND THE SALT AS AN ABRASIVE.)
REMOVE GARLIC. IN THE BOTTOM OF THE BOWL, FIRST
PLACE TOMATOES CUT IN EIGHTHS; ADD ROMAINE LETTUCE,
SLICED IN 1-INCH (2.5 CM) STRIPS.

CONTINUED ON NEXT PAGE...

NOTE: YOU MAY ADD OTHER VEGETABLES TO THIS SALAD IF YOU CHOOSE, BUT REMEMBER TO PUT THE HEAVY VEGETABLES IN FIRST WITH ROMAINE LETTUCE ON TOP. ADD CONDIMENTS.

DRESSING: POUR THE OLIVE OIL INTO A BOWL, ADD LEMON JUICE AND SEASONINGS. ADD CODDLED EGG AND WHIP VIGOROUSLY. WHEN READY TO SERVE, POUR DRESSING OVER SALAD. ADD CROUTONS LAST. TOSS GENEROUSLY. SERVES 6 TO 8.

IT'S SO EASY TO TELL A MARRIED COUPLE THESE DAYS. THE HUSBAND IS THE ONE WHO ENTERS THE CAR FROM THE LEFT OR STREET SIDE. THE WIFE IS THE ONE WHO CLIMBS OVER THE SNOWBANK ON THE RIGHT SIDE.

SALAD ROYALE

I CUP	PITTED RIPE OLIVES, SLICED	250 ML
3 CUPS	FRESH SPINACH, HARD STEMS REMOVED	750 ML
$\frac{1}{2}$ CUP	SLICED FRESH MUSHROOMS	125 ML
2	STALKS GREEN ONION, CHOPPED	2
I TBSP	SESAME SEEDS (TOASTED)	15 ML
8	CHERRY TOMATOES (OPTIONAL)	8
$\frac{1}{4}$ CUP	CATALINA FRENCH DRESSING	50 ML
$\frac{1}{4}$ TSP	CURRY POWDER	I ML

MIX FRENCH DRESSING AND CURRY POWDER. COMBINE FIRST SIX INGREDIENTS AND REFRIGERATE. JUST BEFORE SERVING, ADD DRESSING AND TOSS. SERVES 4 TO 6.

SHRIMP LOUIS SALAD

LADIES LOVE SALADS AT NOON AND THIS
SHOULD PROVE TO BE A POPULAR ONE.

CREAMY MAKE-AHEAD DRESSING

I CUP	CREAM-STYLE COTTAGE CHEESE	250 ML
I	HARD-COOKED EGG, PEELED AND HALVED	I
1/4 CUP	TOMATO JUICE	50 ML
I TSP	PREPARED MUSTARD	5 ML

SALAD

I LB	SHRIMP, COOKED, PEELED AND DEVEINED	500 G
I	LARGE RIPE AVOCADO, PEELED AND SLICED	I
I	CUCUMBER, WASHED AND UNPEELED, SLICED	I
I	LARGE HEAD OF ROMAINE LETTUCE	I
I	CAN (7 1/2 OZ/213 ML) RIPE OLIVES, HALVED	I

DRESSING: COMBINE COTTAGE CHEESE, EGG, TOMATO
JUICE AND MUSTARD IN CONTAINER OF ELECTRIC BLENDER.
WHIRL UNTIL SMOOTH. COVER AND CHILL UNTIL SERVING
TIME. MAKES 1 1/3 CUPS (325 ML).

SALAD: COMBINE SHRIMP, AVOCADO, CUCUMBER, OLIVES
AND LETTUCE IN LARGE SALAD BOWL. TOSS GENTLY AND
POUR CHILLED DRESSING OVER. TOSS AGAIN UNTIL WELL
MIXED. ACCOMPANY SALAD WITH A LIGHT CHILLED WHITE
WINE AND HOT ROLLS. YUMMY! SERVES 8.

BUFFET SEAFOOD SALAD

1	LOAF WHITE SLICED BREAD	1
4	HARD BOILED EGGS	4
6	GREEN ONIONS, CHOPPED	6
1/4 LB	SOFT BUTTER	125 G
2	CANS (EACH 6 1/2 OZ/184 G) CRABMEAT	2
3	CANS (EACH 6 1/2 OZ/184 G) SHRIMP	3
3 CUPS	MAYONNAISE	750 ML

CUT CRUSTS OFF BREAD, BUTTER BOTH SIDES AND CUT INTO 1/2-INCH (1 CM) CUBES. CHOP EGGS AND ONION. PLACE BREAD CUBES, EGGS AND ONION IN PLASTIC BAG. LEAVE IN THE REFRIGERATOR FOR SEVERAL HOURS OR OVERNIGHT. WHEN PREPARING DINNER, DRAIN CRAB AND SHRIMP, PLACE IN LARGE BOWL WITH BREAD MIXTURE AND MAYONNAISE; MIX WELL. SERVE IN WOODEN BOWL OR PLATTER ON LETTUCE LEAVES. SERVES 12 TO 16.

THE MAN WHO WOULD RATHER PLAY GOLF THAN EAT SHOULD MARRY THE WOMAN WHO WOULD RATHER PLAY BRIDGE THAN COOK.

AVOCADO FRUIT SALAD

2	AVOCADOS, PEELED, SLICED	2
2	GRAPEFRUIT, PEELED, CLEANED AND SECTIONED	2
2	ORANGES, PEELED, CLEANED AND SECTIONED	2
1/4 CUP	LEMON JUICE	50 ML
	LETTUCE (ROMAINE OR BUTTER)	
	WATERCRESS (OPTIONAL)	

DIP AVOCADO IN LEMON JUICE (RESERVE JUICE). ARRANGE FRUIT WITH LETTUCE. ADD WATERCRESS. SPOON DRESSING OVER ALL. SERVES 4.

DRESSING

1/3 CUP	CITRUS JUICE (USE LEMON JUICE FROM DIPPING AVOCADO. ADD JUICE FROM FRUIT SECTIONS)	75 ML
1 CUP	SALAD OIL	250 ML
1/2 CUP	SUGAR	125 ML
1 TSP	SALT	5 ML
1 TSP	GRATED ONION	5 ML
1 1/2 TBSP	POPPY SEEDS	22 ML
1/2 TSP	DRY MUSTARD	2 ML

SHAKE ALL INGREDIENTS TOGETHER UNTIL WELL BLENDED.

MY GARDEN'S A LITTLE JEWEL - 14 CARROTS!

MANDARIN ORANGE SALAD

1	CAN (10 OZ/284 ML) MANDARIN ORANGE SECTIONS (DRAINED)	1
1	MEDIUM AVOCADO	1
1	HEAD BUTTER LETTUCE OR ROMAINE	1
	SLICES OF RED ONION (THIN)	
	ITALIAN DRESSING	

AT SERVING TIME, TEAR LETTUCE INTO BITE-SIZE PIECES IN SALAD BOWL. ADD ORANGE SECTIONS AND SLICES OF AVOCADO AND THIN SLICES OF RED ONION. TOSS WITH SALAD DRESSING. THIS IS A COLORFUL, TASTY SALAD THAT SEEMS TO GO ALONG WITH ANY MEAL. SERVES 4.

PINK FROSTY SALAD

1	CAN (14 OZ/398 ML) PINEAPPLE CHUNKS	1
1	CAN (14 OZ/398 ML) WHOLE CRANBERRY SAUCE	1
6 OZ	CREAM CHEESE	175 G
2 TBSP	MAYONNAISE	25 ML
2 TBSP	SUGAR	25 ML
1/2 CUP	CHOPPED WALNUTS OR PECANS	125 ML
1 CUP	WHIPPED CREAM	250 ML

COMBINE CREAM CHEESE AND MAYONNAISE. ADD REMAINING INGREDIENTS AND PLACE IN A LIGHTLY GREASED MOLD. SET IN FREEZER. REMOVE TWO HOURS BEFORE SERVING AND UNMOLD. RETURN TO REFRIGERATOR UNTIL SERVING TIME. SERVES 6 TO 8.

POPPY SEED SALAD DRESSING

1/3 CUP	VINEGAR	75 ML
1/4 CUP	LIME JUICE	50 ML
3/4 CUP	SUGAR	175 ML
1 TSP	SALT	5 ML
1/2 TSP	ONION JUICE	2 ML
1 TSP	POPPY SEEDS	5 ML
1 TSP	DRY MUSTARD	5 ML
1 TSP	PAPRIKA	5 ML
1 CUP	SALAD OIL	250 ML

COMBINE VINEGAR AND LIME JUICE IN PAN, BRING TO A BOIL, THEN ADD ALL OTHER INGREDIENTS BUT OIL AND ONION JUICE, STIRRING TO DISSOLVE. ADD OIL AND JUICE, BEAT UNTIL THICKENED. COVER AND CHILL. SERVE ON FRESH FRUIT SALAD, EITHER AS FIRST COURSE OR DESSERT. MAKES ABOUT 2 CUPS (500 ML).

LADIES, STAY SINGLE. WHO NEEDS A HUSBAND? GET A DOG THAT GROWLS AND SLEEPS ALL DAY, A PARROT THAT SWEARS AND A CAT THAT STAYS OUT ALL NIGHT.

SPAGHETTI WITH EGGPLANT SAUCE

½ CUP	OLIVE OIL	125 ML
½ CUP	FINELY CHOPPED ONION	125 ML
2	CLOVES GARLIC, CRUSHED	2
1	MEDIUM EGGPLANT, PEELED AND CUBED	1
1 CUP	SLIVERED GREEN PEPPER	250 ML
3 CUPS	PEELED CHOPPED TOMATOES	750 ML
½ TSP	DRIED LEAF BASIL	2 ML
½ TSP	SALT	2 ML
¼ TSP	PEPPER	1 ML
½ CUP	SLIVERED RIPE OLIVES	125 ML
1 TBSP	CHOPPED CAPERS	15 ML
	COOKED SPAGHETTI	
	CHOPPED PARSLEY	
	PARMESAN CHEESE	

HEAT OIL IN HEAVY POT. ADD ONION AND GARLIC AND COOK GENTLY, STIRRING OFTEN, FOR 10 MINUTES. ADD EGGPLANT AND GREEN PEPPER AND CONTINUE COOKING FOR 5 MINUTES, STIRRING CONSTANTLY. ADD TOMATOES, BASIL, SALT AND PEPPER. COVER AND SIMMER 30 MINUTES, STIRRING OCCASIONALLY. ADD OLIVES AND CAPERS. COOK 5 MINUTES MORE.

SERVE OVER BUTTERED SPAGHETTI (WITH MEATBALLS IF DESIRED) GARNISH WITH CHOPPED PARSLEY AND PARMESAN CHEESE. SERVES 4 TO 6.

HOW DOES THE GUY WHO DRIVES THE SNOWPLOW GET TO WORK?

SATURDAY NIGHT SPECIAL

. . . OR SUNDAY . . . OR MONDAY . . . OR TUESDAY

1/2 LB	SPAGHETTI, BROKEN IN PIECES	250 G
I LB	GROUND BEEF	500 G
I	SMALL ONION, CHOPPED	I
I	GREEN PEPPER, CHOPPED	I
I CUP	FRESH MUSHROOMS, SLICED	250 ML
I	CAN (12 OZ/341 ML) KERNEL CORN OR I CUP (250 ML) FROZEN CORN	I
I CUP	GRATED CHEDDAR CHEESE	250 ML
I	CAN (10 OZ/284 ML) TOMATO SOUP	I
I	CAN (14 OZ/398 ML) TOMATOES	I
3/4 TSP	SALT	4 ML
1/2 TSP	CHILI POWDER	2 ML
1/2 TSP	WORCESTERSHIRE SAUCE	2 ML

IN A POT, BRING SALTED WATER TO A BOIL AND COOK SPAGHETTI UNTIL TENDER. DRAIN. IN A FRYING PAN, BROWN BEEF AND ONION. ADD GREEN PEPPER AND MUSHROOMS AND COOK UNTIL TENDER. IN A LARGE CASSEROLE, COMBINE BEEF MIXTURE WITH THE OTHER INGREDIENTS AND MIX WELL. BAKE AT 325°F (160°C) FOR 45 MINUTES. SERVE WITH FRENCH BREAD AND A TOSSED SALAD. SERVES 6 TO 8.

TOMORROW IS TODAY'S GREATEST LABOR-SAVING DEVICE.

LASAGNA

EVERYONE HAS A LASAGNA RECIPE,
BUT THIS IS OUR FAVORITE.

1½ LBS	GROUND BEEF	750 G
1	CAN (28 OZ/796 ML) TOMATOES	1
1	CAN (14 OZ/398 ML) SEASONED TOMATO SAUCE	1
2	ENVELOPES SPAGHETTI SAUCE MIX	2
2	CLOVES GARLIC, MINCED	2
8 OZ	LASAGNA OR BREAD NOODLES	250 G
2	PACKAGES (EACH 6 OR 8 OZ/175 OR 250 G) THIN SLICED MOZZARELLA CHEESE	2
1 CUP	CREAMED COTTAGE CHEESE	250 ML
½ CUP	GRATED PARMESAN CHEESE	125 ML

BROWN MEAT SLOWLY; DRAIN OFF EXCESS FAT. ADD NEXT FOUR INGREDIENTS. COVER AND SIMMER 40 MINUTES, STIRRING OCCASIONALLY. SALT TO TASTE. COOK NOODLES IN BOILING SALTED WATER UNTIL TENDER FOLLOWING PACKAGE INSTRUCTIONS. DRAIN. RINSE IN COLD WATER. PLACE HALF THE NOODLES IN 13- X 9-INCH (3 L) BAKING DISH. COVER WITH ONE-THIRD OF THE SAUCE, THEN LAYER HALF THE MOZZARELLA AND HALF THE COTTAGE CHEESE. REPEAT LAYERS ENDING WITH SAUCE. TOP WITH PARMESAN.

BAKE AT 350°F (180°C) FOR 25 TO 30 MINUTES. LET STAND 15 MINUTES. CUT IN SQUARES. SERVE WITH GREEN SALAD AND FRENCH BREAD. SERVES 6 TO 8.

CANNELLONI

PREPARE MINDLESS MEAT SAUCE (SEE PAGE 248)
AND CHICKEN FILLING AHEAD OF TIME AND THIS WILL
SEEM EFFORTLESS. REGARDLESS, THE RESULTS
ARE WORTH THE TIME INVOLVED.

CHICKEN FILLING

3	LARGE CHICKEN BREASTS, COOKED IN OVEN, RESERVE 1/2 CUP (125 ML) PAN JUICES FOR FILLING	3
2 TBSP	OIL	25 ML
1/4 CUP	MINCED ONION	50 ML
1/4 CUP	FINELY CHOPPED CELERY	50 ML
1/4 CUP	FINELY CHOPPED CARROT	50 ML
2 TBSP	MINCED PARSLEY	25 ML
3/4 TSP	SALT	4 ML
1/4 TSP	BASIL	1 ML
1/8 TSP	NUTMEG	0.5 ML
1/2 TSP	WHITE PEPPER	2 ML
1 CUP	RICOTTA OR CREAMED COTTAGE CHEESE	250 ML
2	EGG YOLKS	2
1/2 CUP	FRESH GROUND PARMESAN CHEESE	125 ML
1/2 CUP	CHICKEN BROTH	125 ML

CHEDDAR SAUCE

4 TBSP	MELTED BUTTER	60 ML
5 TBSP	FLOUR	75 ML
1	CAN (10 OZ/284 ML) CHICKEN BROTH	1
	SALT AND PEPPER TO TASTE	
1 CUP	GRATED CHEDDAR CHEESE	250 ML

CONTINUED ON NEXT PAGE...

1 CUP	MINDLESS MEAT SAUCE (PAGE 248)	250 ML
1/2 CUP	LIGHT CREAM	125 ML
1	PACKAGE KNORR'S SWISS HOLLANDAISE SAUCE OR YOUR OWN RECIPE	1
3	PACKAGES (EACH 6 OZ/175 G) MONTEREY JACK CHEESE	3
20	CANNELLONI SHELLS, OR 20 CRÊPES (SEE PAGE 58)	20

CHICKEN FILLING: COOK CHICKEN AND FINELY CHOP OR GRIND MEAT. COMBINE OIL, ONION, CELERY, CARROTS AND PARSLEY IN SAUCEPAN AND COOK FOR 10 MINUTES. BEAT EGG YOLKS IN LARGE BOWL, ADD PARMESAN CHEESE AND RICOTTA OR COTTAGE CHEESE AND BEAT UNTIL SMOOTH. ADD SALT, OREGANO, BASIL, NUTMEG AND PEPPER. ADD CHICKEN, PAN JUICE, CHICKEN BROTH. BEAT UNTIL WELL MIXED. THIS MAY BE COVERED AND REFRIGERATED OR FROZEN UNTIL READY TO USE.

CHEDDAR SAUCE: MELT BUTTER IN SAUCE PAN, ADD FLOUR UNTIL SMOOTH, THEN CAREFULLY ADD CHICKEN BROTH, STIRRING CONSTANTLY. ADD SALT AND PEPPER TO TASTE. STIR IN CHEDDAR CHEESE UNTIL WELL BLENDED AND THICK. NOW ADD PREPARED MEAT SAUCE AND CREAM. (SEE PAGE 248 FOR MINDLESS MEAT SAUCE.)

HOLLANDAISE SAUCE: PREPARE YOUR OWN OR COOK ACCORDING TO PACKAGE INSTRUCTIONS. ADD TO CHEDDAR SAUCE.

CONTINUED ON NEXT PAGE...

COOK CANNELLONI SHELLS IN BOILING, SALTED WATER FOR 8 MINUTES, DRAIN AND RINSE IN COLD WATER, OR HAVE CRÊPES PREPARED. DON'T BE CONCERNED IF SHELLS SPLIT. IT MAKES THEM EASIER TO FILL.

SPOON THIN LAYER OF SAUCE IN TWO 13- X 9-INCH (3 L) PANS. USING APPROXIMATELY 2 TBSP (25 ML) CHICKEN FILLING PER SHELL, SHAPE FILLING IN HANDS AND INSERT IN SHELL OR ROLL UP IN SHELL OR CRÊPE. PLACE IN PANS, SIDE BY SIDE, WITH 5 IN EACH ROW. CAREFULLY SPOON SAUCE AROUND CANNELLONI. COVER EACH CANNELLONI COMPLETELY WITH STRIPS OF MONTEREY JACK CHEESE. YOU REALLY CAN'T USE TOO MUCH. BAKE IN PREHEATED 425°F (220°C) OVEN FOR 10 MINUTES, UNTIL CHEESE IS BUBBLING. SERVE AT ONCE. MAKES 20 CANNELLONI, OR 10 SERVINGS.

NOTE: IF YOU'RE MAKING THE ENTIRE RECIPE IN ADVANCE, PREPARE TO THE BAKING STAGE AND FREEZE. AS THIS IS A RICH MEAL, SERVE WITH A GREEN SALAD AND ROLLS.

VOLUNTEER WORKERS ARE GOOD FOR NOTHING!

BEST SEAFOOD LASAGNA

A TASTY VARIATION OF AN OLD FAVORITE.

8	LASAGNA NOODLES	8
2 TBSP	BUTTER	25 ML
I CUP	CHOPPED ONION	250 ML
I	PACKAGE (8 OZ/250 G) CREAM CHEESE, SOFTENED	I
1½ CUPS	RICOTTA CHEESE	375 ML
I	EGG, BEATEN	I
2 TSP	BASIL	10 ML
½ TSP	SALT	2 ML
⅛ TSP	PEPPER	0.5 ML
2	CANS (EACH 10 OZ/284 ML) CREAM OF MUSHROOM SOUP	2
⅓ CUP	DRY WHITE WINE OR DRY VERMOUTH	75 ML
5 OZ	CRABMEAT	150 G
I LB	SHRIMP, DEVEINED AND COOKED	500 G
¼ CUP	GRATED PARMESAN CHEESE	50 ML
½ CUP	SHREDDED, SHARP (OLD) CHEDDAR CHEESE	125 ML

COOK NOODLES. PLACE 4 NOODLES IN A 13- X 9-INCH (3 L) BAKING DISH. COOK ONION IN BUTTER. ADD CHEESES, EGG, BASIL, SALT AND PEPPER. SPREAD HALF THE CHEESE MIXTURE OVER NOODLES. COMBINE SOUP AND WINE. STIR IN CRAB AND SHRIMP AND SPREAD HALF OVER CHEESE LAYER. REPEAT ALL LAYERS. SPRINKLE WITH PARMESAN AND CHEDDAR. BAKE, UNCOVERED, AT 350°F (180°C) FOR 45 MINUTES. LET STAND 15 MINUTES BEFORE SERVING. SERVES 8 TO 10. FREEZES WELL.

CHOP SUEY

A YUMMY WAY TO USE UP LEFTOVERS.

3 TBSP	SOY SAUCE	45 ML
1 TBSP	BROWN SUGAR	15 ML
2 CUPS	SLICED LEFTOVER ROAST PORK, BEEF OR CHICKEN	500 ML
2 TBSP	CORNSTARCH	25 ML
1 CUP	WATER	250 ML
1/4 CUP	VEGETABLE OIL	50 ML
1	MEDIUM ONION, SLICED	1
2	GARLIC CLOVES, MINCED	2
1	GREEN OR RED PEPPER, SLICED	1
3	CELERY STALKS, SLICED	3
2 CUPS	MUSHROOMS, SLICED	500 ML
	SALT AND PEPPER TO TASTE	
2 CUPS	FRESH BEAN SPROUTS	500 ML

COMBINE SOY SAUCE, BROWN SUGAR AND MIX WITH MEAT. LET STAND FOR 15 MINUTES. MIX CORNSTARCH WITH WATER AND SET ASIDE. NOW, YOU'RE READY TO START COOKING.

IN A WOK OR FRYING PAN OVER HIGH HEAT, HEAT OIL; ADD ONION; STIR FOR 2 MINUTES. ADD GARLIC AND SLICED VEGETABLES; STIR FOR 2 MINUTES. ADD MEAT MIXTURE; STIR FOR 2 MINUTES. ADD CORNSTARCH MIXTURE; STIR FOR 2 MINUTES. ADD BEAN SPROUTS; STIR FOR 2 MINUTES. NOW YOU'RE STIR CRAZY BUT DINNER'S READY! SERVE OVER RICE AND PASS THE SOY SAUCE. SERVES 6 TO 8.

STUFFED ARCTIC CHAR

1	WHOLE ARCTIC CHAR, DEBONED AS MUCH AS POSSIBLE (5 LBS/2.5 KG)	1
1 CUP	SOFTENED BUTTER	250 ML
1	LARGE ONION, CHOPPED	1
4	STALKS CELERY, CHOPPED	4
1	LARGE GREEN PEPPER, CHOPPED	1
	PIMENTO (JUST TO ADD SOME COLOR), SLICED	
	SALT AND PEPPER TO TASTE	

MIX BUTTER, ONION, CELERY, GREEN PEPPER, PIMENTO, SALT AND PEPPER. FILL THE FISH CAVITY WITH MIXTURE. SECURE THE FISH BY TYING IN SEVERAL PLACES WITH STRING. RUB GENEROUSLY WITH BUTTER. WRAP IN FOIL. PLACE IN ROASTING PAN ON TRIVET AND ADD ENOUGH WATER TO COVER THE BOTTOM (ADD MORE WATER AS NEEDED THROUGHOUT COOKING TIME. BAKE FOR 50 MINUTES AT 350°F (180°C). SERVES 6.

BRIDGE WEEKEND CONVERSATION: "I WENT TO BED WITHOUT BRUSHING MY TEETH – I COULDN'T FIND MY TOOTHBRUSH."
REPLY: "I COULDN'T FIND MY TEETH!"

BAKED SOLE ROULADE

1 1/2 LBS	FROZEN RAW SHRIMP	750 G
1 1/2 CUPS	SOFT BREAD CRUMBS	375 ML
1	EGG, BEATEN	1
1/2 TSP	JOHNNY'S SEAFOOD SEASONING	2 ML
6	SOLE FILLETS	6
1/2 TSP	SALT	2 ML
2 TBSP	BUTTER	25 ML
2 TBSP	LEMON JUICE	25 ML
1	PACKAGE "KNORR-SWISS" HOLLANDAISE SAUCE MIX	1

COOK SHRIMP ACCORDING TO PACKAGE DIRECTIONS. DRAIN AND SET 6 ASIDE. CHOP REMAINING SHRIMP AND MIX WITH BREAD CRUMBS, EGG AND SEAFOOD SEASONING. LAY FISH ON WAX PAPER; SPREAD SHRIMP MIXTURE EVENLY OVER EACH FILLET. ROLL UP JELLY-ROLL FASHION AND SECURE WITH TOOTHPICKS. PLACE SEAM-SIDE DOWN IN BAKING DISH. SPRINKLE WITH SALT AND LEMON JUICE. DOT WITH BUTTER. COVER AND BAKE AT 350°F (180°C) FOR 30 MINUTES OR UNTIL FISH FLAKES EASILY. PREPARE HOLLANDAISE SAUCE AND KEEP WARM. LIFT FISH CAREFULLY FROM BAKING DISH AND REMOVE PICKS. SPOON PART OF HOLLANDAISE OVER THE TOPS AND GARNISH WITH SET-ASIDE SHRIMP. SERVE REMAINING SAUCE SEPARATELY. SERVES 6.

MONEY TALKS, BUT IT DOESN'T SAY WHEN IT'S COMING BACK.

YOU GOTTA HAVE "SOLE"

4	SOLE FILLETS (OR ANY WHITE FISH)	4
1/2 CUP	SOFTENED BUTTER	125 ML
I CUP	GRATED PARMESAN	250 ML

SPREAD HALF THE BUTTER IN A SHALLOW BAKING PAN.
SPRINKLE ON HALF THE CHEESE. ARRANGE FILLETS IN
SINGLE LAYER ON TOP, DOT WITH REMAINING BUTTER
AND SPRINKLE ON THE REMAINING CHEESE. BAKE AT
400°F (200°C), BASTING WITH MELTED BUTTER AND
CHEESE UNTIL FISH FLAKES, ABOUT 15 MINUTES. SERVE
WITH DRIPPINGS. SERVES 4.

BAR-B-QUED SALMON STEAKS

*IF THE FAMILY FISHERMAN HAS BEEN SUCCESSFUL,
OR YOU HAVE BEEN GIFTED WITH (OH JOY, OH RAPTURE)
A SALMON, TRY THIS.*

	SALMON STEAKS, CUT AT LEAST I INCH (2.5 CM) THICK	
1/2 CUP	BUTTER	125 ML
I 1/2 TSP	SALT	7 ML
2 TBSP	LEMON JUICE	25 ML
I 1/2 TBSP	MUSTARD POWDER	22 ML
	PEPPER TO TASTE	

COMBINE LAST 5 INGREDIENTS IN A SMALL BOWL. BAR-B-QUE
SALMON ON GRILL 4 INCHES (10 CM) FROM HOT COALS FOR
6 TO 8 MINUTES EACH SIDE. DON'T OVERCOOK. BASTE
FREQUENTLY WITH MIXTURE IN BOWL WITH A PASTRY BRUSH.
SERVE WITH LEMON WEDGES, A HUGE GREEN SALAD AND
FRENCH BREAD - MARVELOUS!

RICE AND OLIVE
STUFFING FOR SALMON

THIS IS A SUPERB STUFFING FOR A 10- TO 12-LB
(5 TO 6 KG) SALMON. IF THERE IS ANY LEFT OVER,
WRAP IN FOIL AND COOK BESIDE FISH.

1/2 CUP	BUTTER	125 ML
1 1/2 CUPS	MINCED ONION	375 ML
2 CUPS	DICED CELERY	500 ML
2 2/3 CUPS	COOKED RICE	650 ML
2 CUPS	CHOPPED STUFFED OLIVES	500 ML
1/2 TSP	SALT	2 ML
1/2 TSP	DRIED SAGE	2 ML
1/2 TSP	PEPPER	2 ML
1/2 TSP	THYME	2 ML

MELT BUTTER IN SKILLET. SAUTÉ ONION AND CELERY
UNTIL TENDER. ADD RICE AND REMAINING INGREDIENTS.
TOSS. SPOON INTO CAVITY OF FISH (DON'T PACK) AND
SEW UP WITH NEEDLE AND THREAD. MESSY JOB - BUT
WORTH IT! SPREAD A LITTLE BUTTER (OR A LOT OF
MAYONNAISE) OVER FISH, TOP WITH 3 OR 4 LEMON
SLICES AND WRAP LOOSELY IN FOIL. SET IN BROILING PAN
AND COOK 10 MINUTES PER INCH OF THICKNESS AT 425°F
(220°C) (OR UNTIL FORK TENDER). SERVES 6 TO 8.

SERVING SUGGESTION: INSTEAD OF SERVING WITH
ADDITIONAL LEMON WEDGES, MAKE A SAUCE USING EQUAL
PROPORTIONS OF MELTED BUTTER AND DRY WHITE WINE.

ALWAYS GET MARRIED EARLY IN THE MORNING. THAT WAY, IF IT
DOESN'T WORK OUT, YOU HAVEN'T WASTED THE WHOLE DAY.

CHILLED SALMON SOUFFLÉ

1½ TBSP	UNFLAVORED GELATIN	22 ML
½ CUP	COLD TOMATO JUICE	125 ML
1	CAN (10 OZ/284 ML) CREAM OF SHRIMP SOUP	1
¾ CUP	MILK	175 ML
4	EGGS, SEPARATED	4
¼ CUP	LEMON JUICE	50 ML
1½ TSP	PREPARED HORSERADISH	7 ML
1½ TSP	SALT	7 ML
1 CUP	WHIPPING CREAM	250 ML
1	CAN (15½ OZ/440 G) SALMON, DRAINED AND FLAKED	1
1 TBSP	SNIPPED PARSLEY	15 ML

SPRINKLE GELATIN OVER TOMATO JUICE AND LET STAND 5 MINUTES TO SOFTEN. ADD SOUP AND MILK AND HEAT TO A SIMMER, STIRRING CONSTANTLY, UNTIL GELATIN IS DISSOLVED. STIR A LITTLE OF THE HOT MIXTURE INTO WELL-BEATEN EGG YOLKS. RETURN TO SAUCE PAN AND COOK 2 MINUTES LONGER. ADD LEMON JUICE, HORSERADISH AND SALT. CHILL UNTIL PARTIALLY SET. BEAT EGG WHITES UNTIL STIFF BUT NOT DRY. WHIP CREAM UNTIL SOFTLY STIFF. FOLD EGG WHITES, CREAM AND SALMON INTO CHILLED MIXTURE. TURN INTO A 4-CUP (1 L) SOUFFLÉ DISH THAT HAS BEEN EXTENDED WITH A 2-INCH (5 CM) PAPER COLLAR. CHILL UNTIL SET. REMOVE COLLAR AND GARNISH WITH PARSLEY. SERVES 6 TO 8.

AFTER ALL IS SAID AND DONE,
MORE IS USUALLY SAID THAN DONE.

COQUILLE DAVID

OUR FRIEND DAVID IS A GREAT COOK. THIS FRENCH CLASSIC IS HIS SIGNATURE DISH.

1 LB	SCALLOPS	500 G
1/2 LB	FRESH MUSHROOMS, SLICED	250 G
1 CUP	DRY WHITE WINE OR 3/4 CUP (175 ML) DRY VERMOUTH	250 ML
1/2 TSP	SALT	2 ML
4	PEPPERCORNS	4
2	SLICES OF ONION	2
1	BAY LEAF	1
1/4 TSP	THYME	1 ML

SAUCE

3 TBSP	BUTTER	45 ML
4 TBSP	FLOUR	60 ML
3/4 CUP	MILK	175 ML
2	EGG YOLKS	2
1/2 CUP	WHIPPING CREAM	125 ML
PINCH	CAYENNE	PINCH
	SALT TO TASTE	
2 TBSP	DRY SHERRY OR BRANDY	25 ML
1/2 CUP	SWISS CHEESE, GRATED	125 ML

RINSE SCALLOPS IN COLD WATER. COMBINE SCALLOPS AND MUSHROOMS IN A SAUCEPAN WITH NEXT 6 INGREDIENTS AND ENOUGH WATER TO BARELY COVER. BRING TO BOIL, COVER AND SIMMER GENTLY FOR 5 MINUTES. REMOVE SCALLOPS AND MUSHROOMS. STRAIN LIQUID AND BOIL

CONTINUED ON NEXT PAGE...

RAPIDLY UNTIL REDUCED TO 1 CUP (250 ML). REMOVE SCALLOPS AND CUT INTO SMALL PIECES.

SAUCE: IN A DOUBLE BOILER, MELT BUTTER AND STIR IN FLOUR. SLOWLY ADD HOT SCALLOP LIQUID AND MILK, STIRRING CONSTANTLY, UNTIL THICK. MIX EGG YOLKS AND CREAM TOGETHER, ADD SOME OF THE HOT SAUCE AND RETURN ALL TO SAUCEPAN. COOK OVER LOW HEAT FOR APPROXIMATELY 5 MINUTES. SEASON TO TASTE WITH SALT AND CAYENNE. FOLD IN SHERRY, MUSHROOMS AND SCALLOPS. SPOON INTO BUTTERED SCALLOP SHELLS (FOR APPETIZERS) OR ONION SOUP BOWLS (FOR MAIN COURSE), AND SPRINKLE WITH SWISS CHEESE. BAKE AT 375°F (190°C) UNTIL LIGHT BROWN AND BUBBLY – ABOUT 15 MINUTES. SERVES 6 AS AN APPETIZER OR 4 AS A MAIN COURSE.

NOTE: $\frac{1}{2}$ CUP (125 ML) BUTTERED BREAD CRUMBS MAY BE SPRINKLED OVER THE CHEESE BEFORE BAKING IF DESIRED. THIS MAY BE MADE AHEAD AND REFRIGERATED BEFORE BAKING.

THE BEST WAY TO GET A GOOD CUP OF COFFEE IN THE MORNING IS TO WAKE UP YOUR SPOUSE FIRST.

SCALLOPS IN WINE

ALWAYS A HIT – AND YOU CAN MAKE IT AHEAD.

2 LBS	SCALLOPS	1 KG
2 CUPS	DRY WHITE WINE	500 ML
1/4 CUP	BUTTER	50 ML
4	FINELY CHOPPED SHALLOTS	4
24	FINELY SLICED MUSHROOM CAPS	24
2 TBSP	MINCED PARSLEY	25 ML
2 TBSP	FLOUR	25 ML
2 TO 4 TBSP	HEAVY CREAM	25 TO 60 ML
	BREAD CRUMBS	

WASH SCALLOPS WELL. SIMMER IN WINE ABOUT 5 MINUTES.
DRAIN AND RESERVE THE LIQUID. MELT BUTTER AND SAUTÉ
SHALLOTS, MUSHROOM CAPS, PARSLEY. STIR IN FLOUR
UNTIL BLENDED. ADD RESERVED LIQUID AND HEAVY CREAM.
ADD SCALLOPS TO HOT SAUCE. PLACE IN SHALLOW
CASSEROLE OR INDIVIDUAL SCALLOP SHELLS AND COVER
WITH DRY BREAD CRUMBS. DOT WITH BUTTER AND PLACE
UNDER BROILER UNTIL GOLDEN BROWN. SERVES 8.

*GIVE A BOY ENOUGH ROPE AND HE'LL BRING HOME
A STRAY DOG ON THE END OF IT.*

OYSTER SCALLOP

2 CUPS	OYSTERS, SLICED, PLUS LIQUID	500 ML
2 TBSP	MILK	25 ML
1/2 CUP	WHITE BREAD CRUMBS (DAY OLD)	125 ML
1 CUP	CRUSHED CRACKERS	250 ML
	SALT AND PEPPER	

IN A 4-CUP (1 L) CASSEROLE ARRANGE FIRST A LAYER OF OYSTERS, THEN BREAD CRUMBS AND CRACKERS, THEN BUTTER AND MILK. REPEAT AND TOP WITH A LAYER OF CRUMBS. BAKE AT 350°F (180°C) FOR 30 MINUTES. SERVES 6.

PARTY SHRIMP

THIS RECIPE MAY BE USED AS AN APPETIZER OR EVENING BRIDGE MENU, DOUBLED, SERVED ALONG WITH HOT ROLLS AND A BEVERAGE.

1/4 CUP	BUTTER OR MARGARINE (MELTED)	50 ML
1/2 CUP	GRATED PARMESAN CHEESE	125 ML
1/2 CUP	DRY BREAD CRUMBS	125 ML
1/4 CUP	LEMON JUICE	50 ML
2/3 CUP	CHOPPED GREEN ONIONS	150 ML
1	GARLIC CLOVE, MINCED	1
1/4 TSP	SALT	1 ML
1 LB	COOKED, PEELED DEVEINED SHRIMP	500 G
	FRESH PARSLEY	

COMBINE ALL INGREDIENTS. PLACE IN FOUR INDIVIDUAL SHELLS OR CASSEROLES. BAKE AT 350°F (180°C) FOR 20 TO 25 MINUTES. GARNISH WITH PARSLEY. SERVES 4.

SHRIMP IN FOIL

2	PACKAGES (EACH 10 OZ/300 G) CHOPPED (FROZEN) SPINACH	2
1 1/2 LBS	SHRIMP (FROZEN COOKED)	750 G
1/4 CUP	BUTTER OR MARGARINE	50 ML
1/4 CUP	FLOUR	50 ML
1 1/2 CUPS	MILK	375 ML
1/2 CUP	WHITE WINE	125 ML
1/2 CUP	SCALLIONS (OR GREEN ONION)	125 ML
	SALT, PEPPER, PAPRIKA	
1 CUP	SHREDDED CHEDDAR CHEESE	250 ML

PREHEAT OVEN TO 350°F (180°C). LINE 9-INCH (23 CM) PIE PLATE WITH HEAVY FOIL. THAW AND DRAIN SPINACH. SPREAD IN PAN AND TOP WITH SHRIMP. IN SAUCE PAN, MELT BUTTER AND STIR IN FLOUR. ADD MILK GRADUALLY WITH WINE AND ONIONS. COOK, STIRRING CONSTANTLY OVER LOW HEAT UNTIL SAUCE BUBBLES AND THICKENS. ADD SALT, PEPPER TO TASTE AND ENOUGH PAPRIKA TO MAKE A ROSY COLOR. POUR OVER SHRIMP AND SPRINKLE WITH CHEESE. BAKE IN OVEN 35 MINUTES OR UNTIL BUBBLY. THIS MAY BE MADE AHEAD AND FROZEN. WHEN READY TO USE, BAKE UNCOVERED FOR 1 HOUR. SERVES 6.

DON'T TRY TO MAKE ENDS MEET. JUST ABOUT THE TIME YOU MANAGE TO MAKE ENDS MEET... YOUR WIFE MOVES THE ENDS.

Frosted Waldorf Salad (page 131)

Spaghetti with Eggplant Sauce (page 143)

Best Seafood Lasagna (page 149)

Seafood Curry (page 168)

SHRIMP STROGANOFF

1/4 CUP	MINCED ONION	50 ML
1/4 CUP	BUTTER	50 ML
1 1/2 LBS	PEELED AND DEVEINED SHRIMP	750 G
1/2 LB	MUSHROOMS (SLICED)	250 G
1 TBSP	FLOUR	15 ML
1 1/2 CUPS	SOUR CREAM	375 ML
1 1/4 TSP	SALT	6 ML
	PEPPER TO TASTE	
1 TBSP	BUTTER	15 ML

IN LARGE SKILLET SAUTÉ MINCED ONION IN 1/4 CUP (50 ML) BUTTER UNTIL SOFTENED. ADD SHRIMP; SAUTÉ FOR 3 TO 5 MINUTES OR UNTIL PINK AND JUST COOKED. TRANSFER MIXTURE TO HEATED DISH AND KEEP WARM. ADD TO SKILLET MUSHROOMS AND 1 TBSP (15 ML) BUTTER. SAUTÉ OVER MEDIUM-HIGH HEAT UNTIL BROWNED. SPRINKLE FLOUR AND COOK, STIRRING FOR 2 MINUTES. REDUCE HEAT TO MEDIUM-LOW AND STIR IN SHRIMP MIXTURE, SOUR CREAM (AT ROOM TEMPERATURE). ADD SALT AND PEPPER. COOK, STIRRING FOR 2 TO 3 MINUTES OR UNTIL SHRIMP ARE HEATED THROUGH. DO NOT BOIL! SERVES 6.

ONLY ONE PERFECT WOMAN EVER EXISTED – THE WOMAN YOUR HUSBAND COULD HAVE MARRIED.

SCAMPI

¼ CUP	BUTTER	50 ML
¼ CUP	SALAD OR OLIVE OIL	50 ML
1 TBSP	GARLIC POWDER	15 ML
1 TSP	SALT	5 ML
PINCH	CAYENNE	PINCH
2 TBSP	LEMON JUICE	25 ML
3	GREEN ONIONS, CHOPPED	3
1 LB	LARGE SHRIMP, PEELED AND DEVEINED	500 G

PREHEAT OVEN TO 400°F (200°C). IN A LARGE OVENPROOF
SKILLET OR SERVING DISH, COMBINE FIRST 7 INGREDIENTS,
MELT AND MIX WELL. ADD SHRIMP AND COAT WITH BUTTER
MIXTURE. BAKE 8 TO 10 MINUTES OR UNTIL TENDER.
GARNISH WITH LEMON WEDGES. SERVES 4.

THE MOON NOT ONLY PULLS THE OCEANS
BACK AND FORTH IN THE TIDES, IT STOPS
CARS ON THE SIDES OF THE ROADS.

CURRIED CRAB TETRAZZINI

GREAT WITH A GREEN SALAD AFTER
A LATE-NIGHT BRIDGE.

2	CANS (EACH 6½ OZ/184 G) CRABMEAT	2
1 TBSP	LEMON JUICE	15 ML
4 TBSP	BUTTER	60 ML
4 TBSP	FLOUR	60 ML
2 CUPS	MILK	500 ML
1 TSP	SALT	5 ML
½ TSP	PEPPER	2 ML
1 TSP	CURRY POWDER	5 ML
¾ CUP	GRATED CHEDDAR	175 ML
1½ CUPS	COOKED FLAT NOODLES, DRAINED	375 ML
½ CUP	CRUMBLED POTATO CHIPS	125 ML

FLAKE CRAB; SPRINKLE WITH LEMON JUICE. MELT BUTTER OVER LOW HEAT. ADD AND BLEND FLOUR. COOK AT LEAST 3 MINUTES. STIR IN MILK SLOWLY. CONTINUE STIRRING UNTIL SAUCE IS SMOOTH, THICKENED. ADD SEASONINGS. ADD ½ CUP (125 ML) CHEESE TO SAUCE. ADD CRAB AND NOODLES AND SPOON INTO BUTTERED 8-CUP (2 L) CASSEROLE. TOP WITH CRUMBLED CHIPS AND REMAINING CHEESE. BAKE AT 350°F (180°C) FOR 30 MINUTES.

SERVES 6.

TWO CAN LIVE AS CHEAPLY AS ONE LARGE FAMILY USED TO.

LOBSTER NEWBURG

THIS IS A SPECIAL DISH AND REQUIRES SPECIAL CARE.
IT _MUST_ BE COOKED SLOWLY AT LOW HEAT OR IT WILL
SEPARATE. IT ALSO SUFFERS WITH REHEATING,
SO SERVE IMMEDIATELY.

1/3 CUP	BUTTER	75 ML
2 TBSP	FLOUR	25 ML
2 CUPS	CREAM	500 ML
4	SLIGHTLY BEATEN EGG YOLKS	4
2	CANS (EACH 5 OZ/142 G) LOBSTER	2
1 CUP	SLICED, FRESH MUSHROOMS (SAUTÉED)	250 ML
1/4 CUP	SHERRY	50 ML
2 TSP	LEMON JUICE	10 ML
1/4 TSP	SALT	1 ML
6	PATTIE SHELLS (FROZEN OR FRESH)	6

IN DOUBLE BOILER, MELT BUTTER AND BLEND IN FLOUR.
GRADUALLY STIR IN CREAM. COOK SLOWLY, STIRRING
CONSTANTLY UNTIL THICKENED. STIR SMALL AMOUNT
OF SAUCE INTO EGG YOLKS. RETURN TO HOT MIXTURE
AND COOK, STIRRING CONSTANTLY FOR ONE MINUTE.
ADD LOBSTER, SHERRY, LEMON JUICE AND SALT AND
MUSHROOMS. HEAT THROUGH AND STIR. DO NOT BOIL!
SERVE OVER PATTIE SHELLS. SPRINKLE WITH PAPRIKA
AND GARNISH WITH CELERY AND BLACK OLIVES.
SERVES 6.

REMEMBER THE GOLDEN RULE:
THOSE THAT HAVE THE GOLD MAKE THE RULES.

CREAMED SEAFOOD

A TASTY DISH TO SERVE TO THE LADIES FOR
LUNCH OR BRIDGE THAT <u>CAN</u> BE REHEATED.

8	PATTIE SHELLS (PEPPERIDGE FARM FROZEN PATTIE SHELLS ARE SUPER - RIGHT THERE IN YOUR FREEZER AND THEY NEVER FAIL!)	8
I LB	SMALL COOKED SHRIMP, KING CRAB OR LOBSTER	500 G
I 1/2 CUPS	SLICED FRESH MUSHROOMS	375 ML
I TBSP	CHOPPED FRESH PARSLEY	15 ML
1/2 CUP	SHERRY	125 ML
4 TBSP	BUTTER	60 ML
4 TBSP	FLOUR	60 ML
2 CUPS	MILK	500 ML
	SALT AND PEPPER TO TASTE	

BROWN MUSHROOMS IN 2 TBSP (25 ML) BUTTER. PREPARE
WHITE SAUCE: MELT BUTTER OVER LOW HEAT. ADD AND
BLEND FLOUR; COOK AT LEAST 3 MINUTES. STIR IN MILK
SLOWLY. CONTINUE STIRRING TILL SAUCE IS SMOOTH
AND THICKENED. ADD SHERRY. ADD SEAFOOD, COOKED
MUSHROOMS AND PARSLEY. HEAT THROUGH. SERVE OVER
PATTIES AND GARNISH WITH A SPRIG OF PARSLEY, RIPE
OLIVES, CARROT CURLS AND CELERY STICKS. TO REHEAT,
PLACE OVER DOUBLE BOILER. SERVES 8.

SPEAK WELL OF YOUR ENEMIES - REMEMBER, YOU MADE THEM.

SHELLFISH PUKÉ

*(THAT'S "POO-KAY.") SERVE WITH GREEN SALAD
AND ROLLS – YOU'LL LOVE IT.*

2	ONIONS, SLICED	2
4 CUPS	WATER	1 L
1	SMALL LEMON, SLICED	1
1½ TSP	SALT	7 ML
1 LB	SCALLOPS	500 G
1 LB	SHRIMP, SHELLED	500 G
½ LB	COOKED CRABMEAT, FLAKED	250 G
2 CUPS	STALE BREAD CRUMBS	500 ML
2 CUPS	MILK	500 ML
2 TBSP	BUTTER	25 ML
⅓ CUP	DRY SHERRY	75 ML
1 TSP	SALT	5 ML
½ TSP	WHITE PEPPER	2 ML
2 OR 3	DROPS TABASCO	2 OR 3
⅓ LB	MONTEREY JACK CHEESE, THINLY SLICED	160 G
3 TBSP	PARMESAN CHEESE	45 ML
2 TBSP	BUTTER, SOFTENED	25 ML

COMBINE 4 CUPS (1 L) WATER, ONE SLICED ONION, LEMON
AND 1½ TSP (7 ML) SALT IN A LARGE SAUCEPAN AND BRING
TO A BOIL. REDUCE HEAT TO MODERATELY LOW AND ADD
SCALLOPS. POACH FOR 2 OR 3 MINUTES AND TRANSFER
WITH A SLOTTED SPOON TO A BOWL. AFTER POACHING,
DON'T THROW OUT LIQUID! ADD SHRIMP TO SAUCEPAN
AND SIMMER 3 MINUTES OR UNTIL PINK. TRANSFER THEM

CONTINUED ON NEXT PAGE...

TO A BOWL. RESERVE COOKING LIQUID, DISCARDING ONION AND LEMON. CUT SCALLOPS INTO $\frac{1}{4}$-INCH (0.5 CM) SLICES. IF LARGE SHRIMP ARE USED, CUT THEM LENGTHWISE. IN A LARGE BOWL, COMBINE SHELLFISH WITH CRABMEAT.

COMBINE BREAD CRUMBS AND MILK IN A SAUCEPAN AND COOK OVER MODERATE HEAT. STIR UNTIL IT IS THE CONSISTENCY OF A PASTE. IN A SMALL SAUCEPAN COOK SECOND ONION IN 2 TBSP (25 ML) BUTTER OVER MODERATE HEAT, UNTIL SOFTENED. ADD THE ONION MIXTURE, SHERRY AND ENOUGH OF THE RESERVED LIQUID TO THE PASTE TO THIN IT TO THE CONSISTENCY OF SOUR CREAM. SEASON WITH 1 TSP (5 ML) SALT, WHITE PEPPER AND TABASCO.

IN BUTTERED CASSEROLE ARRANGE A LAYER OF SEAFOOD, SPREAD WITH A LAYER OF PASTE AND THEN MONTEREY JACK CHEESE. CONTINUE TO LAYER, ENDING WITH CHEESE. SPRINKLE ON PARMESAN AND DOT WITH SOFTENED BUTTER. PREHEAT OVEN TO 350°F (180°C) AND BAKE FOR 30 MINUTES OR UNTIL BUBBLING. (COOKING HINT: WHEN MEASURING SHERRY FOR CREAM SAUCE, MEASURE SOME FOR THE COOK.) SERVES 6.

THE MAN WHO CAN SMILE WHEN THINGS GO WRONG HAS THOUGHT OF SOMEONE ELSE HE CAN BLAME IT ON.

SEAFOOD CURRY

I HAVE A FRIEND WHO WOULD COME OVER ANY TIME OF THE DAY OR NIGHT FOR THIS MALAYSIAN DISH. (SECRETLY, I THINK HE LIKES THE CONDIMENTS BEST!) IT'S A BIT OF A PRODUCTION BUT THE ACCOLADES MAKE UP FOR THE EFFORT.

4 TBSP	BUTTER	60 ML
2 CUPS	CHOPPED (FINE) ONIONS	500 ML
I	MINCED GARLIC CLOVE	I
2 TSP	SALT	10 ML
2 TSP	POWDERED GINGER	10 ML
I TSP	GROUND CORIANDER	5 ML
2 TBSP	GROUND ALMONDS	25 ML
1/4 TSP	CUMIN SEED	I ML
3/4 TSP	DRIED GROUND CHILI PEPPERS	4 ML
I TSP	TURMERIC	5 ML
I	CAN (19 OZ/540 ML) TOMATOES	I
I TBSP	CORNSTARCH	15 ML
2 CUPS	COCONUT MILK (POUR BOILING WATER OVER I PACKAGE UNSWEETENED, SHREDDED COCONUT AND LET STAND I HOUR. STRAIN COCONUT; RESERVE LIQUID)	500 ML
I LB	LOBSTER, SHRIMP OR CRAB, CUBED	500 G
2	CUCUMBERS, PEELED AND CUBED	2
I TBSP	LIME OR LEMON JUICE	15 ML
I TSP	SUGAR	5 ML

PREPARE COCONUT MILK. MELT BUTTER IN A SAUCEPAN. SAUTÉ ONIONS AND GARLIC UNTIL CLEAR. STIR IN SALT, GINGER, CORIANDER, ALMONDS, CUMIN, CHILI PEPPERS,

CONTINUED ON NEXT PAGE...

TURMERIC AND TOMATOES. COVER AND COOK OVER LOW HEAT 4 MINUTES. SPRINKLE WITH CORNSTARCH AND GRADUALLY ADD COCONUT MILK, STIRRING CONSTANTLY UNTIL THICKENED. ADD SEAFOOD AND COOK OVER LOW HEAT 10 MINUTES, ADD CUCUMBERS, LIME JUICE AND SUGAR. COOK 5 MINUTES. SERVE OVER RICE. (BROWN RICE IS BEST.) SERVES 8.

CONDIMENTS TO SERVE WITH CURRY:

1. BANANAS IN GINGER SAUCE: SQUEEZE JUICE OF ONE LEMON. ADD SUGAR AND GINGER TO TASTE. POUR OVER 2 OR 3 BANANAS SLICED INTO STRIPS.

2. MANDARIN ORANGES IN COCONUT: DRAIN ONE CAN (10 OZ/284 ML) MANDARIN ORANGES. ROAST COCONUT ($1/3$ CUP/75 ML) AND SUGAR (2 TSP/10 ML) UNDER BROILER. POUR HOT COCONUT OVER MANDARIN ORANGES AND MIX.

IF YOU CAN SLEEP LIKE A BABY, YOU DON'T HAVE ONE.

JAMBALAYA

A RECIPE THAT REMINDS ME OF EVERY ROMANTIC BOOK ABOUT THE "OLD SOUTH."

2 CUPS	DICED HAM	500 ML
2 TBSP	BUTTER	25 ML
2	CHICKEN BREASTS	2
6	SLICES BACON, COOKED AND CRUMBLED IN LARGE PIECES	6
1	CAN (6½ OZ/184 G) BROKEN SHRIMP	1
1	LARGE ONION, DICE FINELY	1
6	STALKS CELERY, CHOPPED	6
3 CUPS	COOKED RICE	750 ML
1	CAN (28 OZ/796 ML) TOMATOES, WITH JUICE, CHOPPED	1
1 TSP	SALT	5 ML
½ TSP	PEPPER	2 ML
½ TSP	THYME	2 ML
½ TSP	WORCESTERSHIRE SAUCE	2 ML
	TABASCO TO TASTE	

IN LARGE SKILLET, SAUTÉ CHICKEN BREASTS IN BUTTER 20 MINUTES OR UNTIL COOKED. REMOVE DEBONE AND DICE THE CHICKEN. SAUTÉ ONION AND CELERY UNTIL TRANSPARENT. COOK RICE ACCORDING TO PACKAGE DIRECTIONS. COMBINE ALL INGREDIENTS IN SKILLET AND HEAT THROUGH FOR 10 MINUTES. THIS FREEZES WELL; ADD WATER OR TOMATO JUICE IF IT APPEARS DRY. SERVES 6.

WHEN YOUR SHIP FINALLY COMES IN, YOU WILL USUALLY FIND RELATIVES WAITING AT THE DOCK.

CHICKEN IN WINE

VERY QUICK – AND VERY GOOD!

3 LBS	CUT-UP CHICKEN PIECES	1.5 KG
1/2 CUP	SEASONED FLOUR	125 ML
6 TBSP	OIL	90 ML
2 CUPS	SLICED FRESH MUSHROOMS	500 ML
1 TBSP	BUTTER	15 ML
1	CAN (10 OZ/284 ML) MUSHROOM SOUP	1
1/2 CUP	CHICKEN BROTH	125 ML
1/2 CUP	ORANGE JUICE	125 ML
1/2 CUP	DRY WHITE WINE (VERMOUTH IS FINE)	125 ML
1 TBSP	BROWN SUGAR	15 ML
1/2 TSP	SALT	2 ML
4	CARROTS, SLICED	4

WASH AND PAT DRY CHICKEN PIECES. PUT FLOUR IN PLASTIC BAG AND SHAKE CHICKEN IN IT. IN FRYING PAN, HEAT OIL AND BROWN CHICKEN. REMOVE CHICKEN TO LARGE CASSEROLE. COOK MUSHROOMS IN BUTTER AND ADD TO CASSEROLE. COMBINE REMAINING INGREDIENTS; POUR OVER CHICKEN AND MUSHROOMS AND BAKE AT 350°F (180°C) FOR 1 HOUR. SERVE OVER RICE WITH A FRESH GREEN SALAD. SERVES 6.

IF THE SHOE FITS, BUY THE OTHER ONE TOO.

ALMOND CHICKEN

*IF YOU HAVE A WOK IT WILL COME IN HANDY
FOR THIS RECIPE.*

2	CHICKEN BREASTS	2
3 TBSP	OIL	45 ML
4	WATER CHESTNUTS	4
2 CUPS	CHOPPED CELERY	500 ML
I CUP	FRESH MUSHROOMS	250 ML
I CUP	CHOPPED ONION	250 ML
I	PACKAGE (6 OZ/175 G) ALMONDS, SLIVERED	I
I TO 2 TBSP	DRY WHITE WINE	15 TO 25 ML
3 TBSP	SOY SAUCE	45 ML
1/2 CUP	WATER	125 ML
2 TSP	SALT	10 ML
PINCH	PEPPER	PINCH
1/2 TSP	MINCED GARLIC	2 ML
I TBSP	CORNSTARCH	15 ML

REMOVE SKIN AND BONES FROM CHICKEN. WASH, DRAIN
AND DRY. DICE. SPRINKLE WITH WINE, PEPPER AND SALT.
DICE MUSHROOMS, CELERY, ONION AND CHESTNUTS.
DRAIN, DRY AND MIX TOGETHER. SET ASIDE. HEAT FRYING
PAN TO MEDIUM HEAT. ADD I TBSP (15 ML) OIL. BROWN
ALMONDS FOR 2 MINUTES. STIR CONSTANTLY. REMOVE
FROM PAN. HEAT I TBSP (15 ML) OIL, BROWN GARLIC
SLIGHTLY. ADD CHICKEN. STIR AND TOSS I MINUTE.
REMOVE FROM STOVE AND SET ASIDE. HEAT PAN WITH
I TBSP (15 ML) OIL ON HIGH. ADD VEGETABLES. STIR-FRY

CONTINUED ON NEXT PAGE...

3 MINUTES. SPRINKLE WITH SOY SAUCE. ADD WATER.
COVER AND COOK 3 MINUTES. THICKEN WITH CORNSTARCH
AND SPRINKLE WITH ALMONDS. SERVE WITH RICE.
SERVES 4.

LEMON CHICKEN

SO EASY AND SO YUMMY.

4	WHOLE CHICKEN BREASTS (OR THIGHS)	4
1/2 CUP	MELTED BUTTER	250 ML
	SALT AND PEPPER (SPRINKLE TO TASTE)	
1/2 TSP	THYME	2 ML
1	LEMON, UNPEELED, THINLY SLICED	1

HALVE CHICKEN BREASTS AND ARRANGE IN A 13- X 9-INCH
(3 L) SHALLOW, BUTTERED, BAKING DISH. SPRINKLE WITH
SALT AND PEPPER AND THYME. POUR MELTED BUTTER
OVER ALL. ARRANGE LEMON SLICES ON TOP OF CHICKEN
TO COVER ALL PIECES. COOK, UNCOVERED, FOR 1 HOUR AT
350°F (180°C). SERVE WITH RICE, VEGETABLES OR SALAD.
SERVES 4 TO 6.

*IN PREPARING A DISH FOR BEDTIME, CHAMPAGNE
MAKES THE BEST TENDERIZER.*

BARBEQUED CHICKEN MARINADE

½ CUP	SOY SAUCE	125 ML
¼ CUP	SHERRY	50 ML
½ CUP	COOKING OIL	125 ML
	JUICE OF 1 ORANGE	
	GRATED ORANGE ZEST	
	FRESHLY GRATED BLACK PEPPER	
2	CLOVES GARLIC, CHOPPED	2
	FRESHLY GRATED GINGER ROOT	
½ CUP	HONEY	125 ML

MARINATE CHICKEN HALVES OR PIECES FOR SEVERAL HOURS OR OVERNIGHT, TURNING FREQUENTLY. ARRANGE CHICKEN IN SPIT BASKET (SKIN SIDE OUT) AND TURN MOTOR ON. COOK OVER COALS 1½ HOURS. DURING LAST ½ HOUR BASTE WITH MARINADE TO WHICH ½ CUP (125 ML) HONEY HAS BEEN ADDED. MAKES ABOUT 1½ CUPS (375 ML) MARINADE, ENOUGH FOR 3 LBS (1.5 KG) CHICKEN.

THE DIFFERENCE BETWEEN A STOIC AND A CYNIC IS,
THE STOIC IS WHAT BRINGS THE KID AND
A CYNIC IS WHAT YOU WASH HIM IN!

DIVINE CHICKEN DIVAN

*THIS IS ALSO A GOOD WAY TO USE LEFT-OVER
SLICES OF TURKEY BREAST.*

5	WHOLE CHICKEN BREASTS, SPLIT	5
1	LARGE BUNCH OF BROCCOLI (FRESH)	1
1/2 CUP	BUTTER	125 ML
1/2 CUP	FLOUR	125 ML
4 CUPS	CHICKEN STOCK	1 L
3	EGG YOLKS	3
1 CUP	WHIPPING CREAM, WHIPPED	250 ML
6 TBSP	SHERRY	90 ML
	SALT AND PEPPER TO TASTE	
1/2 CUP	GRATED PARMESAN CHEESE (OR MORE IF YOU LIKE)	125 ML

COOK OR GENTLY SAUTÉ CHICKEN BREASTS UNTIL TENDER.
REMOVE AND DEBONE. COOK THE BROCCOLI AND SEASON
LIGHTLY, DRAIN AND SET ASIDE. MELT BUTTER, STIR IN
FLOUR AND THEN ADD THE CHICKEN STOCK. COOK, STIRRING
CONSTANTLY, UNTIL MIXTURE COMES TO A BOIL. SIMMER
GENTLY FOR ABOUT 5 MINUTES. COOL SLIGHTLY, THEN
BEAT IN THE EGG YOLKS. WHIP THE CREAM (NOT TOO STIFF)
AND FOLD IT IN WITH THE SHERRY. PLACE THE BROCCOLI
IN THE BOTTOM OF AN OVEN PROOF DISH. COVER BROCCOLI
WITH HALF THE SAUCE AND COVER WITH GRATED CHEESE.
ARRANGE THE CHICKEN OVER THE CHEESE-COVERED
BROCCOLI AND TOP WITH THE REMAINING SAUCE AND
ADDITIONAL CHEESE IF DESIRED. BAKE AT 350°F (180°C) FOR
20 MINUTES, JUST UNTIL VERY HOT. IF DESIRED YOU CAN
PUT UNDER THE BROILER FOR A MINUTE TO BROWN AT
THE VERY END OF THE HEATING PERIOD. THIS DISH CAN
BE MADE AHEAD AS IT FREEZES WELL. *SERVES 10.*

STUFFED CHICKEN BREASTS WITH MUSHROOM SAUCE

4 TO 6	DE-BONED CHICKEN BREASTS	4 TO 6
2 CUPS	BREAD CRUMBS	500 ML
2 TBSP	MELTED BUTTER	25 ML
2 TBSP	ONION	25 ML
1 TSP	SALT	5 ML
1/4 TSP	POULTRY SEASONING	1 ML
1/4 CUP	HOT WATER	50 ML

HALVE BREASTS AND DUST WITH FLOUR, SALT AND
PAPRIKA. COMBINE OTHER INGREDIENTS, STUFF BREASTS
AND HOLD WITH TOOTHPICK IF NECESSARY. BROWN IN
BUTTER IN FRY PAN. BAKE IN OVEN AT 325°F (160°C) FOR
1 HOUR. SERVE WITH MUSHROOM SAUCE. SERVES 4 TO 6.

MUSHROOM SAUCE

1/2 LB	FRESH MUSHROOMS	250 G
2 TBSP	BUTTER	25 ML
1/4 CUP	MINCED ONION	50 ML
2 TBSP	FLOUR	25 ML
1/2 CUP	SOUR CREAM	125 ML
1 CUP	WHIPPING CREAM	250 ML
	SALT AND PEPPER	

BROWN MUSHROOMS AND ONION. STIR IN FLOUR, SALT
AND PEPPER. COOK VERY SLOWLY ADDING CREAM AND
SOUR CREAM. POUR OVER CHICKEN JUST BEFORE SERVING.

CHICKEN CASSEROLE

2 CUPS	CHICKEN, COOKED AND CUBED	500 ML
I CUP	CHOPPED CELERY	250 ML
I CUP	CHOPPED NUTS (TOASTED, SLIVERED ALMONDS)	250 ML
2 CUPS	COOKED RICE	500 ML
I CUP	MAYONNAISE	250 ML
2 TBSP	CHOPPED ONIONS	25 ML
I	CAN (10 OZ/284 ML) CREAM OF CHICKEN SOUP	I
I	CAN (10 OZ/284 ML) CREAM OF MUSHROOM SOUP	I
$3/4$ TSP	SALT	4 ML
$3/4$ TSP	PEPPER	4 ML
2 TBSP	LEMON JUICE	25 ML
2	CHICKEN BOUILLON CUBES DISSOLVED IN $1/2$ CUP (125 ML) WATER	2

COMBINE ALL INGREDIENTS, MIXING THOROUGHLY. PLACE IN A CASSEROLE. COVER WITH CRUSHED POTATO CHIPS AND ALMONDS. BAKE AT 400°F (200°C) FOR 45 MINUTES OR UNTIL HEATED THROUGH. SERVES 8.

THE HONEYMOON IS REALLY OVER WHEN HE PHONES TO SAY HE'LL BE LATE FOR DINNER, AND SHE HAS ALREADY LEFT A NOTE SAYING IT'S IN THE REFRIGERATOR.

CRAB-STUFFED CHICKEN BREASTS

6	WHOLE CHICKEN BREASTS, BONED AND SKINNED	6

STUFFING

1/2 CUP	HERB-SEASONED STUFFING MIX (MRS. MCCUBBISON'S)	125 ML
1	CAN (5 OZ/142 G) CRABMEAT, DRAINED AND FLAKED	1
1/2 CUP	CHOPPED CELERY	125 ML
1/2 CUP	CHOPPED GREEN ONION	125 ML
3 TBSP	BUTTER	45 ML
3 TBSP	DRY WHITE WINE	45 ML
	PAPRIKA	

SAUCE

1/3 CUP	KRAFT SWISS CHEESE, GRATED	75 ML
1/3 CUP	DRY WHITE WINE	75 ML
3 TBSP	BUTTER	45 ML
3 TBSP	FLOUR	45 ML
2 CUPS	HALF-AND-HALF CREAM	500 ML

PREPARE STUFFING: PLACE BUTTER IN A MIXING BOWL AND MELT IN MICROWAVE FOR 30 SECONDS. ADD ONION AND CELERY AND COOK 2 MINUTES, UNCOVERED, STIRRING ONCE. ADD WINE, STUFFING MIX AND CRABMEAT. MIX WELL. SET ASIDE. POUND CHICKEN TO FLATTEN BY PLACING BETWEEN 2 SHEETS OF WAX PAPER AND POUND WITH A ROLLING PIN, UNTIL QUITE THIN AND UNIFORM. SPRINKLE WITH SALT AND PEPPER. DIVIDE STUFFING MIXTURE AMONG BREASTS, ROLL UP AND SECURE WITH TOOTHPICKS.

CONTINUED ON NEXT PAGE...

SPRINKLE WITH PAPRIKA. COVER WITH WAXED PAPER AND COOK IN MICROWAVE OVEN 10 MINUTES, TURNING DISH ONCE.

PREPARE SAUCE

MELT BUTTER IN SAUCEPAN, ADD FLOUR, STIR UNTIL WELL MIXED. GRADUALLY ADD CREAM AND COOK, STIRRING CONSTANTLY, UNTIL SMOOTH. ADD WINE AND CHEESE AND CONTINUE COOKING UNTIL CHEESE IS MELTED. WHEN READY TO SERVE, REMOVE TOOTHPICKS FROM CHICKEN AND POUR SAUCE OVER. SERVES 6.

NOTE: FOR CONVENTIONAL OVEN, MELT BUTTER AND COOK INGREDIENTS FOR STUFFING IN SAUCEPAN OVER MEDIUM HEAT. BAKE CHICKEN, COVERED, AT 375°F (190°C) FOR 45 MINUTES.

ONE OF THE MAJOR PROBLEMS FACING THIS COUNTRY TODAY IS THAT TOO MANY WOMEN GET ALL EXCITED ABOUT NOTHING... AND THEN MARRY HIM.

CHICKEN AND WILD RICE CASSEROLE

1 CUP	WILD RICE, COOKED	250 ML
1/2 CUP	CHOPPED ONION	125 ML
1/2 CUP	BUTTER	125 ML
1/4 CUP	FLOUR	50 ML
1	CAN (10 OZ/284 ML) SLICED MUSHROOMS	1
1 CUP	CHICKEN BROTH (APPROX.)	250 ML
1 1/2 CUPS	LIGHT CREAM	375 ML
3 CUPS	DICED CHICKEN, COOKED	750 ML
1/4 CUP	DICED PIMENTO	50 ML
2 TBSP	SNIPPED PARSLEY	25 ML
1 1/2 TSP	SALT	7 ML
1/4 TSP	PEPPER	1 ML
1/2 CUP	SLIVERED ALMONDS	125 ML

COOK ONION IN BUTTER UNTIL TENDER BUT NOT BROWN. REMOVE FROM HEAT AND STIR IN FLOUR. DRAIN MUSHROOMS, RESERVING LIQUID. ADD CHICKEN BROTH TO MUSHROOM LIQUID TO MEASURE 1 1/2 CUPS (375 ML). GRADUALLY ADD TO FLOUR MIXTURE. ADD CREAM, COOK AND STIR UNTIL THICK. ADD COOKED WILD RICE, MUSHROOMS, CHICKEN, PIMENTO, PARSLEY, SALT AND PEPPER. PLACE IN AN 8-CUP (2 L) CASSEROLE; SPRINKLE WITH ALMONDS. BAKE IN 350°F (180°C) OVEN FOR 30 MINUTES. SERVES 8.

WHEN MY WIFE HAS AN ACCIDENT IN THE KITCHEN, I GET IT FOR DINNER.

CHICKEN 'N' NOODLE CASSEROLE EXTRAORDINAIRE

THIS IS A QUICK LUNCHEON OR DINNER DISH. PREPARE IN THE MORNING AND REFRIGERATE UNTIL COOKING TIME. SERVE WITH A TOSSED SALAD AND JELLIED SALAD AND DINNER ROLLS.

1	PACKAGE (10 OZ/284 G) UNCOOKED WIDE NOODLES	1
4	CANS (EACH 5 OZ/142 G) BONED CHICKEN OR 2 CUPS (500 ML) COOKED CHICKEN	4
1	CAN (10 OZ/284 ML) CONDENSED CREAM OF MUSHROOM SOUP	1
1	CAN (10 OZ/284 ML) CONDENSED CREAM OF CELERY SOUP	1
1	CAN (10 OZ/284 ML) CONDENSED CREAM OF CHICKEN SOUP	1
1	CAN (4 1/2 OZ/128 ML) CHOPPED RIPE OLIVES	1
1	CAN (10 OZ/284 ML) MUSHROOMS, DRAINED	1
1/2 CUP	WINE OR SHERRY	125 ML
1 LB	CHEDDAR CHEESE, GRATED	500 G
	PAPRIKA	

COOK NOODLES; DRAIN. MIX REMAINING INGREDIENTS WITH NOODLES EXCEPT CHEESE. SPOON INTO A SHALLOW 13- X 9-INCH (3 L) BAKING DISH. TOP WITH GRATED CHEESE. SPRINKLE WITH PAPRIKA. BAKE AT 350°F (180°C) FOR 20 TO 25 MINUTES. CHEESE SHOULD BE MELTED. IF YOU REFRIGERATE THIS CASSEROLE BEFOREHAND, LET IT STAND AT ROOM TEMPERATURE AT LEAST 1 HOUR BEFORE BAKING. SERVES 12 TO 14.

CHICKEN BALLS

(A CHICKEN NEVER DOES!)

1/2 CUP	FLOUR	125 ML
I TSP	ACCENT	5 ML
I TSP	SALT	5 ML
I TO 2	EGGS	I TO 2
2 TO 3	CHICKEN BREASTS OR OTHER PIECES	2 TO 3

CUT CHICKEN IN LONG, NARROW STRIPS AND ROLL INTO A BALL. ROLL CHICKEN PIECES IN EGG THEN DIP IN FLOUR. FRY IN OIL UNTIL LIGHT BROWN.

SAUCE

1/2 CUP	SUGAR	125 ML
1/2 CUP	VINEGAR	125 ML
I TBSP	SOY SAUCE	15 ML
1/2 CUP	PINEAPPLE CHUNKS	125 ML
1/3 CUP	PINEAPPLE JUICE	75 ML
1/4 CUP	KETCHUP	50 ML
SPRINKLE	PEPPER	SPRINKLE
2 TBSP	CORNSTARCH	25 ML

BOIL MIXTURE AND THICKEN WITH CORNSTARCH. POUR OVER BALLS. BAKE AT 250°F (120°C) TO 275°F (140°C) FOR I HOUR. GREAT FOR A BUFFET! SERVES 4.

MISERY IS A LIVE SECRET AND A DEAD TELEPHONE.

CHICKEN FRIED RICE

2 TBSP	COOKING OIL	25 ML
3 CUPS	COOKED RICE	750 ML
1	MEDIUM ONION, CHOPPED FINE	1
1	EGG	1
1/2 TO 1 CUP	DICED MEAT, RAW OR COOKED	125 TO 250 ML
2	CHOPPED GREEN ONIONS	2
	SALT	
	SOY SAUCE TO TASTE	

IN A LARGE, HEAVY SKILLET, HEAT COOKING OIL AT HIGH TEMPERATURE. WHEN HOT, ADD MEAT AND ONION. FRY UNTIL COOKED. BREAK EGG INTO MEAT MIXTURE AND SCRAMBLE, STIRRING CONSTANTLY. TURN HEAT TO LOW, ADD RICE, SALT AND SOY SAUCE TO SUIT YOUR TASTE. BEFORE SERVING ADD GREEN ONIONS. THIS SHOULD BE SERVED IMMEDIATELY, BUT MAY BE KEPT WARM IN CHAFING DISH. SERVES 6.

THE DOCTORS ARE SAYING THAT DRINKING IS BAD FOR US. I DON'T KNOW. YOU SEE A LOT MORE OLD DRUNKS THAN OLD DOCTORS.

CANTONESE CHICKEN

I	CAN (14 OZ/398 ML) PINEAPPLE TIDBITS	I
I CUP	SLICED CELERY	250 ML
I CUP	THINLY SLICED CARROTS	250 ML
¼ CUP	CHOPPED ONIONS	50 ML
¼ CUP	TOASTED SLIVERED ALMONDS	50 ML
¼ CUP	BUTTER	50 ML
I TBSP	ARROWROOT OR CORNSTARCH	15 ML
¼ TSP	GINGER	I ML
⅛ TSP	NUTMEG	0.5 ML
¾ CUP	WATER	175 ML
I TBSP	SOY SAUCE	15 ML
I TSP	LEMON JUICE	5 ML
I TSP	CHICKEN SEASONED STOCK BASE	5 ML
I½ CUPS	CHOPPED, COOKED CHICKEN	375 ML
I	CAN (5 OZ/142 ML) WATER CHESTNUTS, DRAINED AND SLICED THIN	I
	CHOW MEIN NOODLES OR RICE	

DRAIN PINEAPPLE; RESERVE JUICE. SAUTÉ CELERY, CARROTS, ONIONS AND ALMONDS IN BUTTER IN LARGE SKILLET UNTIL ONIONS ARE GOLDEN BROWN. COMBINE ARROWROOT, GINGER, NUTMEG, PINEAPPLE JUICE, WATER, SOY SAUCE, LEMON JUICE AND SEASONED STOCK BASE, MIXING UNTIL WELL BLENDED. ADD TO SAUTÉED VEGETABLES AND COOK UNTIL MIXTURE THICKENS, STIRRING CONSTANTLY. STIR IN PINEAPPLE TIDBITS, CHICKEN AND WATER CHESTNUTS. COVER AND SIMMER 10 TO 15 MINUTES. SERVE OVER CHOW MEIN NOODLES OR RICE. SERVES 4.

POLYNESIAN CHICKEN

I	FRYER, CUT UP	I
1/4 CUP	SOY SAUCE	50 ML
3 TBSP	VEGETABLE OIL	45 ML
I TSP	GINGER	5 ML
2 TBSP	MINCED ONION	25 ML
1/2 CUP	FLOUR	125 ML
I	CAN (14 OZ/398 ML) PINEAPPLE CHUNKS	I
I	CAN (10 OZ/284 ML) MANDARIN ORANGES	I
2 TBSP	CORNSTARCH	25 ML
1/4 CUP	WATER	50 ML
1/4 CUP	TOASTED SLIVERED ALMONDS	50 ML

ARRANGE CHICKEN IN SHALLOW PAN. COMBINE SOY SAUCE, OIL, GINGER, ONION AND MARINATE CHICKEN FOR ONE HOUR. SHAKE CHICKEN IN FLOUR AND BROWN IN OIL IN FRY PAN. DRAIN FRUIT AND SET ASIDE. ADD FRUIT JUICES TO SOY MARINADE. COMBINE CORNSTARCH AND WATER AND ADD TO SOY FRUIT SAUCE. PLACE CHICKEN IN CASSEROLE. POUR SOY FRUIT SAUCE OVER AND BAKE IN A 350°F (180°C) OVEN FOR 45 MINUTES. SHORTLY BEFORE SERVING ADD FRUIT AND ALMONDS. SERVES 4.

BEHIND EVERY GREAT MAN STANDS AN AMAZED MOTHER-IN-LAW.

JAPANESE CHICKEN WINGS

GREAT FOR CROWDS AND KIDS! TASTES GOOD WARMED UP IF THERE'S ANY LEFT.

3 LBS	CHICKEN WINGS, TIPS REMOVED	1.5 KG
1	EGG	1
1/3 CUP	FLOUR	75 ML
1 CUP	BUTTER	250 ML

SAUCE

3 TBSP	SOY SAUCE	45 ML
3 TBSP	WATER	45 ML
1 CUP	WHITE SUGAR	250 ML
1/2 CUP	VINEGAR	125 ML

CUT WINGS IN HALF. DIP IN SLIGHTLY BEATEN EGG AND THEN IN FLOUR. FRY IN BUTTER UNTIL DEEP BROWN AND CRISP. PLACE IN SHALLOW ROASTING PAN. MIX ALL SAUCE INGREDIENTS TOGETHER AND POUR OVER CHICKEN WINGS. BAKE AT 350°F (180°C) FOR 1/2 HOUR. BASTE WINGS WITH SAUCE DURING COOKING. SERVES 6.

WHOEVER SAID "WHERE THERE'S SMOKE, THERE'S FIRE" MUST NEVER HAVE OWNED A FIREPLACE.

CURRIED CHICKEN WINGS

VERY MILD - EVEN THE CHILDREN LIKE THIS ONE.

2	PACKAGE FROZEN CHICKEN WINGS	2
	SEASONED FLOUR	
6 TBSP	COOKING OIL	90 ML
I	MEDIUM ONION, CHOPPED	I
I TSP	CURRY POWDER	5 ML
2	CHICKEN BOUILLON CUBES	2
3 TBSP	FLOUR	45 ML
I½ CUPS	WATER	375 ML

REMOVE TIPS OF CHICKEN WINGS. SHAKE IN SEASONED
FLOUR AND BROWN IN COOKING OIL. REMOVE CHICKEN TO
CASSEROLE AND SPRINKLE WITH CHOPPED ONION. MAKE
GRAVY IN FRYING PAN USING WATER, FLOUR, CHICKEN
BOUILLON CUBES AND CURRY. POUR OVER CHICKEN AND
BAKE AT 325°F (160°C) FOR I½ HOURS. SERVES 8.

GOOD VEGETABLE ACCOMPANIMENT: CARROTS AND CELERY,
SLICED JULIENNE STYLE, COOKED TOGETHER IN SMALL
AMOUNT OF WATER, SERVED IN BUTTER.

MEALTIME? WHEN THE KIDS SIT DOWN TO CONTINUE EATING.

TURKEY CASSEROLE WITH BROCCOLI

2 CUPS	NOODLES	500 ML
I	PACKAGE (IO OZ/300 G) FROZEN BROCCOLI	I
2 CUPS	COOKED TURKEY	500 ML
1/3 CUP	SLIVERED ALMONDS	75 ML

WHITE SAUCE

2 TBSP	BUTTER	25 ML
2 TBSP	FLOUR	25 ML
I TSP	SALT	5 ML
1/4 TSP	PREPARED MUSTARD	I ML
1/4 TSP	PEPPER	I ML
2 CUPS	MILK	500 ML
I CUP	GRATED CHEDDAR CHEESE	250 ML

HEAT OVEN TO 350°F (180°C). COOK NOODLES, THEN BROCCOLI. MAKE WHITE SAUCE; WHEN THICK STIR IN CHEESE. DICE BROCCOLI STEMS LEAVING FLOWERS FOR TOP. PUT NOODLES, BROCCOLI STEMS, TURKEY AND ALMONDS IN CASSEROLE. COVER WITH SAUCE. ARRANGE BROCCOLI FLOWERS ON TOP AND BAKE FOR 15 TO 20 MINUTES. SERVES 4.

A FEED-STORE IS ABOUT THE ONLY PLACE THESE DAYS WHERE YOU CAN GET A CHICKEN DINNER FOR A DIME.

ROAST DUCK WITH PAT'S ORANGE SAUCE

2	DUCKS, WILD OR DOMESTIC	2
1	CARROT	1
2	STALKS CELERY	2
1	LARGE ONION	1
1 CUP	DRY WHITE WINE	250 ML
1 CUP	WATER	250 ML

SOAK CLEANED DUCKS FOR 1/2 HOUR IN BAKING SODA WATER (1/2 CUP/125 ML BAKING SODA MIXED IN SINK OF COLD WATER). RINSE AND DRY CAVITIES AND OUTSIDES OF BIRDS WITH PAPER TOWELS. PLACE IN ROASTING PAN AND FILL CAVITIES AND SURROUND DUCKS WITH SLICES OF ONION, CARROT AND CELERY. (THESE WILL BE DISCARDED AFTER ROASTING.) COVER DUCKS WITH LAYER OF BUTTER. SPRINKLE GENEROUSLY WITH SALT AND PEPPER. POUR WHITE WINE AND 1 CUP (250 ML) WATER OVER DUCKS. COVER AND ROAST AT 350°F (180°C) FOR THE FIRST HOUR AND 300°F (150°C) FOR THE FINAL 3 1/2 HOURS. (THIS IS THE SECRET FOR COOKING ANY WILD FOWL – SLOWLY AND FOR A LONG TIME.) MEAT WILL BE VERY TENDER AND LITERALLY FALL FROM THE CARCASS. YOU MAY WANT TO REMOVE THE MEAT FROM THE BONES AND SERVE IT IN THIS INFORMAL MANNER. SERVE WITH PAT'S SPECIAL ORANGE SAUCE, PAGE 190. SERVES 4.

EXPERIENCE IS DIRECTLY PROPORTIONAL TO THE AMOUNT OF EQUIPMENT RUINED.

PAT'S SPECIAL ORANGE SAUCE

ESPECIALLY FOR ROAST DUCK

1	CAN (10 OZ/284 ML) DRAINED MANDARIN ORANGE SECTIONS	1
4 TBSP	BUTTER	60 ML
4 TBSP	FLOUR	60 ML
2 TBSP	CHICKEN BOUILLON POWDER	25 ML
1 CUP	HOT WATER	250 ML
1 CUP	ORANGE JUICE (MADE FROM UNSWEETENED FROZEN CONCENTRATE)	250 ML
DASH	TABASCO	DASH
3/4 CUP	CREAMED HONEY	175 ML
	SHREDDED ORANGE PEEL	

MELT BUTTER IN A SAUCEPAN, ADD FLOUR AND STIR UNTIL BUBBLY. MIX BOUILLON POWDER, HOT WATER, ORANGE JUICE AND SHREDDED ORANGE PEEL. (USING POTATO PEELER, REMOVE PEEL FROM AN ORANGE AND CUT IN THIN JULIENNE STRIPS.) ADD TO BUTTER MIXTURE. STIR UNTIL THICKENED. ADD HONEY AND TABASCO. KEEP STIRRING AND ADD ORANGE SECTIONS. BEAT UNTIL FAIRLY SMOOTH AND SERVE HOT WITH DUCK. MAKES ABOUT 4 CUPS (1 L).

"WHERE DOES VIRGIN WOOL COME FROM?"
"FROM SHEEP THAT RUN THE FASTEST."

LA CORNEILLE IVRE

PREHEAT OVEN TO 450°F (230°C). PLACE SMALL AMOUNT OF GARLIC-FLAVORED BUTTER IN BOTTOM OF ROASTING PAN. STUFF AND TRUSS ONE MEDIUM-SIZED CROW. ROAST BETWEEN 2 ROCKS FOR 6 HOURS. WHEN YOU CAN PUT A FORK THROUGH THE ROCK, THE CROW IS DONE.

PEACHY PORK

4	PORK STEAKS, FAT REMOVED	4
1 TBSP	OIL	15 ML
1 TSP	BASIL, SALT AND PEPPER TO TASTE	5 ML
1	CAN (28 OZ/796 ML) PEACH SLICES	1
1 TBSP	VINEGAR	15 ML
2	BEEF BOUILLON CUBES, CRUSHED	2

HEAT OIL IN SKILLET. ADD MEAT AND BROWN. DRAIN. DRAIN PEACH SYRUP AND ADD TO IT: BASIL, SALT, PEPPER, VINEGAR AND CRUSHED BEEF CUBES. COMBINE MEAT AND PEACH SYRUP MIXTURE IN SKILLET. COVER AND SIMMER 30 MINUTES. ADD WATER IF NECESSARY. FIVE MINUTES BEFORE SERVING, ADD PEACHES. HEAT THROUGH. SERVE WITH BUTTERED RICE. SERVES 4.

DEFINITION OF A PICNIC: MEADOW LARK

CHINESE PORK ROAST

I TBSP	SUGAR	15 ML
I TBSP	HONEY	15 ML
3 TBSP	CHICKEN BOUILLON	45 ML
I TSP	SALT	5 ML
I TBSP	SOY SAUCE	15 ML
2 LBS	FRESH PORK BUTT OR SHOULDER OF PORK, CUT IN 3 PIECES, LENGTHWISE	I KG

MIX THE MARINADE TOGETHER IN BOWL UNTIL WELL COMBINED. SOAK PORK FOR $3/4$ OF AN HOUR, IN MARINADE, TURNING OCCASIONALLY. REMOVE FROM BOWL AND PLACE ON RACK IN A A ROASTING PAN, ADDING A FEW TABLESPOONS OF WATER TO PREVENT FROM SMOKING. ROAST IN MODERATE OVEN A 350°F (180°C) FOR ABOUT $1\frac{1}{2}$ HOURS, TURNING OCCASIONALLY. SLICE PORK AND SERVE IMMEDIATELY WITH HOT MUSTARD. SERVES 6 TO 8.

YOU DON'T HAVE TO EAT AN APPLE A DAY TO KEEP THE DOCTOR AWAY. HE WON'T COME TO THE HOUSE, ANYWAY.

APRICOTS 'N' HAM

SUPER FOR ANY BUFFET OR CROWD!

10 TO 12 LB	HAM, WHOLE, FULLY COOKED	5 TO 6 KG
1½ CUPS	COARSELY CHOPPED DRIED APRICOTS	375 ML
1 CUP	FINELY CHOPPED PECANS	250 ML
1	CAN (8½ OZ/242 ML) CRUSHED PINEAPPLE, UNDRAINED	1
¼ TSP	THYME	1 ML
1	CAN (12 OZ/341 ML) APRICOT NECTAR	1
½ TSP	GROUND ALLSPICE	2 ML
½ CUP	HONEY	125 ML

HAVE THE BUTCHER REMOVE BONE FROM HAM. GRIND UP ½ LB (250 G) LEAN HAM FROM CAVITY. IN A LARGE BOWL COMBINE GROUND HAM WITH DRIED APRICOTS, PECANS, PINEAPPLE AND THYME. MIX WELL. SPOON INTO CAVITY. COVER END WITH FOIL AND HOLD WITH SKEWERS. (I ALWAYS SEEM TO HAVE TOO MUCH FOR THE CAVITY SO I COOK AND COVER THE REMAINDER IN A CASSEROLE ON THE SIDE.) POUR APRICOT NECTAR OVER HAM, SPRINKLE WITH ALLSPICE. COVER ROASTING PAN WITH FOIL. BAKE 2 HOURS AT 325°F (160°C). REMOVE FROM OVEN AND SPREAD HALF THE HONEY OVER HAM. BAKE, UNCOVERED 30 MINUTES; BRUSH WITH REMAINING HONEY AND BAKE FOR 15 MINUTES LONGER. SERVES 16 TO 20.

FAILURE _MAY_ BE YOUR THING.

SATAY

RAVE NOTICES: A BAR-B-QUED INDONESIAN DISH WE HIGHLY RECOMMEND FOR YOUR NEXT DINNER PARTY OR SUMMER COOKOUT. THERE WON'T BE A SPECK LEFT OVER.

1½ LBS	PORK TENDERLOIN (OR CHICKEN BREAST), IN 1" (2.5 CM) CUBES	750 G
2 TBSP	BUTTER	25 ML
1 TBSP	LEMON JUICE	15 ML
	GRATED ZEST OF 1 LEMON	
½ TSP	TABASCO	2 ML
3 TBSP	GRATED ONION	45 ML
1 TBSP	BROWN SUGAR	15 ML
1 TSP	CORIANDER	5 ML
½ TSP	GROUND CUMIN	2 ML
¼ TSP	GINGER	1 ML
1	GARLIC CLOVE, CRUSHED	1
½ CUP	INDONESIAN SOY SAUCE OR TERIYAKI SAUCE	125 ML
	SALT AND PEPPER TO TASTE	
	WOODEN SKEWERS	

PLACE PORK TENDERLOIN IN SHALLOW DISH. MELT BUTTER IN SAUCEPAN AND ADD REMAINING INGREDIENTS. BRING TO A BOIL AND SIMMER 5 MINUTES. POUR OVER MEAT, COVER AND REFRIGERATE OVERNIGHT. TURN MEAT PERIODICALLY (BUTTER WILL CONGEAL BUT DON'T WORRY). REMOVE MEAT FROM MARINADE (RESERVE) AND PUT 5-6 PIECES ON EACH SKEWER. GRILL ON BAR-B-QUE, TURNING FREQUENTLY, FOR 15 MINUTES (DON'T OVERCOOK).

CONTINUED ON NEXT PAGE...

REHEAT MARINADE AND DRIZZLE OVER MEAT. SET ON A PLATTER ON A BED OF RICE. SERVE WITH FRESH SPINACH SALAD (PAGE 126). SERVES 6 TO 8.

HAM CASSEROLE

THAT'S IT FOR THE LEFTOVER HAM!

2 TBSP	BUTTER	25 ML
1/2 CUP	CHOPPED ONION	125 ML
3 TBSP	FLOUR	45 ML
	SALT AND PEPPER TO TASTE	
1 1/4 CUPS	MILK	300 ML
1/2 CUP	SHREDDED SWISS CHEESE	125 ML
2 CUPS	CUBED COOKED HAM (OR MORE)	500 ML
1 CUP	CUBED COOKED POTATOES	250 ML
1 1/2 CUPS	SOFT BREADCRUMBS	375 ML
2 TBSP	BUTTER	25 ML

IN A FRYING PAN, MELT BUTTER AND SAUTÉ ONION. BLEND IN FLOUR, SALT AND PEPPER. SLOWLY ADD MILK; STIR CONSTANTLY AND COOK UNTIL THICKENED. ADD CHEESE AND STIR UNTIL MELTED. ADD HAM AND POTATOES AND MIX GENTLY. POUR INTO A CASSEROLE. SPRINKLE WITH BREADCRUMBS AND DOT WITH BUTTER. PREHEAT OVEN TO 400°F (200°C) AND BAKE FOR 30 MINUTES. SERVES 6.

SWEET AND SOUR SPARE RIBS

ABSOLUTELY EXCELLENT!

3 TO 4 LBS	PORK SPARE RIBS (PORK BUTTON BONES ARE ALSO GOOD; BITE-SIZE AND MEATY)	1.5 TO 2 KG
1/4 CUP	VINEGAR	50 ML
3 TBSP	SOY SAUCE	45 ML
1 TSP	SUGAR	5 ML
1/2 TSP	PEPPER	2 ML
4 TBSP	FLOUR	60 ML
2 TBSP	COOKING OIL	25 ML

SWEET AND SOUR SAUCE

1/2 CUP	VINEGAR	125 ML
1 1/2 CUPS	BROWN SUGAR	375 ML
1 CUP	WATER	250 ML
1 TBSP	CORNSTARCH DISSOLVED IN 1/2 CUP (125 ML) WATER	15 ML

OPTIONAL

1	CAN (14 OZ/398 ML) PINEAPPLE TIDBITS, REPLACE 1/2 CUP (125 ML) WATER WITH 1/2 CUP (125 ML) PINEAPPLE JUICE	1

CUT RIBS INTO SERVING-SIZED PIECES AND PLACE IN LARGE POT. COVER WITH WATER AND ADD VINEGAR. BRING TO A BOIL AND SIMMER 1 HOUR. DRAIN. MAKE MARINADE OF SOY SAUCE, SUGAR AND PEPPER. POUR OVER RIBS (USE SAME POT) AND TURN FREQUENTLY TO COVER EACH PIECE. REMOVE RIBS AND SHAKE IN BROWN PAPER BAG WITH FLOUR. IN A LARGE SKILLET, ADD COOKING OIL AND BROWN

CONTINUED ON NEXT PAGE...

RIBS (NOT TOO LONG OR THEY'LL DRY OUT). PLACE IN LARGE CASSEROLE DISH. IN A SAUCEPAN, COMBINE SAUCE INGREDIENTS AND COOK OVER MEDIUM HEAT UNTIL SLIGHTLY THICK. (IF USING PINEAPPLE, PLACE TIDBITS IN CASSEROLE WITH RIBS.) POUR OVER RIBS AND SET IN 350°F (180°C) OVEN FOR AT LEAST $\frac{1}{2}$ HOUR. FLOUR ON RIBS WILL THICKEN THE SAUCE. SERVE OVER A BED OF RICE. SERVES 6 TO 8.

AFTER PAYING FOR THE WEDDING, ABOUT ALL A FATHER HAS LEFT TO GIVE AWAY IS THE BRIDE.

SWEET 'N' SOUR RIBS

2 LBS	RIBS, BROWNED	1 KG
SAUCE		
3/4 CUP	BROWN SUGAR	175 ML
1/2 CUP	KETCHUP	125 ML
1/2 CUP	VINEGAR	125 ML
3/4 CUP	WATER	175 ML
2 TBSP	WORCESTERSHIRE SAUCE	25 ML
1/2 TSP	CHILI POWDER	2 ML
1	ONION, DICED	1
	SALT, PEPPER	

POUR OVER RIBS AND BAKE IN A 250°F (120°C) OVEN FOR
3 HOURS, UNCOVERED. SERVES 4.

DRY RIBS
(FROM SWEET 'N' SOUR RIBS)

DIP DESIRED AMOUNT OF RIBS, WHICH HAVE BEEN CUT
INTO 1-INCH (2.5 CM) PIECES, INTO SOY SAUCE AND THEN
INTO FLOUR AND SALT AND PEPPER. FRY IN DEEP FAT AT
385°F (195°C) UNTIL DONE.

*CHILDHOOD IS THAT WONDERFUL TIME WHEN ALL YOU
HAVE TO DO TO LOSE WEIGHT IS TO TAKE A BATH.*

SWEET 'N' SOUR CHILI RIBS

*THE AROMA OF THESE RIBS WILL BRING
YOUR FAMILY RUNNING.*

4 LBS	PORK RIBS	2 KG
SAUCE		
3/4 CUP	BROWN SUGAR	175 ML
1/2 CUP	KETCHUP	125 ML
1/2 CUP	WHITE VINEGAR	125 ML
2 TBSP	WORCESTERSHIRE SAUCE	25 ML
1 TSP	CHILI POWDER	5 ML
3/4 CUP	WATER	175 ML
1	ONION, DICED	1

PARBOIL RIBS IN A LARGE POT FOR 30-45 MINUTES.
PLACE RIBS IN A LARGE SHALLOW BAKING PAN.

TO MAKE SAUCE: IN A MEDIUM BOWL, COMBINE
INGREDIENTS.

POUR SAUCE OVER RIBS. BAKE, UNCOVERED, AT 250°F
(120°C) FOR 3 HOURS. SERVES 4 TO 6.

*WE REALLY DON'T NEED ANY CALENDARS.
WHEN IT RAINS, IT'S SUNDAY.*

TOURTIÈRE

THIS IS A VERY OLD FRENCH CANADIAN RECIPE FOR
MEAT PIES. IT IS PARTICULARLY GOOD BECAUSE THE
MEAT IS CHOPPED, NOT GROUND, AND MOST OF THE
FAT HAS BEEN REMOVED. THIS RECIPE USUALLY MAKES
ABOUT SIX PIES, BUT THIS CAN VARY WITH THE AMOUNT
OF MEAT USED. ALWAYS USE A COMBINATION PORK (OR
HAM) AND BEEF. THE ADDITION OF BREAST OF CHICKEN
LENDS A FULLER FLAVOR. SEVERAL PIES CAN BE
PREPARED AND FROZEN UNCOOKED IN <u>DEEP</u> ALUMINUM
PIE PLATES (9- X 1½-INCH/23 X 4 CM). ALWAYS SERVE
WITH RHUBARB RELISH, RECIPE INCLUDED. A TOURTIÈRE
AND A JAR OF RELISH IS A SPECIAL GIFT AT CHRISTMAS
TIME. THIS TAKES LOTS OF TIME, SO PROCEED AT
A LEISURELY PACE AND ENJOY YOURSELF
(A GLASS OF WINE HELPS.)

6 LBS	MEAT (THIS SHOULD BE A TOTAL WEIGHT AFTER REMOVAL OF BONE AND FAT. START WITH APPROXIMATELY 12 LBS/6 KG)	3 KG
	PORK (BOSTON BUTT) OR FRESH HAM, OR MIXTURE OF BOTH	
	BEEF: POT ROAST	
	CHICKEN: BREAST OF SMALL CHICKEN	
	BUTTER (ENOUGH TO BROWN ALL MEAT)	
I TBSP	ALLSPICE	15 ML
I TBSP	SAVORY	15 ML
2	MEDIUM ONIONS	2
2	GARLIC CLOVES, MINCED	2
I CUP	BREAD OR CRACKER CRUMBS SALT, PEPPER, CHILI POWDER, POULTRY SEASONING TO TASTE	250 ML

CONTINUED ON NEXT PAGE...

CUT MEAT INTO BITE-SIZE CUBES, REMOVING ALL EXCESS FAT. BROWN MEAT IN BUTTER, SAUTE ONIONS AND GARLIC, ADD SEASONING. COVER WITH HOT WATER AND SIMMER UNCOVERED FOR 3 HOURS. ALLOW TO COOL. SKIM OFF ANY EXCESS FAT. DRAIN OFF WATER, CORRECT SEASONING, ADD CRUMBS IN LAST HALF HOUR TO THICKEN, AND PLACE IN UNBAKED PIE SHELLS. COVER WITH TOP CRUST. BAKE AT 350°F (180°C) UNTIL CRUST IS GOLDEN. MAKES ABOUT 6 PIES.

NOTE: FOR RHUBARB RELISH TO SERVE WITH THIS RECIPE, SEE PAGE 252!

FRANKS IN SILVER

2 CUPS	MINCED FRANKFURTERS	500 ML
1/4 CUP	GRATED CHEESE	50 ML
1 1/2 TSP	PREPARED MUSTARD	7 ML
2	HARD BOILED EGGS, CHOPPED	2
1 TSP	WORCESTERSHIRE SAUCE	5 ML
2 TBSP	SWEET PICKLE RELISH	25 ML
1/4 TSP	CHILI POWDER	1 ML
2 TBSP	MAYONNAISE	25 ML

COMBINE MINCED FRANKFURTERS AND NEXT INGREDIENTS. FILL FRANKFURTER ROLLS. WRAP SECURELY IN FOIL. PLACE ON BARBECUE FOR 15 TO 20 MINUTES. TURN OFTEN. SERVES 4.

CHINESE HAMBURGER

CASUAL, DELICIOUS AND VERY EASY TO MAKE.

1	CAN (10 OZ/284 ML) CREAM OF MUSHROOM SOUP	1
1	CAN (10 OZ/284 ML) CREAM OF CHICKEN SOUP	1
1	CAN (10 OZ/284 ML) CHICKEN GUMBO SOUP	1
1	CAN (10 OZ/284 ML) MUSHROOM BITS AND PIECES (DRAINED)	1
1	LARGE CAN DRIED NOODLES	1
2	STALKS CELERY, CHOPPED	2
1	SMALL ONION (CHOPPED)	1
1½ LBS	GROUND BEEF	750 G

BROWN BEEF WITH ONION AND CELERY IN SMALL AMOUNT OF COOKING OIL. DRAIN. SPOON INTO LARGE CASSEROLE. ADD ALL CANNED INGREDIENTS AND MIX THOROUGHLY. SPRINKLE WITH A FEW DRIED NOODLES. COOK UNCOVERED FOR ONE HOUR AT 300°F (150°C) OR UNTIL HEATED THROUGH. SERVES 6.

IT'S PERFECTLY SAFE TO SAY YOUR WIFE IS UNREASONABLE, PROVIDED, OF COURSE, YOU DO NOT SAY IT TO HER.

FANDANGO

1 LB	GROUND BEEF	500 G
1	MEDIUM ONION, CHOPPED	1
1	CAN (10 OZ/284 ML) MUSHROOMS, DRAINED	1
1 TO 2	GARLIC CLOVES, CRUSHED	1 TO 2
1 TSP	OREGANO	5 ML
1 TO 2	PACKAGES (EACH 10 OZ/300 G) CHOPPED SPINACH, THAWED AND DRAINED	1 TO 2
1	CAN (10 OZ/284 ML) CREAM OF CELERY SOUP	1
1 CUP	SOUR CREAM	250 ML
1 TBSP	UNCOOKED MINUTE RICE	15 ML
	SALT AND PEPPER	
1	PACKAGE (6 OZ/175 G) MOZZARELLA CHEESE	1

BROWN MEAT, ONIONS, MUSHROOMS, GARLIC AND OREGANO IN FRYING PAN. STIR IN SPINACH, SOUP, SOUR CREAM, RICE AND SALT AND PEPPER TO TASTE. PLACE CHEESE (GRATED OR CUT IN STRIPS) ON TOP. BAKE IN 350°F (180°C) OVEN FOR 35 TO 45 MINUTES. IF YOU ARE A CHEESE FAN, DOUBLE THE AMOUNT CALLED FOR AND LAYER THIS IN THE MIDDLE OF THE CASSEROLE. SERVES 6.

FOR EVERY PROBLEM THERE IS A NEAT, SIMPLE SOLUTION – AND IT'S ALWAYS WRONG.

EUREKA! ENCHILADAS

1/2 CUP	OLIVE OIL	125 ML
2	CLOVES GARLIC (AS MUCH AS YOU CAN STAND), MINCED	2
I	CAN (14 OZ/398 ML) DARK PITTED OLIVES (RESERVE JUICE)	I
I	CAN (10 OZ/284 ML) TOMATO SAUCE	I
I	CAN (10 OZ/284 ML) WATER	I
2 TBSP	CHILI POWDER (ROUNDED TABLESPOONS)	25 ML
I TSP	CUMIN	5 ML
2 TSP	SALT	10 ML
2	LARGE ONIONS, DICED	2
I LB	MONTEREY JACK CHEESE	500 G
I LB	LEAN GROUND BEEF	500 G
18	TORTILLAS (FROZEN ARE BEST)	18

SAUCE: SAUTÉ MINCED GARLIC IN OLIVE OIL. ADD OLIVE JUICE, TOMATO SAUCE, WATER, CHILI POWDER, CUMIN AND SALT. SIMMER 10 MINUTES.

FILLING: SAUTÉ DICED ONIONS, DICED OLIVES AND GROUND BEEF IN I TBSP (15 ML) OLIVE OIL UNTIL ONIONS ARE TRANSPARENT. ADD 3/4 LB (375 G) GRATED CHEESE, REMOVE FROM HEAT AND ALLOW CHEESE TO MELT THROUGH THE FILLING MIXTURE.

TORTILLAS: FRY TORTILLAS ONE AT A TIME IN 3 TBSP (45 ML) OLIVE OIL AT HIGH TEMPERATURE, TURNING ONCE. REMOVE FROM HEAT. DRY BETWEEN PAPER TOWELS. SPREAD WITH SMALL AMOUNT OF SAUCE. PLACE I HEAPING TBSP (15 ML) OF FILLING ON EACH TORTILLA. ROLL UP LIKE

CONTINUED ON NEXT PAGE...

A CRÊPE AND LAY IN A RECTANGULAR OVEN DISH. ADD REMAINING SAUCE. SPRINKLE REMAINING FILLING AND REMAINING 1/4 LB (125 G) GRATED CHEESE OVER THE ROLLED TORTILLAS.

BAKE AT 350°F (180°C) FOR 30 MINUTES. SERVES 8.

"ARE YOU MARRIED?"
"NO, I WAS HIT BY A CAR."

ASIAN MEATBALLS

1/2 CUP	COOKING OIL	125 ML
1 1/2 LBS	GROUND BEEF	750 G
1	SMALL CLOVE GARLIC, CRUSHED	1
1 TSP	SALT	5 ML
1/4 TSP	PEPPER	1 ML
2	EGGS	2
1/4 CUP	FLOUR	50 ML
1 TSP	SALT	5 ML
1/4 TSP	PEPPER	1 ML
1/2 CUP	CHICKEN STOCK (OR BOUILLON)	125 ML
1	CAN (14 OZ/398 ML) PINEAPPLE CHUNKS, DRAINED, RESERVE JUICE	1
3 TBSP	CORNSTARCH	45 ML
1/2 CUP	SUGAR	125 ML
1/2 CUP	PINEAPPLE JUICE	125 ML
1/2 CUP	VINEGAR	125 ML
3 TBSP	SOY SAUCE	45 ML

OPTIONAL

1	LARGE TOMATO, PEELED AND CHOPPED	1
2	LARGE GREEN PEPPERS, 1-INCH (2.5 CM) SQUARES	2

HEAT OIL IN FRYING PAN. COMBINE BEEF, GARLIC, SALT AND PEPPER; SHAPE INTO SIZE OF MEATBALLS DESIRED. BEAT EGGS, FLOUR, AND SALT AND PEPPER TOGETHER, ADDING WATER IF NECESSARY TO MAKE THIN BATTER.

DIP MEATBALLS IN BATTER WITH TONGS, SHAKING OFF EXCESS AND DROP INTO HOT OIL. COOK SLOWLY TO

CONTINUED ON NEXT PAGE...

BROWN ON ALL SIDES. REMOVE MEATBALLS AS THEY BROWN AND DISCARD ALL BUT 1 TBSP (15 ML) OF OIL AS WELL AS ANY PIECES OF BATTER. ADD CHICKEN STOCK, GREEN PEPPER, IF DESIRED, AND PINEAPPLE CHUNKS TO PAN. COVER AND SIMMER 5 MINUTES. RETURN MEAT TO PAN AND SIMMER 3 MINUTES MORE. MIX CORNSTARCH, SUGAR PINEAPPLE JUICE, GINGER AND SOY SAUCE TOGETHER UNTIL SMOOTH. ADD TO PAN, STIRRING CONSTANTLY, UNTIL THICKENED. IF SERVING TOMATO PIECES, ADD JUST BEFORE SERVING.

THESE MAY BE MADE AS APPETIZERS AND KEPT WARM IN A CHAFING DISH, OR SERVED AS AN ENTREE OVER RICE. THIS WILL FREEZE WELL AND MAY BE MADE WELL IN ADVANCE. SERVES 6 TO 8.

YOU CANNOT MAKE A HUSBAND TENDER BY KEEPING HIM IN HOT WATER.

STROGANOFF MEATBALLS

A GUARANTEED FAMILY HIT!

MEATBALLS

2 LBS	LEAN GROUND BEEF	1 KG
1 1/2 CUPS	BREAD CRUMBS	375 ML
1/4 CUP	MILK	50 ML
1/4 CUP	FINELY CHOPPED ONION	50 ML
2	EGGS, BEATEN	2
	SALT AND PEPPER TO TASTE	

SOUR CREAM SAUCE

1 CUP	CHOPPED ONION	250 ML
1/4 CUP	BUTTER	50 ML
1/4 CUP	FLOUR	50 ML
1/4 CUP	KETCHUP	50 ML
2	CANS (EACH 10 OZ/284 ML) CONSOMMÉ (UNDILUTED)	2
2 CUPS	FAT-FREE SOUR CREAM	500 ML

TO MAKE MEATBALLS: COMBINE ALL INGREDIENTS IN LARGE BOWL. MIX WELL AND ROLL IN BALLS OF DESIRED SIZE. PLACE ON EDGED COOKIE SHEET AND BAKE AT 375°F (190°C) FOR 25-30 MINUTES. REMOVE FROM OVEN, DRAIN AND SET ASIDE.

TO MAKE SAUCE: BROWN ONION IN BUTTER. ADD FLOUR AND MIX WELL. ADD KETCHUP AND CONSOMMÉ, COOKING SLOWLY UNTIL THICKENED. ADD SOUR CREAM, THEN MEATBALLS. PLACE IN CASSEROLE AND KEEP WARM IN 250°F (120°C) UNTIL SERVING TIME. SERVE OVER BROAD EGG NOODLES. SERVES 6.

CHINESE STEAK

PREPARE YOUR INGREDIENTS AND COOK THIS AT THE TABLE IN A WOK WITH YOUR GUESTS LOOKING ON. USE ROUND OR SIRLOIN STEAK. YOU CAN USE ELECTRIC FRY PAN OR WOK.

1 LB	STEAK STRIPS (1/4 INCH/0.5 CM THICK)	500 G
1/2 TSP	GINGER, SALT AND PEPPER	2 ML
1/4 CUP	SALAD OIL	50 ML
1	GREEN PEPPER, COARSELY CHOPPED	1
1 CUP	CELERY, COARSELY CHOPPED	250 ML
1/2 CUP	ONION, COARSELY CHOPPED	125 ML

SAUCE

2 TBSP	CORNSTARCH	25 ML
1/3 CUP	SOY SAUCE	75 ML
1 CUP	HOT WATER	250 ML
1	CUBE BEEF BOUILLON	1

BROWN MEAT IN FRY PAN AND PUSH TO ONE SIDE. ADD VEGETABLES AND STIR-FRY. POUR SAUCE OVER AND SIMMER. LASTLY, ADD CHUNKS OF TOMATOES AND SERVE ON RICE. SERVES 4.

MARRIAGE IS A LOT LIKE A BOXING EVENT... SOMETIMES THE PRELIMINARIES ARE BETTER THAN THE MAIN EVENT.

BAKED STEAK

2½-INCH	SIRLOIN STEAK	6 CM
	SALT AND FRESHLY GROUND PEPPER TO TASTE	
1	MEDIUM ONION, FINELY CHOPPED	1
1 CUP	KETCHUP	250 ML
3 TBSP	BUTTER, MELTED	45 ML
1 TBSP	LEMON JUICE	15 ML
1	SMALL GREEN PEPPER, SLICED	1
1	SMALL BUNCH FRESH CHOPPED PARSLEY	1
	FEW DROPS WORCESTERSHIRE SAUCE	

PREHEAT BROILER. PLACE STEAK 4 INCHES (10 CM) BELOW BROILER. SEAR BOTH SIDES. REMOVE AND DRAIN FAT. SEASON WITH SALT AND PEPPER. MIX ALL INGREDIENTS AND POUR OVER STEAK IN PAN. PLACE IN 425°F (220°C) OVEN FOR 30 MINUTES. REMOVE FROM OVEN. POUR MUSTARD SAUCE OVER AND SPRINKLE PARSLEY ON TOP AND SERVE. SERVES 6 TO 8.

FOR MUSTARD SAUCE, SEE PAGE 250!

THE MAN WHO SAYS THAT MARRIAGE IS A
50-50 PROPOSITION DOESN'T UNDERSTAND
TWO THINGS 1) WOMEN, 2) FRACTIONS.

ENGLISH SPICED BEEF

*THIS IS TRADITIONAL CHRISTMAS FARE. PRODUCES A
PINK AND HAM-LIKE TEXTURE THAT, SLICED THINLY,
IS A GREAT FAVORITE FOR HOLIDAY FEASTING.
WELL WORTH THE TROUBLE!*

	PIECE OF LEAN BEEF, UP TO 25 LBS (12.5 KG) DEBONED AND ROLLED	
1½ OZ	SALTPETER	45 G
1½ CUPS	BROWN SUGAR	375 ML
1½ CUPS	SALT	375 ML
4 TBSP	BLACK PEPPER	60 ML
4 TBSP	GROUND ALLSPICE	60 ML
2 TBSP	MACE	25 ML
2 TBSP	NUTMEG	25 ML
2 TBSP	CLOVES	25 ML

MIX INGREDIENTS TOGETHER AND RUB ROUND OF BEEF.
COVER LOOSELY WITH FOIL. SET IN A COOL PLACE (A
CROCK POT IS IDEAL) AND TURN EVERY 2 OR 3 DAYS
FOR 3 WEEKS. BEFORE BOILING, PUT IN A PIECE OF SUET
WHERE BONE WAS TAKEN OUT. TIE FIRMLY WITH CORD
UNTIL IT IS OF UNIFORM SHAPE. SIMMER GENTLY FOR
5 TO 7 HOURS TURNING AT HALF TIME. DO NOT WASH OFF
SPICES BEFORE BOILING. FOR SMALLER PIECE OF BEEF
(10 TO 12 LBS/5 TO 6 KG) USE SAME AMOUNT OF SPICES
BUT REDUCE PICKLING TIME TO 12 DAYS AND REDUCE
BOILING TIME TO 3 TO 5 HOURS.

THE COST OF LIVING IS HIGH, BUT CONSIDER THE ALTERNATIVE.

BEEF BOURGUIGNON

AN ELEGANT FRENCH STEW FOR 8 GOOD FRIENDS.
SERVE WITH BEAUCOUP BAGUETTES ... C'EST SI BON!

1/2 LB	THICK-SLICED BACON	250 G
12 TO 15	SMALL WHOLE ONIONS, PEELED, OR 4 HANDFULS PEARL ONIONS, SKINS REMOVED	12 TO 15
3 LBS	LEAN BEEF CHUCK, CUT INTO 1-INCH (2.5 CM) PIECES	1.5 KG
	OLIVE OIL	
2	CLOVES GARLIC, MINCED	2
3 TBSP	FLOUR	45 ML
	SALT AND PEPPER TO TASTE	
3 CUPS	DRY RED WINE	750 ML
2 CUPS	BEEF BROTH	500 ML
	BAY LEAF	
1/2 TSP	DRIED THYME	2 ML
2 CUPS	SLICED MUSHROOMS	500 ML
4 TO 6	LARGE CARROTS, PEELED AND CUT IN BITE-SIZED PIECES	4 TO 6
2 TBSP	BUTTER	25 ML
	CHOPPED FRESH PARSLEY FOR GARNISH	

PREHEAT OVEN TO 300°F (150°C). IN A DUTCH OVEN,
SAUTÉ BACON UNTIL CRISP. REMOVE, COOL AND COARSELY
CHOP. RESERVE 1 TO 2 TBSP (15 TO 25 ML) BACON DRIPPINGS.
ADD ONIONS AND SAUTÉ LIGHTLY; REMOVE TO ANOTHER
DISH. ADD BEEF TO POT (AND SOME OIL IF NECESSARY)
AND BROWN OVER MEDIUM-HIGH HEAT FOR 5 MINUTES;
ADD GARLIC FOR THE LAST MINUTE (BE CAREFUL NOT
TO BURN). SPRINKLE WITH FLOUR, SALT AND PEPPER;

CONTINUED ON NEXT PAGE...

STIR UNTIL FLOUR BEGINS TO BROWN. ADD WINE, BEEF BROTH, BAY LEAF AND THYME. STIR TO LOOSEN BROWNED BITS ON BOTTOM OF POT, ADD ONIONS, COVER AND PLACE IN OVEN FOR AT LEAST 2 HOURS.

MEANWHILE, LIGHTLY SAUTÉ MUSHROOMS AND CARROTS IN BUTTER AND SET ASIDE. REMOVE POT FROM OVEN, ADD SAUTÉED VEGGIES AND RETURN TO OVEN FOR ANOTHER $\frac{1}{2}$ HOUR. IF MORE LIQUID IS NEEDED, ADD BEEF BROTH. GARNISH WITH PARSLEY. SERVES 8.

HE WHO LAUGHS LAST USUALLY HAS A TOOTH MISSING.

STONED STEW

3 LBS	STEWING BEEF, CUT UP	1.5 KG
1/4 CUP	FLOUR	50 ML
1/2 TSP	SALT	2 ML
1/2 TSP	SEASONED PEPPER	2 ML
1/4 CUP	OIL	50 ML
2	LARGE ONIONS, THINLY SLICED	2
1	CAN (10 OZ/284 ML) SLICED MUSHROOMS	1
1	CAN (10 OZ/284 ML) BEEF BROTH	1
1	BOTTLE (12 OZ/341 ML) BEER	1
2 TBSP	VINEGAR	25 ML
2 TBSP	SUGAR	25 ML
2	CLOVES GARLIC, MINCED	2
1 TSP	THYME	5 ML
3	BAY LEAVES	3
2 TBSP	DRIED PARSLEY	25 ML

IN PLASTIC BAG COMBINE FLOUR, SALT AND PEPPER. TRIM BEEF CUBES AND SHAKE IN FLOUR MIXTURE. HEAT OIL IN SKILLET AND BROWN MEAT, TURNING OFTEN. ADD SLICED ONIONS, MUSHROOMS WITH LIQUID, BEEF BROTH, BEER, VINEGAR, SUGAR, GARLIC, THYME AND BAY LEAVES. SIMMER, COVERED, ADDING WATER IF NECESSARY, FOR 2 HOURS. ADD PARSLEY. SERVE OVER HOT BUTTERED NOODLES. SERVES 8.

SIGN IN A BANKRUPT STORE WINDOW:
"WE UNDERSOLD EVERYONE."

GINGER'S BEEF STROGANOFF

GREAT FOR LARGE CROWDS (ADJUST RECIPE ACCORDINGLY). FREEZES BEAUTIFULLY, BUT DON'T ADD SOUR CREAM AND SHERRY UNTIL DAY OF SERVING.

1 LB	BEEF SIRLOIN, CUT AGAINST GRAIN INTO 1- X 1/4-INCH (2.5 X 0.5 CM) PIECES	500 G
2 TBSP	BUTTER	25 ML
1 CUP	SLICED FRESH MUSHROOMS	250 ML
1/2 CUP	CHOPPED ONION	125 ML
1	GARLIC CLOVE, MINCED	1
3 TBSP	FLOUR	45 ML
1 TBSP	TOMATO PASTE	15 ML
1	CAN (10 OZ/284 ML) BEEF BOUILLON	1
1/2 TSP	SALT	2 ML
1 CUP	SOUR CREAM	250 ML
2 TBSP	SHERRY	25 ML

BROWN MEAT QUICKLY IN A HOT SKILLET. REMOVE TO CASSEROLE DISH. REDUCE SKILLET HEAT AND ADD MUSHROOMS, ONIONS AND GARLIC (ADD MORE BUTTER IF NECESSARY). COOK 3 TO 4 MINUTES UNTIL ONION IS CLEAR. REMOVE AND ADD TO THE CASSEROLE DISH. NOW MAKE THE SAUCE IN THE SKILLET. MELT BUTTER, ADD FLOUR, SALT AND TOMATO PASTE. STIR IN BEEF BOUILLON AND COOK UNTIL THICK. ADD SAUCE TO CASSEROLE. WHEN READY TO SERVE ADD SOUR CREAM AND SHERRY TO CASSEROLE AND HEAT IN 275°F (140°C) OVEN FOR 1/2 HOUR OR UNTIL WARMED THROUGH. DON'T LET IT BOIL OR SOUR CREAM WILL CURDLE. SERVES 4 TO 6.

GOULASH

2 LBS	HAMBURGER	1 KG
2	PACKAGES MACARONI AND CHEESE	2
1 CUP	CELERY, SLICED	250 ML
1	ONION, CHOPPED	1
2	CANS (EACH 10 OZ/284 ML) MUSHROOMS	2
1 TBSP	HP SAUCE	15 ML
DASH	TABASCO	DASH
4	CANS (EACH 10 OZ/284 ML) TOMATO SOUP	4
1	LARGE GREEN PEPPER, SLICED	1
2	CANS (EACH 10 OZ/284 ML) MUSHROOM SOUP	2
1	CAN (10 OZ/284 ML) CORN KERNELS	1
1 TBSP	WORCESTERSHIRE SAUCE	15 ML
1 TBSP	CURRY POWDER (OPTIONAL)	15 ML

BROWN HAMBURGER AND ONION. DRAIN OFF EXCESS FAT.
COOK MACARONI AND CHEESE. COMBINE EVERYTHING.
BAKE AT 325°F (180°C) FOR 1 HOUR. SERVES 10.

HE WHO HESITATES IS NOT ONLY LOST,
BUT MILES FROM THE NEXT EXIT.

BONES

MOST BUTCHER SHOPS NOW SELL THE RIB BONES
CUT FROM THE PRIME OR STANDING RIB-ROASTS.
A TREAT! SERVE 2 PER PERSON.

	RIB BONES	
	GARLIC SALT AND SEASONED PEPPER (LOTS OF BOTH)	
2 TBSP	DRY MUSTARD	25 ML
3 TBSP	CREAM	45 ML
	BREAD CRUMBS	
3 TBSP	BUTTER, MELTED	45 ML

PREHEAT BROILER. GENEROUSLY SPRINKLE BONES WITH
GARLIC SALT AND SEASONED PEPPER. MAKE A PASTE OF
MUSTARD AND CREAM. BRUSH EACH RIB WITH PASTE AND
SPRINKLE EACH WITH FINE BREAD CRUMBS. PLACE RIBS
ON BROILER PAN AND BROIL THREE MINUTES PER SIDE,
BRUSHING WITH MELTED BUTTER WHILE TURNING, 10 TO
12 MINUTES IN TOTAL OR UNTIL WELL BROWNED AND
CRISPY. SERVE WITH BAKED POTATOES AND VEGETABLES.
REALLY DELICIOUS.

IF YOU REALLY LOOK LIKE YOUR PASSPORT PHOTO,
CHANCES ARE YOU'RE NOT WELL ENOUGH TO TRAVEL.

VEAL SCALOPPINI

ITALIAN IN ORIGIN, THIS FAMOUS RECIPE IS PARTY FARE.

1½ LBS	VEAL STEAK (½ INCH/1 CM THICK)	750 G
1 TSP	SALT	5 ML
1 TSP	PAPRIKA	5 ML
½ CUP	SALAD OIL	125 ML
¼ CUP	LEMON JUICE	50 ML
1	CLOVE GARLIC (SPLIT)	1
1 TSP	PREPARED MUSTARD	5 ML
¼ TSP	NUTMEG	1 ML
½ TSP	SUGAR	2 ML
¼ CUP	FLOUR	50 ML
¼ CUP	OIL	50 ML
1	MEDIUM ONION, SLICED THIN	1
1	GREEN PEPPER CUT IN STRIPS	1
1	CAN (10 OZ/284 ML) CHICKEN BROTH	1
¼ LB	MUSHROOMS, SLICED	125 G
1 TBSP	BUTTER	15 ML
6	PIMENTO OLIVES, SLICED	6

SAUCE: COMBINE SALT, PAPRIKA, OIL, LEMON JUICE, GARLIC, MUSTARD, NUTMEG AND SUGAR IN A JAR. SHAKE TO COMBINE THOROUGHLY. CUT VEAL INTO SERVING PIECES. SPREAD VEAL IN SHALLOW DISH, POUR SAUCE OVER, COAT WELL AND LET STAND 20 MINUTES. REMOVE GARLIC. HEAT OIL IN LARGE SKILLET. LIFT VEAL FROM SAUCE AND DIP IN FLOUR. BROWN IN SKILLET AND ADD ONION AND GREEN PEPPER. COMBINE CHICKEN BROTH

CONTINUED ON NEXT PAGE...

WITH REMAINING SAUCE AND POUR OVER VEAL. CONTINUE COOKING SLOWLY (COVERED) UNTIL VEAL IS TENDER. (ABOUT 30 MINUTES) BROWN MUSHROOMS LIGHTLY IN BUTTER. ADD MUSHROOMS AND OLIVES TO VEAL. SERVE ON LARGE PLATTER SURROUNDED WITH NOODLES AND GARNISH WITH PARSLEY AND LEMON WEDGES. SERVES 6.

A LOT OF PEOPLE DON'T CARE WHO WEARS THE PANTS IN THE FAMILY AS LONG AS THERE IS MONEY IN THE POCKETS.

SHORT RIBS IN BEER

A PERENNIAL FAVORITE. MY RECIPE CARD IS COVERED WITH GREASE AND DULLED FROM YEARS OF USE.

8	SHORT RIBS (3 LBS/1.5 KG, TRIMMED)	8
1/2 CUP	FLOUR	125 ML
1/4 TSP	PEPPER	1 ML
1/4 TSP	GINGER	1 ML
1 TSP	SALT	5 ML
1/2 TSP	DRY MUSTARD	2 ML
1 TSP	CHOPPED PARSLEY	5 ML
2 TBSP	OIL	25 ML
1	MEDIUM ONION, SLICED	1
1	CLOVE GARLIC	1
12 OZ	BEER	341 ML
5	CARROTS	5

WASH AND DRY SHORT RIBS. COMBINE FLOUR, PEPPER, GINGER, SALT, DRY MUSTARD AND PARSLEY. DREDGE SHORT RIBS IN THE MIXTURE. BROWN MEAT IN OIL WITH ONION. ADD GARLIC, BEER (AND WATER IF NECESSARY TO MAKE 1 INCH (2.5 CM) OF LIQUID). COVER AND BAKE AT 300°F (150°C) FOR 2 1/2 HOURS OR UNTIL MEAT IS TENDER. ADD CARROTS DURING THE LAST 20 MINUTES. REMOVE GARLIC. SERVE WITH RICE AND SALAD. SERVES 4 TO 6.

IF IT IS SUCH A SMALL WORLD, WHY DOES IT COST SO MUCH TO RUN IT?

YEAR-ROUND GREENS

I	HEAD CAULIFLOWER, BROKEN IN TO FLORETS	I
I	CELERY HEART, CUT IN 2-INCH (5 CM) DIAGONAL SLICES	I
2	STALKS BROCCOLI, BROKEN INTO FLORETS	2
3	MEDIUM GREEN PEPPERS, CUT IN 2-INCH (5 CM) SQUARES	3
4 TBSP	OIL	60 ML
I	SPANISH ONION, CUT IN SIXTHS	I
2	CANS (EACH 10 OZ/284 ML) WHOLE MUSHROOMS	2
1½ TBSP	LEMON JUICE	22 ML
¼ TO ½ CUP	SOY SAUCE	50 TO 125 ML

FILL 3-QUART (3 L) SAUCEPAN ⅔ FULL WITH WATER, BRING TO BOIL AND PLACE CAULIFLOWER IN BOILING WATER. COOK 3 MINUTES, REMOVE AND SET ASIDE. PLACE CELERY IN BOILING WATER AND BOIL 3 MINUTES. REMOVE AND SET ASIDE. IN SIMILAR MANNER COOK BROCCOLI FOR 2 MINUTES AND GREEN PEPPER FOR I MINUTE. DRAIN VEGETABLES WELL. IN LARGE FRYING PAN OR WOK, HEAT OIL. ADD COOKED VEGETABLES, MUSHROOMS AND ONIONS. STIR-FRY 2 MINUTES. POUR LEMON JUICE AND SOY SAUCE OVER MIXTURE. COVER AND COOK OVER LOW HEAT 6 MINUTES OR UNTIL TENDER. SERVES 8 TO 10.

MY WIFE'S T.V. DINNERS MELT IN YOUR MOUTH. I WISH SHE'D DEFROST THEM FIRST.

BEAN STUFF

A TASTY VARIATION OF CHILI!

6	SLICES BACON	6
I LB	LEAN GROUND BEEF	500 G
I	ONION, CHOPPED	I
I	GREEN PEPPER, CHOPPED	I
I	GARLIC CLOVE, MINCED	I
2 TBSP	MOLASSES	25 ML
2 TBSP	BROWN SUGAR	25 ML
I TSP	DRY MUSTARD	5 ML
$\frac{1}{3}$ CUP	VINEGAR	75 ML
I	CAN (19 OZ/540 ML) TOMATOES	I
I	CAN (14 OZ/398 ML) KIDNEY BEANS	I
I	CAN (14 OZ/398 ML) LIMA BEANS, DRAINED	I
I	CAN (14 OZ/398 ML) PORK AND BEANS	I
I TSP	WORCESTERSHIRE SAUCE	5 ML
	SALT, PEPPER AND TABASCO SAUCE, TO TASTE	

FRY BACON UNTIL CRISP. CRUMBLE. BROWN BEEF AND ONION. COMBINE WITH REMAINING INGREDIENTS IN A LARGE CASSEROLE. BAKE AT 300°F (150°C) OVEN FOR 2 HOURS. SERVE WITH CAESAR SALAD (PAGE 135). SERVES 4 TO 6.

A HUSBAND WHO GETS HIS BREAKFAST IN BED
IS IN THE HOSPITAL.

GREEN BEAN CASSEROLE

THIS RECIPE YOU CAN MAKE AHEAD, SET IN THE REFRIGERATOR AND HEAT JUST BEFORE DINNER. TRY WITH HAM OR CORNED BEEF.

2	PACKAGES (EACH 12 OZ/375 G) FROZEN FRENCH-CUT BEANS (COOKED AND DRAINED)	2
1	CAN (5 OZ/142 ML) WATER CHESTNUTS, DRAINED, SLICED	1
½ CUP	TOASTED, SLIVERED ALMONDS	125 ML
½ CUP	BUTTER	125 ML
1 LB	FRESH MUSHROOMS, SLICED	500 G
¼ CUP	FLOUR	50 ML
2 CUPS	MILK	500 ML
1 CUP	CREAM	250 ML
1½ CUPS	GRATED SHARP (OLD) CHEDDAR CHEESE	375 ML
⅛ TSP	TABASCO SAUCE	0.5 ML
2 TSP	SOY SAUCE	10 ML
1 TSP	SALT	5 ML
½ TSP	PEPPER	2 ML

SAUTÉ SLICED ONION AND MUSHROOM IN BUTTER. ADD FLOUR AND MIX. ADD MILK AND CREAM, STIR UNTIL THICKENED. ADD REMAINING INGREDIENTS AND SIMMER UNTIL CHEESE MELTS. ADD COOKED BEANS, MIX WELL. POUR INTO GREASED SHALLOW CASSEROLE. SPRINKLE WITH TOASTED SLIVERED ALMONDS. BAKE AT 350°F (180°C) FOR 35 TO 45 MINUTES. SERVES 8.

SESAME BROCCOLI

2 LBS	FRESH BROCCOLI	1 KG
2 TBSP	SALAD OIL	25 ML
2 TBSP	VINEGAR	25 ML
2 TBSP	SOY SAUCE	25 ML
4 TBSP	SUGAR	60 ML
2 TBSP	TOASTED SESAME SEEDS	25 ML

POUR BOILING WATER OVER BROCCOLI AND LET STAND 5 MINUTES. DRAIN. HEAT REMAINING INGREDIENTS AND POUR OVER BROCCOLI IN A CASSEROLE. HEAT IN OVEN BEFORE SERVING. SERVES 8.

EASTER BROCCOLI

THIS MAY BE MADE AHEAD AND HEATED THROUGH.

2 CUPS	PARTIALLY COOKED BROCCOLI (FRESH IS BEST)	500 ML
1 CUP	CHOPPED CELERY	250 ML
1	SMALL JAR PIMENTOS, CHOPPED	1
1	CAN (10 OZ/284 ML) CREAM OF MUSHROOM SOUP	1
1 CUP	SOUR CREAM	250 ML
	GRATED CHEESE TO COVER	

MIX SOUP AND CREAM TOGETHER. IN SEPARATE BOWL, MIX VEGETABLES. POUR SOUP MIXTURE OVER VEGETABLES AND BAKE AT 325°F (160°C) FOR 30 MINUTES. THIS RECIPE CAN BE DOUBLED, BUT CUT DOWN ON SOUR CREAM, AS IT GOES RUNNY. SERVES 6.

Polynesian Chicken (page 185)

Japanese Chicken Wings (page 186)

Peachy Pork (page 191)

Beef Bourguignon (page 212)

RED CABBAGE

EXCELLENT WITH FOWL AND A MUST WITH WILD GAME!

3 LBS	RED CABBAGE	1.5 KG
2	GREEN APPLES, PEELED AND CHOPPED	2
1	ONION, FINELY CHOPPED	1
1/4 CUP	WHITE SUGAR	50 ML
1/4 CUP	VINEGAR	50 ML
2 TBSP	BACON FAT	25 ML
1 TSP	SALT	5 ML
	FRESHLY GROUND PEPPER	
1/2 CUP	BOILING WATER	125 ML

SHRED CABBAGE AND PLACE IN A LARGE SAUCEPAN WITH
REMAINING INGREDIENTS. BRING TO A BOIL; REDUCE HEAT;
COVER AND SIMMER FOR 1 HOUR. STIR OCCASIONALLY.
SERVES 6 TO 8.

*DON'T BE TOO FUSSY. LOTS OF PEOPLE WAIT SO LONG FOR
THEIR SHIP TO COME IN, THEIR PIER COLLAPSES.*

CORN SOUFFLÉ

A LOVELY CHANGE FOR THE CORN - ALWAYS GOOD WHEN SERVED WITH HAM. MUST BE PREPARED AND SERVED JUST BEFORE DINNER OR SOUFFLÉ WILL FALL. DON'T FORGET THE SALT!

1	CAN (10 OZ/284 ML) CREAMED CORN	1
4	EGGS	4
2 TBSP	FLOUR	25 ML
1 TBSP	SUGAR	15 ML
2 TBSP	BUTTER	25 ML
1/4 TSP	SALT	1 ML

SEPARATE EGGS INTO 2 MEDIUM BOWLS. BEAT TOGETHER YOLKS, SUGAR AND CORN. MELT BUTTER AND FLOUR, BEAT INTO CORN MIXTURE. BEAT EGG WHITES UNTIL STIFF AND FOLD INTO CORN. POUR INTO SOUFFLÉ DISH OR CASSEROLE. BAKE AT 350°F (180°C) FOR 45 MINUTES. SERVE AT ONCE. SERVES 4 TO 6.

NEVER PUT ALL YOUR EGGS IN YOUR POCKET.

DEVILED CORN

GOOD FOR BUFFETS AND GOES WITH
PRACTICALLY EVERYTHING.

4 TBSP	BUTTER	60 ML
2 TBSP	FLOUR	25 ML
1 TSP	DRY MUSTARD	5 ML
1 TBSP	LEMON JUICE	15 ML
1/2 TSP	SALT	2 ML
PINCH	PEPPER	PINCH
1/2 CUP	MILK	125 ML
3	SLICES BACON, COOKED AND CRUMBLED	3
2	HARD-COOKED EGGS, CHOPPED	2
1	CAN (14 OZ/398 ML) CORN KERNELS, DRAINED	1
1	CAN (14 OZ/398 ML) CREAMED CORN	1
1/2 CUP	GRATED PARMESAN CHEESE	125 ML
1/2 CUP	CRACKER CRUMBS	125 ML
1 TBSP	BUTTER, MELTED	15 ML
2	HARD-COOKED EGGS, SLICED	2
	SLICED RIPE OLIVES, PITTED	

IN LARGE SAUCEPAN, MELT BUTTER AND ADD FLOUR,
MUSTARD, LEMON JUICE, SALT AND PEPPER. MIX WELL.
ADD MILK AND STIR UNTIL THICK AND BUBBLY. REMOVE
PAN FROM HEAT AND STIR IN BACON, CHOPPED EGGS
AND BOTH CANS OF CORN. SPOON INTO 6-CUP (1.5 L)
CASSEROLE AND SPRINKLE WITH PARMESAN CHEESE.
COMBINE CRUMBS AND MELTED BUTTER AND SPRINKLE
OVER CHEESE. BAKE AT 350°F (180°C) FOR 45 MINUTES.
GARNISH WITH EGGS AND OLIVES. SERVES 6.

FESTIVE MUSHROOMS

A VERY RICH DISH FOR SPECIAL OCCASIONS. SERVE SMALL HELPINGS! GOOD WITH ROAST BEEF.

2 LBS	FRESH MUSHROOMS, CUT INTO "T'S"	1 KG
3 TBSP	BUTTER	45 ML
1	CAN (14 OZ/398 ML) PITTED RIPE OLIVES, SLICED	1
1 CUP	GRATED, OLD CHEDDAR CHEESE	250 ML
2 TBSP	FLOUR	25 ML
2 TBSP	BUTTER	25 ML
1/2 CUP	SOFT BREAD CRUMBS	125 ML
1 TBSP	MELTED BUTTER	15 ML

SAUTÉ MUSHROOMS IN 3 TBSP (45 ML) BUTTER, UNTIL JUICY. IN A MEDIUM CASSEROLE, ADD A LAYER OF MUSHROOMS AND SLICED OLIVES. SPRINKLE WITH CHEDDAR CHEESE AND FLOUR; DOT WITH BUTTER. CONTINUE LAYERS IN THIS ORDER, AND TOP LAST LAYER WITH BUTTERED CRUMBS. BAKE AT 350°F (180°C) FOR 30 MINUTES. SERVES 8 TO 10.

AN IDEALIST IS ONE WHO, ON NOTICING THAT A ROSE SMELLS BETTER THAN A CABBAGE, CONCLUDES THAT IT WILL ALSO MAKE BETTER SOUP.

PICKLED ONIONS

GREAT WITH ROAST BEEF SANDWICHES. SERVES A CROWD.

4	LARGE YELLOW ONIONS, THINLY SLICED	4
1½ CUPS	WHITE VINEGAR	375 ML
1½ CUPS	WATER	375 ML
1 CUP	WHITE SUGAR	250 ML
¼ CUP	FRESH LEMON JUICE	50 ML
¼ TSP	TABASCO SAUCE	1 ML
1 TSP	SALT	5 ML
½ TSP	SEASONED PEPPER	2 ML
2	GARLIC CLOVES, MINCED	2
1 CUP	SOUR CREAM (FAT-FREE IS OKAY)	250 ML
1 TSP	CELERY SEED	5 ML

COMBINE ALL INGREDIENTS, EXCEPT SOUR CREAM AND CELERY SEED. MARINATE OVERNIGHT. BEFORE SERVING, DRAIN AND STIR IN SOUR CREAM AND CELERY SEED. PLACE IN A PRETTY BOWL – THERE'S NOTHING BEAUTIFUL ABOUT AN ONION! *MAKES ABOUT 3 CUPS (750 ML).*

TO PREVENT A HEAD COLD FROM GOING TO YOUR CHEST, JUST TIE A KNOT IN YOUR NECK.

CASSEROLE PEAS

2 TBSP	BUTTER	25 ML
1/2 LB	FRESH MUSHROOMS, SLICED	250 G
2	PACKAGES (EACH 10 OZ/284 G) FROZEN PEAS	2
1	CAN (10 OZ/284 ML) MUSHROOM SOUP	1
1	CAN BEAN SPROUTS, WELL DRAINED	1
1	CAN (4 OZ/114 ML) WATER CHESTNUTS, SLICED	1
	TOASTED SLIVERED ALMONDS, OR FRENCH ONION RINGS	

HEAT BUTTER. ADD MUSHROOMS, SAUTÉ 5 MINUTES, COMBINE WITH PEAS, SOUP, BEAN SPROUTS AND CHESTNUTS. PLACE IN LIGHTLY BUTTERED CASSEROLE. BAKE AT 350°F (180°C) FOR 20 TO 25 MINUTES. PAT ALMONDS ON TOP OR MIX THEM IN OR PUT CHINESE NOODLES ON TOP. MAY BE WATERY BUT YOU CAN SERVE IT WITH A SLOTTED SPOON. SERVES 8 TO 10.

MIDDLE AGE IS WHEN THE PHONE RINGS ON A SATURDAY NIGHT AND YOU HOPE IT'S THE WRONG NUMBER.

TURNIP PUFF

IDEAL FOR THANKSGIVING AND CHRISTMAS DINNERS.

6 CUPS	CUBED TURNIPS	1.5 L
2 TBSP	BUTTER	25 ML
2	EGGS, BEATEN	2
3 TBSP	FLOUR	45 ML
1 TBSP	BROWN SUGAR	15 ML
1 TSP	BAKING POWDER	5 ML
	SALT AND PEPPER TO TASTE	
PINCH	NUTMEG	PINCH
1/2 CUP	FINE BREAD CRUMBS	125 ML
2 TBSP	BUTTER, MELTED	25 ML

COOK TURNIPS UNTIL TENDER. DRAIN AND MASH. ADD BUTTER AND EGGS. BEAT WELL. (THIS MUCH CAN BE DONE THE DAY AHEAD.) COMBINE FLOUR, SUGAR, BAKING POWDER, SALT, PEPPER AND NUTMEG. STIR INTO TURNIPS. BUTTER A CASSEROLE AND PUT IN TURNIP MIXTURE. COMBINE CRUMBS AND BUTTER. SPRINKLE ON TOP. BAKE AT 375°F (190°C) FOR 25 MINUTES, OR UNTIL LIGHT BROWN ON TOP. SERVES 6.

MOST WOMEN DON'T PLAY BRIDGE SKILLFULLY,
BUT THEY ALWAYS PLAY FLUENTLY.

TURNIPS 'N' APPLES

EVERYBODY WHO TRIES THIS WANTS THE RECIPE –
YOU'VE GOT IT!

I	LARGE TURNIP	I
I TBSP	BUTTER	15 ML
2	APPLES	2
1/4 CUP	BROWN SUGAR	50 ML
PINCH	CINNAMON	PINCH

CRUST

1/3 CUP	FLOUR	75 ML
1/3 CUP	BROWN SUGAR	75 ML
2 TBSP	BUTTER	25 ML

PEEL, DICE, COOK, DRAIN AND MASH THE TURNIP WITH BUTTER. PEEL AND SLICE APPLES. TOSS WITH BROWN SUGAR AND CINNAMON. ARRANGE IN GREASED CASSEROLE, TURNIPS AND APPLES IN ALTERNATE LAYERS BEGINNING AND ENDING WITH TURNIPS. COMBINE CRUST INGREDIENTS TO A CRUMBLY TEXTURE AND PAT ON TOP OF CASSEROLE. BAKE AT 350°F (180°C) FOR I HOUR. SERVES 6 TO 8.

SHE TRIED TO BAKE A BIRTHDAY CAKE,
BUT THE CANDLES MELTED IN THE OVEN.

ZUCCHINI CASSEROLE

1 1/2 LBS	ZUCCHINI	750 G
4	EGGS	4
1/2 CUP	MILK	125 ML
1 LB	JACK OR MOZZARELLA CHEESE, GRATED	500 G
1 TSP	SALT	5 ML
2 TSP	BAKING POWDER	10 ML
3 TBSP	FLOUR	45 ML
1/2 CUP	BREAD CRUMBS	125 ML
	BUTTER OR MARGARINE	

PREHEAT OVEN TO 350°F (180°C). WASH AND CUT THE ZUCCHINI INTO 1/2-INCH (1 CM) SLICES. COOK IN A SMALL AMOUNT OF WATER UNTIL BARELY TENDER (5 MINUTES). DRAIN AND COOL. BEAT EGGS SLIGHTLY AND ADD MILK, GRATED CHEESE, SALT, BAKING POWDER AND FLOUR. STIR ZUCCHINI INTO EGG MIXTURE. PLACE IN BUTTERED CASSEROLE. SPRINKLE WITH CRUMBS AND DOT WITH BUTTER. BAKE FOR 35 TO 40 MINUTES. TO BRING OUT THE FLAVOR OF ZUCCHINI, CUT AND LET STAND IN A DISH OF SALTED WATER FOR 15 TO 30 MINUTES. SERVES 6.

WHAT A WONDERFUL NIGHT. THE MOON WAS OUT
AND SO WERE HER PARENTS.

SWEET POTATO SUPREME

GREAT WITH HAM OR TURKEY.

4 CUPS	COOKED, MASHED SWEET POTATOES	1 L
2 TBSP	CREAM OR MILK	25 ML
1 TSP	SALT	5 ML
1/4 TSP	PAPRIKA	1 ML
1/2 CUP	BROWN SUGAR, PACKED	125 ML
1/3 CUP	BUTTER	75 ML
1 CUP	PECAN HALVES, TO COVER CASSEROLE	250 ML

THOROUGHLY MIX POTATOES, CREAM, SALT AND PAPRIKA. SPREAD IN GREASED CASSEROLE. MAKE THE TOPPING BY HEATING BROWN SUGAR AND BUTTER OVER LOW HEAT, STIRRING CONSTANTLY, UNTIL BUTTER IS BARELY MELTED. (IT IS IMPORTANT NOT TO COOK AFTER BUTTER IS MELTED, OR THE TOPPING WILL HARDEN WHEN CASSEROLE IS HEATED.) SPREAD TOPPING OVER POTATOES AND COVER WITH PECAN HALVES. REFRIGERATE UNTIL READY TO HEAT. THIS CASSEROLE MAY BE WARMED IN AN OVEN OF ANY TEMPERATURE. SHOULD BE BUBBLING HOT BEFORE SERVING. SERVES 6 TO 8.

WHEN LIFE HANDS YOU A LEMON, MAKE LEMONADE!

ELSIE'S POTATOES

A MUST WITH TURKEY DINNER . . . CAN BE MADE AHEAD
AND FROZEN.

5 LBS	POTATOES (ABOUT 9 LARGE)	2.5 KG
8 OZ	LOW-FAT CREAM CHEESE	250 G
1 CUP	FAT-FREE SOUR CREAM	250 ML
2 TSP	ONION SALT	10 ML
1 TSP	SALT	5 ML
PINCH	PEPPER	PINCH
2 TBSP	BUTTER	25 ML

COOK AND MASH POTATOES. ADD ALL INGREDIENTS, EXCEPT
BUTTER, AND COMBINE. PUT INTO LARGE GREASED
CASSEROLE. DOT WITH BUTTER. BAKE, COVERED, AT 350°F
(180°C). FOR 30 MINUTES. IF MAKING AHEAD, COVER AND
REFRIGERATE OR FREEZE. THAW BEFORE BAKING. SERVES
10 TO 12.

ONE SEVENTH OF YOUR LIFE IS SPENT ON MONDAYS.

CHEESY SCALLOPED POTATOES

THIS RECIPE CAN ALL BE MADE IN A FOOD PROCESSOR.

6	MEDIUM POTATOES, PEELED AND SLICED	6
1/4 CUP	DICED ONION	50 ML
1/4 CUP	CELERY LEAVES	50 ML
2	SPRIGS PARSLEY	2
3 TBSP	FLOUR	45 ML
1/4 CUP	BUTTER	50 ML
1 1/2 TSP	SALT	7 ML
1/4 TSP	PEPPER	1 ML
1 1/2 CUPS	MILK	375 ML
1 TO 2 CUPS	GRATED SHARP (OLD) CHEDDAR CHEESE	250 TO 500 ML
PINCH	PAPRIKA	PINCH

BLEND ONION, CELERY LEAVES, PARSLEY, FLOUR, BUTTER, SALT, PEPPER AND MILK IN A BLENDER, MIXING THOROUGHLY. ARRANGE POTATO SLICES IN BUTTERED 8-CUP (2 L) BAKING DISH. POUR MIXTURE OVER POTATOES; SPRINKLE WITH GRATED CHEESE AND PAPRIKA. BAKE IN 350°F (180°C) OVEN FOR APPROXIMATELY 50 MINUTES. THIS CAN BE FROZEN AND REHEATED. SERVES 8.

LOVE IS AN ITCH AROUND YOUR HEART THAT YOU CAN'T SCRATCH.

CREAMY WHIPPED POTATOES

THIS IS A DIFFERENT TWIST TO STANDARD POTATOES.
SERVE WITH STEAK, CHICKEN OR HAM. YUMMY!

8	MEDIUM POTATOES	8
I TSP	SALT	5 ML
2 CUPS	WHIPPING CREAM (2 CARTONS)	500 ML
$\frac{1}{2}$ LB	GRATED SHARP (OLD) CHEDDAR CHEESE	250 G

BOIL POTATOES WITH THE SALT. MASH AND MIX WITH
I CUP (250 ML) OF WHIPPING CREAM UNTIL THICK AND
CREAMY. ADD SALT AND PEPPER TO TASTE AND A SPRINKLE
OF THE GRATED CHEESE. PUT IN A 13- X 9-INCH (3 L)
CASSEROLE. LAYER TOP WITH I CUP (250 ML) CREAM,
WHIPPED; SPRINKLE GRATED CHEESE ON TOP AND BAKE
AT 300°F (150°C) FOR I$\frac{1}{2}$ HOURS. SERVES 6 TO 8.

DOGS IN SIBERIA ARE THE FASTEST IN THE WORLD,
BECAUSE THE TREES ARE SO FAR APART.

MASHED POTATOES ALMANDINE

THIS CASSEROLE CAN BE MADE A DAY AHEAD AND KEPT IN THE REFRIGERATOR. JUST HEAT BEFORE SERVING. A GREAT ACCOMPANIMENT FOR ANY ROAST.

4	MEDIUM POTATOES, COOKED AND MASHED	4
1½ CUPS	COTTAGE CHEESE	375 ML
¼ CUP	SOUR CREAM	50 ML
2 TBSP	CHOPPED GREEN ONION	25 ML
1½ TSP	SALT	7 ML
	PEPPER TO TASTE	
2 TBSP	MELTED BUTTER	25 ML
¼ CUP	SLIVERED ALMONDS	50 ML

PLACE COOKED POTATOES IN LARGE BOWL AND MASH WITH ELECTRIC BEATER. ADD COTTAGE CHEESE, SOUR CREAM, ONION, SALT AND PEPPER. BEAT UNTIL SMOOTH AND PLACE IN SHALLOW CASSEROLE. SPRINKLE WITH ALMONDS AND BRUSH WITH MELTED BUTTER. BAKE AT 350°F (180°C) FOR 30 MINUTES. SERVES 6 TO 8.

MANY A WOMAN MARRIES A MAN FOR LIFE THEN FINDS OUT HE DOESN'T HAVE ANY.

SCHWARTIES HASH BROWNS

GREAT FOR BUFFETS! FREEZES WELL.

2 LBS	FROZEN HASH BROWNS	1 KG
2 CUPS	FAT-FREE SOUR CREAM	500 ML
2	CANS (EACH 10 OZ/284 ML) MUSHROOM SOUP	2
1/4 CUP	MELTED BUTTER	50 ML
	GRATED ONION AND SALT TO TASTE	
2 CUPS	GRATED LIGHT CHEDDAR CHEESE	500 ML
2 TBSP	PARMESAN CHEESE	25 ML

THAW POTATOES SLIGHTLY. MIX FIRST 6 INGREDIENTS IN A 13- X 9-INCH (3 L) BAKING DISH. SPRINKLE PARMESAN ON TOP. BAKE AT 350°F (180°C) FOR 1 HOUR. SERVES 8 TO 10.

FIFTH LAW OF APPLIED TERROR: IF YOU ARE GIVEN AN OPEN-BOOK EXAM, YOU WILL FORGET YOUR BOOK. IF YOU ARE GIVEN A TAKE-HOME EXAM, YOU WILL FORGET WHERE YOU LIVE.

SAVORY RICE

THIS CAN BE DOUBLED AND TRIPLED.

1 TBSP	BUTTER	15 ML
1 TBSP	ONION, CHOPPED	15 ML
1 CUP	CELERY	250 ML
1	CAN (10 OZ/284 ML) CREAM OF MUSHROOM SOUP	1
1	CAN (10 OZ/284 ML) CONSOMMÉ	1
1	CAN (10 OZ/284 ML) CHICKEN WITH RICE SOUP	1
1	CAN (10 OZ/284 ML) MUSHROOMS, SLICED	1
1/2 CUP	BLANCHED ALMONDS	125 ML
1 CUP	LONG-GRAIN RICE	250 ML

SAUTÉ ONION AND CELERY IN BUTTER UNTIL TRANSPARENT. PUT IN CASSEROLE. MIX ALL INGREDIENTS, EXCEPT ALMONDS. SAUTÉ THEM IN BUTTER. BAKE AT 300°F (150°C) FOR 45 MINUTES. COVER WITH ALMONDS. BAKE A FURTHER 30 MINUTES. THIS MAY BE KEPT WARM FOR A LONG TIME. SERVES 4 TO 6.

THE ONLY TIME SOME GIRLS DRAW A LINE IS WHEN THEY USE AN EYEBROW PENCIL.

RICE PILAF

*GREAT WITH ANY MEAL! CAN BE FROZEN AND
REHEATED WITH NO ILL EFFECTS.*

1 CUP	LONG-GRAIN RICE	250 ML
1 CUP	PEARL BARLEY	250 ML
1/4 CUP	BUTTER	50 ML
8	GREEN ONIONS, CHOPPED	8
2	CANS (EACH 10 OZ/284 ML) CONSOMMÉ	2
2	CANS (EACH 10 OZ/284 ML) WATER	2
1	CAN (10 OZ/284 ML) WHOLE MUSHROOMS WITH LIQUID	1

BROWN RICE AND BARLEY IN BUTTER UNTIL GOLDEN, THEN
ADD GREEN ONIONS, CONSOMMÉ, WATER AND MUSHROOMS
WITH LIQUID. COOK EITHER ON TOP OF STOVE IN COVERED
DUTCH OVEN FOR 30 MINUTES OR IN A COVERED
CASSEROLE IN 350°F (180°C) OVEN FOR ONE HOUR OR
UNTIL LIQUID IS ABSORBED. TOSS AND SERVE. SERVES
10 TO 12.

*ALL MEN ARE NOT HOMELESS, BUT SOME
ARE HOME LESS THAN OTHERS.*

RICE CASSEROLE

3 TO 4	SLICES BACON	3 TO 4
1/2 CUP	MINCED ONION	125 ML
I CUP	DICED CELERY	250 ML
1/2	GREEN PEPPER, CHOPPED (OPTIONAL)	1/2
I	CAN (10 OZ/284 ML) MUSHROOM SOUP	I
1/2	CAN'S WORTH WATER	1/2
2 CUPS	RICE	500 ML
I TSP	SALT	5 ML

COOK RICE. COOK THE BACON UNTIL CRISP, BREAK INTO CRUMBS. COOK THE ONION, CELERY AND GREEN PEPPER IN THE BACON FAT UNTIL THE CELERY IS TENDER. DRAIN. MIX ALL THE INGREDIENTS IN A CASSEROLE DISH. BAKE AT 300°F (150°C) FOR I HOUR. SERVES 6.

IF YOU HAVE TROUBLE GOING TO SLEEP AT NIGHT, LIE AT THE VERY EDGE OF THE BED... YOU'LL SOON DROP OFF.

WILD RICE BROCCOLI CASSEROLE

THIS COMPLEMENTS ANY MEAT OR FOWL.

1	PACKAGE (6 OZ/170 G) WILD RICE MIXTURE	1
2	HEADS BROCCOLI, CUT INTO FLORETS	2
2	CANS (EACH 10 OZ/284 ML) MUSHROOM SOUP	2
2 CUPS	GRATED CHEDDAR CHEESE	500 ML

COOK RICE MIXTURE AS DIRECTED. COOK BROCCOLI UNTIL CRUNCHY. MIX SOUP AND 1½ CUPS (375 ML) CHEESE. BUTTER A CASSEROLE. ALTERNATE SOUP MIXTURE, BROCCOLI AND RICE IN LAYERS. SPRINKLE WITH REMAINING ½ CUP (125 ML) CHEESE. COOK AT 350°F (180°C) FOR 1 HOUR. SERVES 6.

A BABY FIRST LAUGHS AT THE AGE OF FOUR WEEKS. BY THAT TIME HIS EYES FOCUS WELL ENOUGH TO SEE YOU CLEARLY.

BROCCOLI RICE CASSEROLE

4 1/2 CUPS	COOKED RICE	1.125 L
1	PACKAGE (10 OZ/300 G) CHOPPED BROCCOLI	1
1 CUP	CHOPPED CELERY	250 ML
1/2 CUP	CHOPPED ONIONS	125 ML
4 TBSP	BUTTER	60 ML
2	CANS (EACH 10 OZ/284 ML) CREAM OF MUSHROOM SOUP	2
1 CUP	MILK	250 ML
1	JAR (10 OZ/284 ML) CHEEZ WHIZ	1

COOK RICE AND BROCCOLI. SAUTÉ CELERY AND ONION IN BUTTER. COMBINE SOUP, MILK AND CHEESE. PUT ALL INGREDIENTS INTO A CASSEROLE. BAKE AT 350°F (180°C) FOR 40 TO 50 MINUTES. SERVES 12 TO 16.

ONE SMALL BOY TO ANOTHER: "OF COURSE I KNOW THE FACTS OF LIFE; EAT YOUR VEGETABLES AND WASH YOUR HANDS."

BROCCOLI CASSEROLE

1	CLOVE GARLIC, MINCED	1
1	LARGE ONION, CHOPPED	1
1/4 CUP	BUTTER	50 ML
4 CUPS	BROCCOLI, BITE-SIZE PIECES	1 L
1	CAN (10 OZ/284 ML) CREAM OF MUSHROOM SOUP	1
1	ROLL (7 OZ/200 G) SHARP CHEESE SNACK OR 7 OZ (200 G) CHEEZ WHIZ	1
1	CAN (10 OZ/284 ML) SLICED MUSHROOMS, DRAINED, OR 1/4 LB (125 G) FRESH MUSHROOMS (SAUTÉ WITH ONION)	1
1/4 CUP	CHOPPED ALMONDS	50 ML
1/2 CUP	BUTTERED BREAD CRUMBS	125 ML
1/4 CUP	CHOPPED ALMONDS	50 ML

SAUTÉ ONION AND GARLIC IN BUTTER. SPOON INTO LARGE GREASED CASSEROLE. COOK BROCCOLI UNTIL CRUNCHY. ADD TO CASSEROLE. ADD MUSHROOMS AND CHOPPED ALMONDS. IN A SEPARATE BOWL, BLEND MUSHROOM SOUP AND CHEESE. FOLD INTO CASSEROLE. TOP WITH ALMONDS AND BUTTERED BREAD CRUMBS. BAKE AT 350°F (180°C) FOR 45 MINUTES. SERVES 10.

HOME REPAIR IS LIKE CASINO GAMBLING – THE HOUSE ALWAYS WINS.

HOT CURRIED FRUIT

GOOD WITH BAKED HAM OR PORK.

1 CUP	BROWN SUGAR	250 ML
1/4 TSP	SALT	1 ML
1 TBSP	CURRY	15 ML
1/2 CUP	BUTTER	125 ML
3	CANS (EACH 14 OZ/398 ML) FRUIT, DRAINED (CHOOSE A COMBINATION OF PINEAPPLE, PEARS, PEACHES, APRICOTS OR MANDARIN ORANGES)	3
	MARASCHINO CHERRIES FOR COLOR	

COMBINE FIRST FOUR INGREDIENTS IN A SAUCEPAN AND BRING TO A BOIL. COOK FOR 5 MINUTES. POUR OVER FRUIT IN BUTTERED CASSEROLE. BAKE AT 300°F (150°C) FOR 20 TO 25 MINUTES. *SERVES 6 TO 8.*

MAN WILL NEVER FEEL LONELY EATING SPAGHETTI... THERE'S TOO MUCH TO DO.

THE GAFFER'S SPAGHETTI SAUCE

1 LB	LEAN GROUND BEEF	500 G
1	ONION, FINELY CHOPPED	1
1	CAN (10 OZ/284 ML) BUTTON MUSHROOMS, RESERVE LIQUID	1
	SALT, PEPPER AND GARLIC SALT TO TASTE	
1	CAN (14 OZ/398 ML) TOMATO SAUCE	1
1	CAN (28 OZ/796 ML) TOMATOES, CUT UP	1
3/4 CUP	CHILI SAUCE (SEE PAGE 38)	175 ML
1/4 TO 1/2 TSP	EACH OREGANO, MARJORAM, THYME (ANY OR ALL, AS YOU WISH)	1 TO 2 ML
1/4 CUP	DRY RED WINE	50 ML

SAUTÉ BEEF, ONION, MUSHROOMS, SALT, PEPPER AND GARLIC SALT, CRUMBLING MEAT AS FINELY AS POSSIBLE UNTIL BROWNED. IF YOUR MEAT IS NOT LEAN, BE SURE TO DRAIN ANY EXCESS FAT. ADD MUSHROOM LIQUID, TOMATO SAUCE, TOMATOES, CHILI SAUCE, OREGANO, MARJORAM, THYME AND SALT TO TASTE. IF YOU DON'T HAVE THE CHILI SAUCE MADE UP, SUBSTITUTE 1 TBSP (15 ML) BROWN SUGAR, 2 TBSP (25 ML) KETCHUP AND 1 RED CHILI PEPPER, CRUSHED. COOK OVER LOW HEAT FOR 1 HOUR UNTIL ALL INGREDIENTS GET TO KNOW EACH OTHER. SOME WATER MAY BE ADDED AS THIS THICKENS. DON'T BE AFRAID TO PLAY WITH THE SPICES A BIT TO SUIT YOUR OWN TASTE. ADD THE RED WINE BEFORE SERVING. SERVES 8.

MINDLESS MEAT SAUCE

MINDLESS, BECAUSE OF ITS SIMPLICITY.

1½ LBS	LEAN GROUND BEEF	750 G
¼ TSP	SAGE	1 ML
¼ TSP	OREGANO	1 ML
1 TBSP	SALT	15 ML
½ TSP	PEPPER	2 ML
1	MEDIUM ONION, FINELY CHOPPED	1
15	LARGE MUSHROOMS, FINELY CHOPPED	15
3	CLOVES GARLIC, MINCED	3
1	CAN (28 OZ/796 ML) TOMATOES, CHOPPED, WITH JUICE	1
1	CAN (10 OZ/284 ML) TOMATO SAUCE	1
1	CAN (5½ OZ/156 ML) TOMATO PASTE	1

PREHEAT OVEN TO 350°F (180°C). IN LARGE ROASTING PAN, SPREAD GROUND BEEF. COOK FOR 30 MINUTES, STIRRING OCCASIONALLY TO SEPARATE. MEANWHILE, COMBINE SAGE, OREGANO, SALT, PEPPER, ONION, MUSHROOMS AND GARLIC IN SAUCEPAN AND COOK AT MEDIUM HEAT UNTIL ONIONS ARE TRANSPARENT. SPREAD OVER MEAT AND CONTINUE COOKING IN OVEN FOR 15 MINUTES MORE. REMOVE FROM OVEN AND ADD CANNED TOMATOES, TOMATO SAUCE AND PASTE. BRING TO BOIL, THEN SIMMER FOR 1 HOUR OR LONGER. ADD SALT TO TASTE. STORE IN CONTAINERS AND FREEZE. USE IT IN ANY RECIPE CALLING FOR MEAT SAUCE, SUCH AS SPAGHETTI, LASAGNA OR CANNELLONI. SERVES 6.

MUSTARD SAUCE FOR HAM

2	EGG YOLKS	2
1/2 CUP	SUGAR	125 ML
2	DESSERT SPOONS OF DRY MUSTARD	2
1/3 CUP	WHITE VINEGAR	75 ML

COMBINE INGREDIENTS AND BRING TO BOIL. IDEAL FOR
SERVING WITH HAM FOR BUFFET; EITHER FOR HOT HAM
OR FOR SANDWICHES. MAKES ABOUT 1/2 CUP (125 ML).

IF WE COULD TRAIN OURSELVES TO BREATHE THROUGH
OUR EARS, WE COULD PUT OUR FACES RIGHT DOWN
INTO THE SOUP AND NOT REQUIRE SPOONS.

MUSTARD SAUCE FOR STEAK

2 TBSP	BUTTER	25 ML
2 TBSP	BAR-B-QUE SAUCE (ANY COMMERCIAL BRAND)	25 ML
2 TSP	WORCESTERSHIRE SAUCE	10 ML
2 TSP	DRY MUSTARD	10 ML
2 TBSP	CREAM	25 ML

MIX ALL INGREDIENTS EXCEPT CREAM TO MELTED BUTTER. HEAT OVER MEDIUM HEAT. ADD CREAM AND HEAT AGAIN OVER MEDIUM HEAT. MAKES ABOUT 1/3 CUP (75 ML).

TERIYAKI SAUCE FOR STEAK

BLEND THE FOLLOWING IN A BLENDER:

1	ONION	1
2	CLOVES GARLIC	2
2 TSP	GINGER	10 ML
1/2	FRESH MASHED PAPAYA (OPTIONAL)	1/2
1/2 CUP	WATER	125 ML

ADD:

2 1/2 TBSP	BROWN SUGAR	32 ML
3 CUPS	SOY SAUCE	750 ML
1 1/2 CUPS	WATER	375 ML

STORE IN REFRIGERATOR INDEFINITELY. FOR FLANK STEAK OR THE CHEAPER CUTS OF MEAT, MARINATE FOR 24 HOURS. USE ON CHICKEN AND ANY STEAKS. MAKES ABOUT 7 CUPS (1.75 L).

GINGER SOY SAUCE FOR BEEF

1/2 CUP	SOY SAUCE	125 ML
1 TSP	GROUND GINGER	5 ML

MIX TOGETHER AND BRING TO BOIL. MAKES 1/2 CUP (125 ML). THIS IS A MARVELOUS DIP FOR FONDUE, OR EVEN IN PLACE OF WORCESTERSHIRE WITH STEAK. FOR ASIAN STIR-FRIED DINNERS, PLACE INDIVIDUAL SAUCE DISHES AT EACH PLACE.

CRANBERRY BURGUNDY SAUCE

THIS IS A DELICIOUS CHANGE FOR A GLAZED HAM OR CHICKEN GLAZE.

1	LARGE CAN CRANBERRY SAUCE	1
1 CUP	BROWN SUGAR	250 ML
1/2 CUP	BURGUNDY (DRY RED WINE)	125 ML
2 TSP	PREPARED MUSTARD	10 ML

MIX INGREDIENTS IN SAUCEPAN AND HEAT TO BOILING. STIR UNTIL SUGAR HAS DISSOLVED. SPOON OVER HAM OR CHICKEN WHILE THEY COOK AND USE REMAINING SAUCE FOR ACCOMPANYING THE DINNER. MAKES 2 TO 3 CUPS (500 TO 750 ML).

IF LOOKS COULD KILL, A LOT OF PEOPLE WOULD DIE WITH BRIDGE CARDS IN THEIR HANDS.

RHUBARB RELISH

THIS IS VERY EASY.

8 CUPS	CUT RHUBARB	2 L
1 CUP	CHOPPED COOKING ONION	250 ML
1/2 TSP	CINNAMON	2 ML
1/2 TSP	ALLSPICE	2 ML
1/2 TSP	CLOVES	2 ML
1 CUP	VINEGAR (WHITE)	250 ML
2 CUPS	WHITE SUGAR	500 ML
1 TBSP	SALT	15 ML

SIMMER UNCOVERED APPROXIMATELY 4 HOURS (SOMETIMES MORE) UNTIL QUITE THICK. WATCH CLOSELY AS IT BURNS EASILY. LADLE INTO HOT, STERILIZED JARS, LEAVING 1/2 INCH (1 CM) HEADSPACE. WIPE RIMS AND SEAL WITH TWO-PIECE CANNING LIDS. PROCESS IN A BOILING WATER CANNER FOR 10 MINUTES. CHECK SEALS AND REFRIGERATE ANY JARS THAT ARE NOT SEALED. MAKES ABOUT NINE 8-OZ (250 ML) JARS.

A BOILED EGG IS HARD TO BEAT!

THE MAYOR'S WIFE'S
BLUE PLUM RELISH

A CONSTANT FAVORITE THAT GOES WITH PRACTICALLY EVERYTHING. (SUNDAY SANDWICHES, CHRISTMAS MORNING WIFE SAVER.)

5 LBS	FRESH, BLUE PRUNE PLUMS	2.5 KG
3	LARGE ONIONS	3
4 LBS	COOKING APPLES, PEELED	2 KG
4 CUPS	VINEGAR	1 L
4 LBS	WHITE SUGAR	2 KG
1/2 LB	PRESERVED OR CANDIED GINGER, GRATED	250 G
1 TBSP	ALLSPICE (HEAPING TABLESPOON)	15 ML
1 TBSP	GROUND CLOVES (HEAPING TABLESPOON)	15 ML
2 TBSP	CORNSTARCH DISSOLVED IN 1/4 CUP (50 ML) WATER	25 ML
	SALT AND PEPPER	

PIT AND MINCE PRUNE PLUMS AND GRATE ONION AND COOKING APPLES. PLACE IN LARGE POT, ADD VINEGAR AND BOIL TOGETHER FOR 1/2 HOUR. ADD SUGAR AND BRING TO BOIL AGAIN. SIMMER AT LEAST 15 MINUTES. ADD GINGER AND CONTINUE TO SIMMER AT LEAST 15 MINUTES MORE. JUST BEFORE REMOVING FROM HEAT, ADD ALLSPICE, GROUND CLOVES AND DISSOLVED CORNSTARCH. SALT AND PEPPER TO TASTE. LADLE INTO HOT, STERILIZED JARS, LEAVING 1/2 INCH (1 CM) HEADSPACE. WIPE RIMS AND SEAL WITH TWO-PIECE CANNING LIDS. PROCESS IN A BOILING WATER CANNER FOR 10 MINUTES. CHECK SEALS AND REFRIGERATE ANY JARS THAT ARE NOT SEALED. BEST AGED 3 TO 6 MONTHS. MAKES ABOUT TWENTY-FOUR 8-OZ (250 ML) JARS.

GREEN TOMATO RELISH

YOU MADE IT YOURSELF? – AREN'T YOU WONDERFUL DEAR!

7½ LBS	GREEN TOMATOES, THINLY SLICED	3.25 KG
5	GREEN PEPPERS, QUARTERED, SEEDED AND SLICED	5
4	RED PEPPERS, QUARTERED, SEEDED AND SLICED	4
4	LARGE ONIONS, HALVED AND SLICED	4
1 CUP	SALT	250 ML
4 CUPS	VINEGAR	1 L
6 CUPS	SUGAR	1.5 L
1 TSP	CINNAMON	5 ML
1 TSP	GROUND CLOVES	5 ML
1 TBSP	TURMERIC	15 ML
2 TBSP	MIXED PICKLING SPICES	25 ML

PLACE SLICED TOMATOES, PEPPERS AND ONIONS IN A LARGE POT. COVER WITH SALT AND LET STAND OVERNIGHT. DRAIN AND RINSE WELL. RETURN TO POT AND ADD REMAINING INGREDIENTS. BRING TO A BOIL, REDUCE TO SIMMER AND COOK UNTIL DESIRED CONSISTENCY, APPROXIMATELY 30 MINUTES. LADLE INTO HOT, STERILIZED JARS, LEAVING ½ INCH (1 CM) HEADSPACE. WIPE RIMS AND SEAL WITH TWO-PIECE CANNING LIDS. PROCESS IN A BOILING WATER CANNER FOR 15 MINUTES. CHECK SEALS AND REFRIGERATE ANY JARS THAT ARE NOT SEALED. *MAKES ABOUT TEN 2-CUP (500 ML) JARS.*

TOMATO ASPIC

2 TSP	CIDER OR RED WINE VINEGAR	10 ML
1/2 TSP	EACH SALT, BASIL AND ACCENT	2 ML
1	PACKAGE (3 OZ/85 G) LEMON JELL-O	1
1	CAN (10 OZ/284 ML) TOMATO SOUP AND WATER TO MAKE 2 CUPS (500 ML) LIQUID	1
2	STALKS CELERY, CHOPPED	2
1	MEDIUM ONION, CHOPPED FINE (OR 3 GREEN ONIONS)	1
4	CLOVES	4
HANDFUL	FROZEN GREEN PEAS	HANDFUL
1	CAN (6 1/2 OZ/184 G) MEDIUM CLEANED SHRIMP	1

BRING JELL-O AND LIQUID TO BOIL. ADD ALL INGREDIENTS EXCEPT SHRIMP AND CELERY AND COOK FOR 5 MINUTES. REMOVE CLOVES AND ADD SHRIMP AND CELERY.

POUR INTO LIGHTLY OILED MOLD AND CHILL UNTIL SET. SERVE ON LETTUCE LINED PLATE, GARNISHED WITH EXTRA SHRIMP, OLIVES AND MAYONNAISE, ALONG WITH CHEESE STICKS IF SERVING FOR BRIDGE. SERVES 8.

OUT OF THE MOUTHS OF BABES TOO OFTEN, COMES CEREAL.

CHUTNEY

30	RIPE TOMATOES	30
6	PEACHES	6
6	PEARS	6
4	ONIONS	4
3 TBSP	SALT	45 ML
2	RED PEPPERS	2
2	GREEN PEPPERS	2
4 CUPS	VINEGAR	1 L
4 CUPS	BROWN SUGAR	1 L
2 TBSP	WHOLE CLOVES (WRAP IN CHEESECLOTH WITH CINNAMON)	25 ML
2	1-INCH (2.5 CM) PIECES CINNAMON STICK	2

SCALD, PEEL AND CHOP TOMATOES, PEACHES, PEARS AND ONIONS. MIX WITH OTHER INGREDIENTS (EXCEPT SPICES). SIMMER 2 HOURS. ADD SPICES DURING LAST 15 MINUTES. REMOVE SPICES. LADLE INTO HOT, STERILIZED JARS, LEAVING $\frac{1}{2}$ INCH (1 CM) HEADSPACE. WIPE RIMS AND SEAL WITH TWO-PIECE CANNING LIDS. PROCESS IN A BOILING WATER CANNER FOR 15 MINUTES. CHECK SEALS AND REFRIGERATE ANY JARS THAT ARE NOT SEALED. MAKES TWENTY TO TWENTY-FOUR 8-OZ (250 ML) JARS.

NOTE: DELICIOUS SERVED WITH ANY MEAT. PLACE THIS ON YOUR BUFFET WHEN HAVING "MAKE YOUR OWN SANDWICHES."

CHRISTMAS MARMALADE

A FRIEND ONCE LEFT THIS ON MY DOORSTEP CHRISTMAS EVE (IT WAS A WARM NIGHT!) AND I'VE MADE IT EVER SINCE. WHY NOT MAKE A BATCH FOR YOUR FRIENDS?

3	MEDIUM ORANGES	3
2	LEMONS	2
1½ CUPS	COLD WATER	375 ML
1	BOTTLE (6 OZ/170 ML) PRESERVED GINGER	1
6 CUPS	SUGAR	1.5 L
1	BOTTLE (6 OZ/170 ML) MARASCHINO CHERRIES, DRAINED AND CHOPPED (ADD EXTRA GREEN CHERRIES AS WELL – COLORFUL!)	1
1	POUCH LIQUID PECTIN	1

WASH ORANGES AND LEMONS. SLICE PAPER THIN. DISCARD SEEDS. PUT INTO LARGE KETTLE. ADD WATER AND BRING TO A BOIL. TURN DOWN HEAT, COVER AND SIMMER ABOUT 30 MINUTES UNTIL RINDS ARE TENDER AND TRANSPARENT. STIR OCCASIONALLY. DRAIN GINGER, SAVING SYRUP. CHOP GINGER FINELY. ADD SUGAR, CHOPPED GINGER, GINGER SYRUP AND CHERRIES TO ORANGE-LEMON MIXTURE. TURN HEAT TO HIGH AND BRING TO A FULL, ROLLING BOIL, STIRRING CONSTANTLY. BOIL HARD ONE MINUTE. REMOVE FROM HEAT AND STIR IN PECTIN. CONTINUE STIRRING AND SKIMMING FOR 5 MINUTES. LADLE INTO HOT, STERILIZED JARS, LEAVING ¼ INCH (0.5 CM) HEADSPACE. WIPE RIMS AND SEAL WITH TWO-PIECE CANNING LIDS. PROCESS IN A BOILING WATER CANNER FOR 5 MINUTES. CHECK SEALS AND REFRIGERATE ANY JARS THAT ARE NOT SEALED. MAKES ABOUT TEN 8-OZ (250 ML) JARS.

PART III
GOODIES

PIES AND TARTS

OTHER DESSERTS

CONTINUED ON NEXT PAGE...

ICINGS AND SAUCES

CHOCOLATE CHIP COOKIES

DELICIOUS, ESPECIALLY RIGHT OUT OF THE OVEN!

1 CUP	BUTTER	250 ML
3/4 CUP	BROWN SUGAR, FIRMLY PACKED	175 ML
1/4 CUP	WHITE SUGAR	50 ML
1 TSP	VANILLA	5 ML
1 1/2 CUPS	FLOUR	375 ML
1/2 TSP	SALT	2 ML
1 TSP	BAKING SODA	5 ML
1/3 CUP	BOILING WATER	75 ML
2 CUPS	ROLLED OATS	500 ML
1/2 CUP	CHOPPED NUTS	125 ML
3/4 CUP	CHOCOLATE CHIPS	175 ML

BEAT BUTTER UNTIL SOFT. ADD SUGARS AND BEAT UNTIL FLUFFY. ADD VANILLA. ADD FLOUR AND SALT AND MIX WELL. DISSOLVE BAKING SODA IN BOILING WATER. BLEND INTO MIXTURE. STIR IN THE ROLLED OATS, NUTS AND CHOCOLATE CHIPS. ROLL IN BALLS AND FLATTEN WITH FORK DIPPED IN COLD WATER. BAKE AT 350°F (180°C) FOR 10 TO 12 MINUTES. MAKES 4 TO 5 DOZEN COOKIES.

BY THE TIME A MAN CAN READ WOMEN LIKE A BOOK, HE'S TOO OLD TO START A LIBRARY.

FORGOTTEN COOKIES

2	EGG WHITES	2
3/4 CUP	SUGAR	175 ML
1/2 TSP	VANILLA	2 ML
6 OZ	SEMI-SWEET CHOCOLATE CHIPS	175 G
I CUP	CHOPPED PECANS	250 ML

PREHEAT OVEN TO 350°F (180°C). BEAT EGG WHITES UNTIL STIFF, ADD SUGAR GRADUALLY. BEAT AT HIGH SPEED 5 MINUTES. FOLD IN VANILLA, CHIPS AND PECANS. DROP FROM TEASPOON ONTO FOIL-LINED COOKIE SHEET. PUT IN OVEN AND TURN OFF HEAT. LEAVE OVERNIGHT OR AT LEAST 8 HOURS. YOU CAN ADD A FEW DROPS OF FOOD COLORING (WITH NUTS AND CHIPS) IF YOU WANT THEM COLORED. MAKES ABOUT 3 DOZEN MERINGUE-LIKE COOKIES.

MISERY IS THE INABILITY TO CONCEAL THE FACT THAT YOU'VE HAD A FOURTH MARTINI.

SOFT RAISIN COOKIES

3 CUPS	SEEDLESS RAISINS	750 ML
1½ TSP	CINNAMON	7 ML
1½ TSP	NUTMEG	7 ML
1½ TSP	GINGER	7 ML
½ CUP	SHORTENING	125 ML
1½ CUPS	WHITE SUGAR	375 ML
2	EGGS	2
2 TSP	BAKING SODA	10 ML
1 TSP	SALT	5 ML
3½ CUPS	FLOUR	825 ML

PLACE RAISINS AND SPICES IN SAUCEPAN AND COVER
WITH WATER TO 1 INCH (2.5 CM) ABOVE RAISINS. COOK
ABOUT 20 MINUTES UNCOVERED OR UNTIL WATER IS
REDUCED TO LEVEL OF RAISINS. COOL SLIGHTLY. COMBINE
THE REMAINING INGREDIENTS. MIXTURE WILL BE DRY AND
MEALY BUT DO NOT DESPAIR, ADD RAISIN MIXTURE AND
YOU'RE THERE! (IF TOO DRY, ADD ADDITIONAL WATER
CAREFULLY.) DROP FROM DESSERT SPOON ONTO COOKIE
SHEET. BAKE AT 350°F (180°C) FOR 15 TO 20 MINUTES.
MAKES ABOUT 48 LARGE COOKIES.

BACHELORS ARE LIKE DETERGENTS;
BOTH WORK FAST AND LEAVE NO RINGS.

HERMITS – SPICED DROP COOKIES

THESE FAMILY FAVORITES WERE ALWAYS INCLUDED IN OUR "CARE PACKAGES" FROM HOME. WILL KEEP FOR AGES AND ARE BETTER AFTER A FEW DAYS – IF THEY LAST THAT LONG!

3/4 CUP	BUTTER	175 ML
1 1/2 CUPS	BROWN SUGAR	375 ML
2	EGGS	2
1 TSP	VANILLA	5 ML
2 CUPS	FLOUR	500 ML
1/2 TSP	BAKING POWDER	2 ML
1/2 TSP	NUTMEG	2 ML
1/2 TSP	GINGER	2 ML
1/2 TSP	MACE	2 ML
1 TSP	CINNAMON	5 ML
1 CUP	RAISINS	250 ML
1 CUP	CHOPPED DATES	250 ML
1 CUP	WALNUTS	250 ML

CREAM BUTTER AND SUGAR. BEAT IN EGGS. ADD VANILLA. SIFT FLOUR, BAKING POWDER, BAKING SODA AND SPICES. RESERVE 1/3 CUP (75 ML) OF THIS DRY MIXTURE AND TOSS WITH RAISINS, DATES AND NUTS. (THIS WILL KEEP THEM FROM SINKING TO THE BOTTOM OF THE COOKIE.) ADD REMAINING FLOUR MIXTURE TO BATTER AND BLEND. ADD FLOURED RAISINS, DATES AND NUTS TO DOUGH. DROP BY SPOONFULS ONTO GREASED BAKING SHEETS. BAKE AT 365°F (185°C) FOR 10 MINUTES. DON'T OVERCOOK – SHOULD BE SOFT AND CHEWY. MAKES AT LEAST 5 DOZEN COOKIES.

PECAN MACAROONS

THIS IS A PRETTY CHRISTMAS COOKIE AND IS GOOD TOO!

1/2 CUP	WHITE SUGAR	125 ML
1/4 CUP	BOILING WATER	50 ML
2	EGG WHITES	2
1/2 CUP	BROWN SUGAR	125 ML
1 1/2 CUPS	COCONUT	375 ML
2 TBSP	CARAMEL SYRUP (SEE BELOW)	25 ML
1/2 CUP	GLACÉ CHERRIES, WHOLE	125 ML
1 CUP	WHOLE PECANS	250 ML

TO MAKE CARAMEL SYRUP: MELT 1/2 CUP (125 ML) OF WHITE SUGAR IN POT OVER MEDIUM HEAT. CAREFULLY ADD 1/4 CUP (50 ML) BOILING WATER. (MIXTURE OF HOT SUGAR AND WATER CAN "EXPLODE" IF NOT ADDED AWAY FROM HEAT AND WITH CAUTION!) SUGAR WILL HARDEN, BUT THE LIQUID WILL MAKE AT LEAST 2 TBSP (25 ML) SYRUP. COOL COMPLETELY.

COOKIES: BEAT EGG WHITES, ADDING PINCH OF SALT. ADD ADDITIONAL INGREDIENTS AND 2 TBSP (25 ML) COOLED SYRUP. BAKE AT 300°F (150°C) FOR 20 MINUTES OR UNTIL LIGHTLY BROWNED. COOKIES WILL SLIGHTLY RUN TOGETHER ON SHEET; THEREFORE, WHILE STILL HOT, PUSH COOKIE BACK TOGETHER WITH A SPOON. COOL ON COOKIE SHEET. MAKES ABOUT 3 DOZEN COOKIES.

DIAMONDS

1 CUP	BUTTER	250 ML
1 CUP	BROWN SUGAR	250 ML
1	EGG YOLK	1
1 CUP	FLOUR	250 ML
6	MILK CHOCOLATE BARS (1 OZ/30 G EACH)	6
2/3 CUP	SLICED FILBERTS OR ALMONDS	150 ML

CREAM BUTTER, SUGAR AND EGG YOLK. ADD FLOUR.
SPREAD DOUGH ON A GREASED 15- X 10- X 1-INCH (38 X 25 X
2.5 CM) PAN. BAKE AT 350°F (180°C) FOR 15 TO 20 MINUTES.
REMOVE FROM OVEN AND LAY CHOCOLATE BARS ON TOP.
SPREAD WHEN MELTED. SPRINKLE WITH NUTS. WHILE WARM,
CUT INTO 75 BARS OR DIAMONDS. MAKES 75 COOKIES.

PRALINES

3 TBSP	MELTED BUTTER	45 ML
1	EGG	1
4 TBSP	FLOUR	60 ML
1 CUP	PECANS, CHOPPED	250 ML
1 TSP	VANILLA	5 ML

MIX ALL INGREDIENTS WELL AND DROP WITH SMALL
TEASPOON ONTO GREASED SHEET. BAKE 5 MINUTES
AT 350°F (180°C). REMOVE IMMEDIATELY. MAKES ABOUT
3 DOZEN COOKIES.

SWEDISH PASTRY

½ CUP	BUTTER	125 ML
¼ CUP	BROWN SUGAR	50 ML
1 CUP	FLOUR (OR ENOUGH TO MAKE A COOKIE DOUGH)	250 ML
1	EGG, SEPARATED	1
PINCH	SALT	PINCH

MIX TOGETHER, RESERVING EGG WHITE, AND ROLL INTO BALLS. DIP IN SLIGHTLY BEATEN EGG WHITE AND ROLL IN CRUSHED WALNUTS. PLACE ON A GREASED PAN. PRESS IN CENTER WITH A THIMBLE. BAKE AT 325°F (160°C) FOR A FEW MINUTES, THEN REMOVE FROM OVEN AND PRESS WITH THIMBLE AGAIN. RETURN TO OVEN AND BAKE UNTIL NICELY BROWNED. FILL CENTERS WITH JAM OR HALF A CHERRY. MAKES ABOUT 2 DOZEN COOKIES.

IN THE 16TH CENTURY, EXERCISING WAS CONSIDERED SINFUL. IN THE 21ST CENTURY, SIN IS CONSIDERED A FORM OF GOOD EXERCISE!

MONA'S MOTHER'S MOTHER'S BEST FRIEND'S FAVORITE

THIS IS A VERRRY OLD RECIPE!

1 CUP	BUTTER	250 ML
1 CUP	WHITE SUGAR	250 ML
1/2 CUP	BROWN SUGAR	125 ML
1	EGG	1
1 1/2 CUPS	FLOUR	375 ML
1 TSP	BAKING POWDER	5 ML
1 TSP	BAKING SODA	5 ML
1 1/4 CUPS	ROLLED OATS	300 ML
3/4 CUP	COCONUT	175 ML

CREAM BUTTER AND SUGARS. ADD EGG AND BEAT WELL. MIX IN FLOUR, BAKING POWDER AND SODA UNTIL JUST BLENDED. STIR IN OATS AND COCONUT. ROLL INTO 1-INCH (2.5 CM) BALLS AND PRESS WITH A FORK DIPPED IN WATER. BAKE AT 350°F (180°C) FOR 12-15 MINUTES. MAKES 3 DOZEN COOKIES.

THE YEARS A WOMAN SUBTRACTS FROM HER AGE ARE NOT LOST; THEY ARE ADDED TO THE AGES OF OTHER WOMEN.

MISSION CRYBABIES

1 CUP	SHORTENING	250 ML
1 CUP	SUGAR	250 ML
2	EGGS	2
1/2 CUP	MOLASSES	125 ML
1 TBSP	VINEGAR	15 ML
1 CUP	STRONG COFFEE	250 ML
2 TSP	BAKING SODA	10 ML
2 CUPS	RAISINS	500 ML
4 CUPS	FLOUR	1 L
2 TSP	CINNAMON	10 ML
1 TSP	GINGER	5 ML
1/2 TSP	SUGAR	2 ML

POUR HOT COFFEE OVER RAISINS, ADD SODA AND LET STAND. IN LARGE BOWL MEASURE SHORTENING AND SUGAR AND BEAT UNTIL LIGHT. ADD EGGS AND BEAT UNTIL LIGHT AND PALE. BEAT IN VINEGAR AND MOLASSES. THEN ADD RAISIN MIXTURE. SIFT FLOUR, SALT AND SPICES AND ADD TO MIXTURE. DROP BY SPOONFULS ONTO GREASED COOKIE SHEET AT LEAST 2 INCHES (5 CM) APART. BAKE AT 375°F (190°C) FOR 7 TO 9 MINUTES. DO NOT OVERBAKE! MAKES ABOUT 10 DOZEN COOKIES.

ALWAYS DO RIGHT - IT WILL GRATIFY SOME PEOPLE AND ASTONISH OTHERS.

CANDIED ALMONDS

¼ CUP	WATER	50 ML
½ CUP	SUGAR	125 ML
I CUP	ALMONDS (OR PECANS)	250 ML

PLACE INGREDIENTS IN CAST IRON FRYING PAN. (THIS RECIPE DOUBLED FITS WELL INTO A 10-INCH (25 CM) PAN.)

COOK ABOUT 10 MINUTES STIRRING CONSTANTLY WITH WOODEN SPOON. MIXTURE WILL BECOME POWDERY WHITE, THEN GLAZE WILL BEGIN.

KEEP STIRRING UNTIL NUTS ARE COVERED WITH THE GLAZE. TURN OUT ON BREADBOARD AND SEPARATE – BE CAREFUL AS NUTS ARE VERY HOT. MAKES I CUP (250 ML).

THESE MAKE NICE CHRISTMAS GIFTS IN LITTLE BOWLS OR JARS.

OF COURSE THERE'S SUCH A THING AS LUCK – HOW ELSE COULD YOU EXPLAIN YOUR ENEMIES' SUCCESSES?

SNOWBALLS

1/2 CUP	BUTTER (NOT MARGARINE)	125 ML
1 TBSP	SUGAR	15 ML
1 CUP	FINELY GROUND PECANS (BE SURE THEY ARE FRESH)	250 ML
7/8 CUP	FLOUR	220 ML
1 TSP	VANILLA	5 ML
PINCH	SALT	PINCH
1 CUP	ICING SUGAR	250 ML

CREAM BUTTER AND SUGAR. ADD NUTS, FLOUR, VANILLA AND SALT. MIX, BUT DO NOT OVERBEAT. FORM SMALL BALLS AND BAKE ON UNGREASED SHEET AT 325°F (160°C) FOR 12 TO 15 MINUTES, UNTIL BARELY BROWN. COOL. COAT THOROUGHLY IN ICING SUGAR. MAKES ABOUT 4 DOZEN.

CHOCOLATE SNOWBALLS

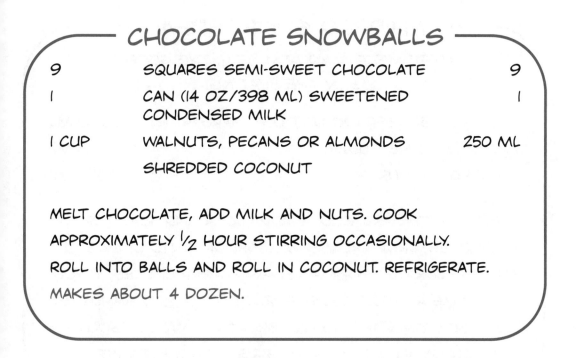

9	SQUARES SEMI-SWEET CHOCOLATE	9
1	CAN (14 OZ/398 ML) SWEETENED CONDENSED MILK	1
1 CUP	WALNUTS, PECANS OR ALMONDS	250 ML
	SHREDDED COCONUT	

MELT CHOCOLATE, ADD MILK AND NUTS. COOK APPROXIMATELY 1/2 HOUR STIRRING OCCASIONALLY. ROLL INTO BALLS AND ROLL IN COCONUT. REFRIGERATE. MAKES ABOUT 4 DOZEN.

CHOCOLATE FUDGE BALLS

3	SQUARES UNSWEETENED CHOCOLATE	3
3 TBSP	BUTTER	45 ML
1/3 CUP	MASHED POTATOES	75 ML
1/8 TSP	SALT	0.5 ML
I TSP	VANILLA	5 ML
3 CUPS	ICING SUGAR	750 ML
3/4 CUP	FINELY CHOPPED WALNUTS (COCONUT MAY BE USED)	175 ML

MELT CHOCOLATE AND BUTTER IN TOP OF DOUBLE BOILER. ADD POTATOES, SALT AND VANILLA. MIX WELL. BLEND IN SUGAR, ONE CUP AT A TIME, THOROUGHLY MIX, AND KNEAD GENTLY. SHAPE INTO SMALL BALLS AND ROLL IN WALNUTS. SET ON WAX PAPER, DRY BEFORE STORING. MAKES ABOUT 4 DOZEN.

WHIPPED SHORTBREAD

THESE MELT IN YOUR MOUTH. THE SECRET IS IN THE BEATING.

I CUP	BUTTER (DO NOT USE MARGARINE)	250 ML
1/2 CUP	ICING SUGAR	125 ML
1 1/2 CUPS	FLOUR	375 ML

CREAM BUTTER AND SUGAR; ADD FLOUR AND BEAT FOR 10 MINUTES. DROP FROM SMALL SPOON ONTO COOKIE SHEET. DECORATE WITH MARASCHINO CHERRY PIECES, IF YOU WISH. BAKE AT 350°F (180°F) FOR ABOUT 10 TO 12 MINUTES, UNTIL BOTTOMS ARE LIGHTLY BROWNED. MAKES ABOUT 3 DOZEN SMALL COOKIES. THIS RECIPE DOUBLES WELL.

SHORTBREAD

1 LB	BUTTER	500 G
1 CUP	SUGAR	250 ML
4 TO 5 CUPS	FLOUR	1 TO 1.25 L

CREAM BUTTER WITH SUGAR. ADD FLOUR, BEATING FOR 5 MINUTES. CUT OUT COOKIES USING A 2-INCH (5 CM) COOKIE CUTTER. BAKE AT 300°F (150°C) FOR 10 TO 15 MINUTES OR UNTIL LIGHTLY GOLDEN. MAKES ABOUT 4 DOZEN COOKIES.

JEWISH SHORTBREAD

1 CUP	BUTTER, ROOM TEMPERATURE (NEVER USE MARGARINE)	250 ML
1/3 CUP	WHITE SUGAR	75 ML
1 TSP	VANILLA	5 ML
1/2 CUP	FINELY GROUND WALNUTS OR PECANS	125 ML
1 2/3 CUPS	FLOUR	400 ML
PINCH	SALT	PINCH
1/2 CUP	WHITE SUGAR	125 ML
4 TSP	CINNAMON	20 ML

CREAM TOGETHER BUTTER AND SUGAR. ADD VANILLA, NUTS, FLOUR AND SALT AND BEAT WELL. SHAPE INTO CRESCENTS AND PLACE 1 INCH (2.5 CM) APART ON AN UNGREASED COOKIE SHEET. BAKE AT 325°F (160°C) FOR 15-20 MINUTES. WHILE STILL WARM, COAT WITH SUGAR AND CINNAMON OR FOR VARIETY COAT WITH ICING SUGAR. MAKES 2 TO 3 DOZEN COOKIES.

FRUIT AND NUT SHORTBREAD

A COLORFUL ADDITION TO YOUR CHRISTMAS BAKING.

1/2 LB	BUTTER	250 G
I CUP	BROWN SUGAR	250 ML
I	EGG YOLK	I
2 CUPS	FLOUR	500 ML
2/3 CUP	GLACÉ CHERRIES, HALVED	150 ML
1/2 CUP	WALNUTS, CHOPPED	125 ML

CREAM BUTTER AND SUGAR. ADD YOLK AND FLOUR. CUT IN FRUIT AND NUTS. SHAPE DOUGH INTO TWO ROLLS 2 INCHES (5 CM) IN DIAMETER AND ROLL IN WAX PAPER. CHILL OVERNIGHT. WHILE STILL COLD AND WAX PAPER STILL ON, TAKE A SHARP KNIFE AND CUT THIN SLICES (1/8 INCH/3 MM). SET ON GREASED COOKIE SHEETS, REMOVE WAX PAPER AND BAKE AT 375°F (190°C) FOR 10 MINUTES. (SLIGHTLY BROWN EDGES). *MAKES ABOUT 4 DOZEN COOKIES.*

NOTE: TWIST COOKIES OFF SHEET.

CHEESE SHORTBREAD

1/2 LB	SOFT EXTRA-SHARP CHEDDAR CHEESE	250 G
1/2 LB	BUTTER	250 G
2 CUPS	FLOUR	500 ML
2 TBSP	LIGHT BROWN SUGAR	25 ML

MIX INGREDIENTS TOGETHER AND KNEAD. FORM INTO A ROLL. SLICE THIN AND BAKE AT 250°F (120°C) TO 275°F (140°C) FOR 1 HOUR. *MAKES ABOUT 4 DOZEN COOKIES.*

THESE ARE PARTICULARLY GOOD TO SERVE WITH DRINKS.

LEMON BARS

ANOTHER CLASSIC!

CRUST

I CUP	FLOUR	250 ML
1/2 CUP	BUTTER	125 ML
1/4 CUP	SUGAR	50 ML
PINCH	SALT	PINCH

LEMON CUSTARD

I CUP	SUGAR	250 ML
2 TBSP	FLOUR	25 ML
1/4 TSP	BAKING POWDER	I ML
	ZEST OF I LEMON, FINELY GRATED	
	JUICE OF I LEMON, 3 TBSP (45 ML)	
2	EGGS, BEATEN	2

SPRINKLING OF ICING SUGAR

TO MAKE CRUST: CUT BUTTER INTO DRY INGREDIENTS AND PRESS INTO UNGREASED 9-INCH (2.5 L) SQUARE PAN. BAKE AT 350°F (180°C) FOR 20 MINUTES.

TO MAKE CUSTARD: BEAT ALL INGREDIENTS TOGETHER AND POUR OVER CRUST. BAKE AT 350°F (180°C) FOR 25 MINUTES. COOL AND SPRINKLE WITH ICING SUGAR. CUT INTO BARS. MAKES 24.

"I READ YOUR NEW BOOK. WHO WROTE IT FOR YOU?"
"WHO READ IT TO YOU?"

PEPPERMINT BARS

BASE

1/2 CUP	BUTTER	125 ML
2	EGGS, BEATEN	2
1 CUP	WHITE SUGAR	250 ML
1 TSP	SALT	5 ML
1/2 TSP	PEPPERMINT EXTRACT	2 ML
2	SQUARES UNSWEETENED CHOCOLATE	2
1/2 CUP	FLOUR	125 ML

MELT BUTTER AND CHOCOLATE. REMOVE FROM HEAT, ADD EGGS AND BEAT WELL. ADD SUGAR, PEPPERMINT, FLOUR AND SALT. BEAT WELL. POUR INTO GREASED 9-INCH (2.5 L) SQUARE PAN. BAKE AT 350°F (180°C) FOR 20 MINUTES. COOL.

2ND LAYER

1 CUP	ICING SUGAR	250 ML
2 TBSP	BUTTER (HEAPING TABLESPOONS)	25 ML
1 TBSP	MILK OR CREAM	15 ML
1 TBSP	PEPPERMINT EXTRACT	15 ML
	FEW DROPS GREEN FOOD COLORING, IF DESIRED	

MIX SUGAR AND BUTTER UNTIL SMOOTH. MIX IN REMAINING INGREDIENTS. SPREAD ON BASE AND LET SET.

TOP LAYER

2	SQUARES SEMI-SWEET CHOCOLATE	2
2 TBSP	BUTTER	25 ML

MELT TOGETHER. COOL AND DRIZZLE OVER SECOND LAYER. MAKES 24.

PEANUT BUTTER SLICES

A REAL HIT WITH CHILDREN.

1/2 CUP	BUTTER	125 ML
I CUP	PEANUT BUTTER	250 ML
2	PACKAGES (EACH 12 OZ/341 G) BUTTERSCOTCH CHIPS	2
2 CUPS	MINIATURE MARSHMALLOWS	500 ML

MELT BUTTER, PEANUT BUTTER AND CHIPS IN TOP OF DOUBLE BOILER. COOL AND ADD MARSHMALLOWS. PUT IN 8-INCH (2 L) SQUARE PAN. REFRIGERATE. *MAKES 16.*

PEANUT BUTTER CRUNCHES

I CUP	PEANUT BUTTER	250 ML
1/2 CUP	CORN SYRUP	125 ML
1/2 CUP	BROWN SUGAR	125 ML
I TSP	SALT	5 ML
2 CUPS	CORNFLAKES	500 ML
I CUP	RICE KRISPIES	125 ML

PLACE SUGAR AND SYRUP IN DOUBLE BOILER, MELT. ADD PEANUT BUTTER, CORN FLAKES AND KRISPIES. PAT IN 8-INCH (2 L) GREASED SQUARE PAN AND REFRIGERATE. *MAKES 16.*

DREAM SLICES

ALWAYS A HIT – ADD TO YOUR CHRISTMAS BAKING.

CRUST

1 1/3 CUPS	FLOUR	325 ML
1 TBSP	SUGAR	15 ML
3/4 CUP	BUTTER	175 ML

FILLING

2	EGGS	2
1 CUP	BROWN SUGAR	250 ML
1 TSP	VANILLA	5 ML
3 TBSP	FLOUR	45 ML
1 TSP	BAKING POWDER	5 ML
PINCH	SALT	PINCH
1 CUP	SHREDDED COCONUT	250 ML
2/3 CUP	CHOPPED WALNUTS	150 ML
1/4 CUP	SNIPPED GLACÉ CHERRIES	50 ML

BUTTER ICING

1/4 CUP	BUTTER, ROOM TEMPERATURE	50 ML
2 1/2 CUPS	ICING (CONFECTIONER'S) SUGAR	625 ML
3 TBSP	CREAM	45 ML

TO MAKE CRUST: PREHEAT OVEN TO 350°F (180°C). COMBINE FLOUR AND SUGAR. CUT IN BUTTER WITH PASTRY BLENDER UNTIL CRUMBLY. PRESS FIRMLY INTO A LIGHTLY GREASED 8-INCH (2 L) SQUARE PAN. BAKE FOR 20 MINUTES.

CONTINUED ON NEXT PAGE...

TO MAKE FILLING: BEAT EGGS IN A LARGE BOWL, GRADUALLY ADD SUGAR AND VANILLA. MIX FLOUR, BAKING POWDER AND SALT TOGETHER, THEN ADD TO SUGAR MIXTURE. ADD REMAINING INGREDIENTS. SPREAD OVER CRUST.

RETURN TO OVEN - LOWER TEMPERATURE TO 300°F (150°C). BAKE FOR 25-30 MINUTES, UNTIL TOP IS SET AND LIGHTLY BROWN. COOL.

TO MAKE ICING: BEAT INGREDIENTS TOGETHER AND SPREAD OVER COOLED SQUARE. FREEZES WELL. MAKES 36.

CHEESE SQUARES

1/4 LB	BUTTER	125 G
1/4 LB	VELVEETA CHEESE	125 G
1/4 CUP	BROWN SUGAR	50 ML
1 3/4 CUPS	FLOUR	425 ML
1 1/2 TSP	BAKING POWDER	7 ML
1/2 TSP	SALT	2 ML
	JELLY (CRABAPPLE, APPLE OR RASPBERRY)	

COMBINE INGREDIENTS. PAT 3/4 OF MIXTURE IN AN 8-INCH (2 L) SQUARE PAN. COVER WITH JAM OR JELLY. CRUMBLE REST OF MIXTURE ON TOP. BAKE 25 MINUTES AT 300°F (150°C). MAKES 16 TO 24.

RASPBERRY SQUARES

I CUP	FLOUR	250 ML
I TBSP	MILK	15 ML
I	EGG	I
1/2 TSP	SALT	2 ML
I TSP	BAKING POWDER	5 ML
1/2 CUP	BUTTER	125 ML
	RASPBERRY OR STRAWBERRY JAM	

MIX INGREDIENTS LIKE A PIE DOUGH AND ROLL OUT TO FIT SNUGLY IN A 13- X 9-INCH (3 L) PAN. SPREAD A THIN LAYER OF JAM ON TOP.

I CUP	WHITE SUGAR	250 ML
1/4 CUP	BUTTER, MELTED	50 ML
I TSP	VANILLA	5 ML
1 1/2 CUPS	COCONUT	375 ML
I	BEATEN EGG	I

MIX INGREDIENTS WELL AND SPREAD OVER JAM. BAKE IN 350°F (180°C) OVEN FOR 25 MINUTES. CUT INTO SQUARES WHEN WARM. MAKES 36 TO 48.

YOU CAN TELL MALE PANCAKES FROM FEMALE PANCAKES BY NOTICING WHICH ONES ARE STACKED.

CARAMEL BARS

ANOTHER CHILDREN'S FAVORITE!

64	SOFT CARAMELS (14-OZ/398 G PACKAGE)	64
1 CUP	EVAPORATED MILK	250 ML
2 CUPS	FLOUR	500 ML
2 CUPS	OATMEAL	500 ML
1 1/2 CUPS	BROWN SUGAR	375 ML
1 TSP	SODA	5 ML
1 TSP	SALT	5 ML
1 1/2 CUPS	BUTTER	375 ML
1	PACKAGE (12 OZ/341 G) CHOCOLATE CHIPS	1
1/2 CUP	WALNUTS, CHOPPED	125 ML

MELT CARAMELS WITH EVAPORATED MILK IN DOUBLE BOILER. MIX FLOUR, OATMEAL, BROWN SUGAR, SODA, SALT AND BUTTER. PRESS 1/2 OF MIXTURE ONTO 18- X 15-INCH (45 X 38 CM) JELLYROLL PAN OR A 15- X 10-INCH (38 X 25 CM) COOKIE SHEET AND AN 8-INCH (2 L) SQUARE PAN. (BAR SHOULD BE 3/4 INCH/2 CM THICK WHEN COOKED). BAKE 5 MINUTES AT 350°F (180°C). SPRINKLE CHOCOLATE CHIPS AND WALNUTS OVER COOKED CRUST. SPREAD CARAMEL MIXTURE OVER THAT, AND SPRINKLE THE OTHER HALF OF THE CRUMB MIXTURE ON TOP. BAKE 15 TO 20 MINUTES AT 350°F (180°C), UNTIL GOLDEN BROWN. CUT WHILE WARM. MAKES 48.

TIME MAY BE A GREAT HEALER, BUT IT'S A LOUSY BEAUTICIAN.

MRS. LARSON'S BARS

GREAT FAVORITE WITH CHILDREN.

CRUST

1 CUP	BUTTER	250 ML
2 CUPS	BROWN SUGAR	500 ML
2	EGGS, BEATEN	2
2 TSP	VANILLA	10 ML
2½ CUPS	FLOUR	625 ML
1 TSP	SODA	5 ML
1 TSP	SALT	5 ML
3 CUPS	OATMEAL	750 ML

FILLING

1	PACKAGE (12 OZ/341 G) CHOCOLATE CHIPS	1
1	CAN (14 OZ/398 ML) SWEETENED CONDENSED MILK	1
2 TBSP	BUTTER	25 ML
½ TSP	SALT	2 ML
½ TSP	VANILLA	2 ML

CRUST: CREAM BUTTER AND SUGAR. ADD EGGS AND VANILLA AND MIX WELL. SIFT FLOUR, SALT AND SODA. ADD TO BATTER AND MIX WELL. SIFT FLOUR, SALT AND SODA. ADD TO BATTER AND MIX. ADD OATMEAL AND MIX INTO A CRUMBLY TEXTURE. RESERVE ¼ OF THIS OATMEAL MIXTURE FOR TOPPING. PAT REMAINDER INTO BOTTOM OF AN 18- X 15-INCH (4 L) JELLYROLL PAN OR TWO 13- X 9-INCH (3 L) PANS. (BAR SHOULD BE ¾ INCH/2 CM THICK WHEN COOKED.)

CONTINUED ON NEXT PAGE...

FILLING: COMBINE INGREDIENTS IN TOP OF DOUBLE BOILER AND HEAT AND STIR UNTIL MELTED. SPREAD FILLING IN THIN LAYER OVER CRUST AND SPRINKLE TOP WITH RESERVED OATMEAL MIXTURE. BAKE AT 350°F (180°C) FOR APPROXIMATELY 20 MINUTES OR UNTIL GOLDEN BROWN. MAKES 36 TO 48.

MAGIC COOKIE BARS

DON'T MAKE THESE IF YOU CAN'T AVOID TEMPTATION –
THEY'RE TOO YUMMY.

2 CUPS	CRUSHED CORN FLAKES	500 ML
3 TBSP	SUGAR	45 ML
1/2 CUP	BUTTER	125 ML

MIX INGREDIENTS THOROUGHLY AND PAT INTO A 9-INCH (2.5 L) SQUARE PAN.

I CUP	CHOCOLATE CHIPS	250 ML
1 1/2 CUPS	COCONUT	375 ML
I CUP	CHOPPED PECANS	250 ML
I	CAN (14 OZ/398 ML) SWEETENED CONDENSED MILK	I

SPRINKLE ABOVE INGREDIENTS OVER FIRST MIXTURE IN ORDER, THEN DRIZZLE CONDENSED MILK OVER ALL. BAKE AT 350°F (180°C) FOR 30 TO 35 MINUTES. MAKES 24.

VERNA'S CHOCOLATE SQUARES

18	COCONUT (OR PLAIN) COOKIES	18
5 TBSP	BUTTER, MELTED	75 ML
2	SQUARES SEMI-SWEET CHOCOLATE	2
1/4 CUP	MELTED BUTTER	50 ML
1 1/2 CUPS	ICING SUGAR	375 ML
1 TSP	VANILLA	5 ML
1	EGG, BEATEN	1
1 CUP	CHOPPED WALNUTS	250 ML

CRUSH COOKIES, ADD MELTED 1/4 CUP (50 ML) BUTTER AND PUT 2/3 INTO PAN. BAKE 5 MINUTES AT 300°F (150°C). MIX CHOCOLATE SQUARES AND 1/4 CUP (50 ML) MELTED BUTTER. ADD ICING SUGAR, VANILLA, EGG AND WALNUTS. SPREAD OVER FIRST LAYER AND SPRINKLE WITH REMAINING CRUMBS. REFRIGERATE. MAKES 16.

FUDGE SCOTCH SQUARES

1 1/2 CUPS	GRAHAM CRACKER CRUMBS	375 ML
1	CAN (14 OZ/398 ML) SWEETENED CONDENSED MILK	1
1 CUP	SEMI-SWEET CHOCOLATE CHIPS	250 ML
1 CUP	BUTTERSCOTCH CHIPS	250 ML
1 CUP	COARSELY CHOPPED WALNUTS	250 ML

MIX WELL AND PAT MIXTURE INTO A WELL-GREASED 9-INCH (2.5 L) SQUARE PAN. BAKE AT 350°F (180°C) FOR 30 TO 35 MINUTES. COOL BEFORE SERVING. MAKES 16.

NANAIMO BARS

FIRST LAYER

1/2 CUP	BUTTER, MELTED	125 ML
1/4 CUP	BROWN SUGAR	50 ML
3 TBSP	COCOA POWDER	45 ML
1	EGG, BEATEN	1
2 CUPS	GRAHAM WAFER CRUMBS	500 ML
1 CUP	FLAKED COCONUT	250 ML
1/2 CUP	CHOPPED WALNUTS	125 ML

SECOND LAYER

2 CUPS	ICING SUGAR	500 ML
1/4 CUP	BUTTER, SOFTENED	50 ML
1/4 CUP	CREAM OR MILK	50 ML
2 TBSP	CUSTARD POWDER	25 ML

THIRD LAYER

3	1-OZ (30 G) CHOCOLATE SQUARES (SWEET OR SEMISWEET)	3
1/4 CUP	BUTTER	50 ML

TO MAKE FIRST LAYER: COMBINE INGREDIENTS AND PAT INTO A 9-INCH (2.5 L) SQUARE UNGREASED PAN. CHILL FOR 1/2 HOUR.

TO MAKE SECOND LAYER: BEAT ALL INGREDIENTS UNTIL SMOOTH AND FLUFFY. SPREAD CAREFULLY ON TOP OF FIRST LAYER.

TO MAKE THIRD LAYER: MELT CHOCOLATE AND BUTTER TOGETHER. SPREAD OVER SECOND LAYER AND CHILL. CUT INTO SMALL BARS – VERY RICH AND VERY DELICIOUS! MAKES 81.

BROWNIES

OUR "BEST"!

1 CUP	SUGAR	250 ML
1/3 CUP	BUTTER	75 ML
PINCH	SALT	PINCH
2	EGGS, BEATEN	2
1/4 CUP	COCOA POWDER	50 ML
2/3 CUP	FLOUR	150 ML
1/3 CUP	MILK OR CREAM	75 ML
1 TSP	VANILLA	5 ML
1/2 CUP	CHOPPED WALNUTS OR PECANS	125 ML

MOCHA ICING

3 TBSP	COCOA POWDER	45 ML
2 TBSP	BUTTER, SOFTENED	25 ML
3 TBSP	COFFEE (LIQUID)	45 ML
2 TSP	VANILLA	10 ML
	ICING (CONFECTIONER'S) SUGAR	

PREHEAT OVEN TO 350°F (180°C). IN A LARGE BOWL, CREAM TOGETHER SUGAR AND BUTTER. STIR IN SALT, EGGS, COCOA, FLOUR, MILK, VANILLA AND WALNUTS. POUR INTO A GREASED 8-INCH (2 L) SQUARE PAN AND BAKE FOR 20–25 MINUTES, OR UNTIL A KNIFE COMES OUT CLEAN WHEN INSERTED IN THE CENTER. COOL ON A WIRE RACK. MAKES 16 TO 20.

TO MAKE ICING: BEAT COCOA, BUTTER, COFFEE, VANILLA AND ENOUGH ICING SUGAR TO REACH DESIRED CONSISTENCY. SPREAD ON COOLED BROWNIES. THIS RECIPE DOUBLES WELL. USE A 13- X 9-INCH (3 L) PAN.

FANTASTIC FUDGE BROWNIES

MEN LOVE THEM – SO DO CHILDREN, (AND MOMS NOT ON DIETS!).

BROWNIES

I CUP	BUTTER	250 ML
2 CUPS	SUGAR	500 ML
1/4 CUP	COCOA POWDER	50 ML
4	EGGS, BEATEN	4
I TSP	VANILLA	5 ML
I CUP	FLOUR	250 ML
I CUP	CHOPPED WALNUTS OR PECANS	250 ML

ICING

2 CUPS	ICING SUGAR	500 ML
2 TBSP	BUTTER	25 ML
2 TBSP	COCOA POWDER	25 ML
2 TBSP	BOILING WATER	25 ML
2 TSP	VANILLA	10 ML

TO MAKE BROWNIES: CREAM TOGETHER BUTTER, SUGAR AND COCOA POWDER. MIX IN BEATEN EGGS AND VANILLA. ADD FLOUR AND STIR. FOLD IN NUTS. BAKE IN A GREASED 13- X 9-INCH (3 L) PAN AT 350°F (180°C) FOR 40 TO 45 MINUTES. TOP WILL APPEAR TO BE UNDERDONE (FALLS IN MIDDLE) BUT DON'T OVERCOOK. SHOULD BE MOIST AND CHEWY.

TO MAKE ICING: BEAT ALL INGREDIENTS TOGETHER WHILE BROWNIES ARE BAKING. POUR ON TOP AS SOON AS BROWNIES COME OUT OF THE OVEN. IT WILL MELT INTO A SHINY GLAZE. MAKES 36 TO 48.

CHOCOLATE FUDGE

1	PACKAGE (12 OZ/341 G) CHOCOLATE CHIPS	1
2 CUPS	WHITE SUGAR	500 ML
2/3 CUP	EVAPORATED MILK	150 ML
12	MARSHMALLOWS (REGULAR SIZE)	12
1/2 CUP	BUTTER	125 ML
PINCH	SALT	PINCH
1 TSP	VANILLA	5 ML

COOK ALL INGREDIENTS EXCEPT CHOCOLATE CHIPS AND VANILLA, STIRRING OVER MEDIUM HEAT UNTIL MIXTURE COMES TO A BOIL. BOIL FOR 5 MINUTES. REMOVE FROM HEAT; ADD CHOCOLATE CHIPS AND VANILLA. POUR INTO A 8-INCH (2 L) SQUARE PAN. COOL AND CUT INTO SQUARES. THIS IS A SUPER TREAT FOR YOUR SWEET TOOTH. MAKES 48 TO 64 PIECES.

"DARLING WHAT YOU DOING, STANDING SO STILL?"
"SHH! I'M TRYING OUT A NEW RECIPE. THE BOOK SAYS
I MUSTN'T STIR FOR FIFTEEN MINUTES."

Red Cabbage (page 225)

Diamonds (page 266)

Snowballs (page 271)
Chocolate Fudge Balls (page 272)

Fruit and Nut Shortbread (page 274)

CHEESECAKE CUPCAKES

24	PAPER MUFFIN CUPS	24
1	PACKAGE (8½ OZ/242 G) ROUND VANILLA WAFERS	1
1 CUP	SUGAR	250 ML
3	PACKAGES (EACH 8 OZ/250 G) CREAM CHEESE, SOFTENED	3
4	EGGS	4
2 TSP	LEMON JUICE	10 ML
	CHERRY PIE FILLING (OR BLUEBERRY OR RASPBERRY)	

PREHEAT OVEN TO 350°F (180°C). MIX SUGAR, CHEESE, EGGS AND LEMON JUICE UNTIL SMOOTH. LINE CUPCAKE PANS WITH PAPERS. PLACE ONE VANILLA WAFER IN THE BOTTOM OF EACH. SPOON CHEESE MIXTURE OVER WAFERS TO FILL CUPS 3/4 FULL. BAKE IN PREHEATED OVEN FOR 18 TO 20 MINUTES. COOL. CUPCAKES WILL SINK IN THE MIDDLE WHILE COOLING. SPOON PIE FILLING ON EACH CUPCAKE, AND REFRIGERATE AT LEAST ONE HOUR. THESE MAY BE TOPPED WITH A WHIPPED TOPPING IF DESIRED. SERVES 24.

EVERY YEAR IT TAKES LESS TIME TO FLY ACROSS THE OCEAN, AND LONGER TO DRIVE TO WORK.

BEST OF BRIDGE CLASSIC CHEESECAKE

CRUST

1 3/4 CUPS	GRAHAM WAFER CRUMBS	425 ML
1/4 CUP	FINELY CHOPPED WALNUTS	50 ML
1/2 TSP	CINNAMON	2 ML
1/2 CUP	BUTTER, MELTED	125 ML

FILLING

2	PACKAGES (EACH 8 OZ/250 G) CREAM CHEESE	2
1 CUP	SUGAR	250 ML
3	EGGS	3
2 1/2 CUPS	SOUR CREAM	625 ML
2 TSP	VANILLA	10 ML

TOPPING

1	PACKAGE (15 OZ/426 G) FROZEN SLICED STRAWBERRIES WITH JUICE, THAWED	1

TO MAKE CRUST: COMBINE INGREDIENTS AND PRESS INTO A LIGHTLY GREASED 10-INCH (25 CM) SPRINGFORM PAN.

TO MAKE FILLING: PREHEAT OVEN TO 325°F (160°C). BLEND CHEESE, SUGAR AND EGGS. ADD SOUR CREAM AND VANILLA. MIX WELL AND POUR ONTO CRUST. BAKE FOR 1 1/2 HOURS.

SERVE WEDGES WITH STRAWBERRY TOPPING. SERVES 8 TO 12.

SOME MEN ARE ATTRACTED BY A WOMAN'S MIND. OTHERS ARE ATTRACTED BY WHAT SHE DOESN'T MIND.

WAR CAKE

THIS RECIPE WAS A FAVORITE WITH OUR MOTHERS
DURING THE EARLY FORTIES WHEN EGGS WERE
RATIONED. AN ECONOMICAL AND VERY EASY SPICE CAKE.

1 CUP	RAISINS	250 ML
2 CUPS	WATER	500 ML
1 TSP	SODA	5 ML
1 TBSP	LARD	15 ML
1 CUP	SUGAR	250 ML
1 TSP	CLOVES	5 ML
1 TSP	NUTMEG	5 ML
1 TBSP	CINNAMON	15 ML
PINCH	SALT	PINCH
1 1/2 CUPS	FLOUR	375 ML
1/2 CUP	CHOPPED WALNUTS (OPTIONAL)	125 ML
1/2 CUP	COCONUT (OPTIONAL)	125 ML

COMBINE RAISINS AND WATER IN A SAUCEPAN, BRING TO A
BOIL AND SIMMER FOR 20 MINUTES. ADD SODA AND LARD,
LET COOL. ADD RAISIN MIXTURE TO DRY INGREDIENTS AND
MIX WELL. POUR INTO GREASED 8-INCH (2 L) SQUARE PAN
AND BAKE AT 350°F (180°C) FOR 20 TO 25 MINUTES.
SERVES 6 TO 8.

A FOOL AND HIS MONEY ARE SOON POPULAR.

ANGEL MOCHA TORTE

A CLASSIC ENTERTAINING DESSERT.

MERINGUES

1 CUP	SLICED ALMONDS	250 ML
4	EGG WHITES	4
PINCH	SALT	PINCH
1 CUP	BROWN SUGAR	250 ML

MOCHA FILLING

1 CUP	WHIPPING CREAM	250 ML
$\frac{1}{2}$ CUP	BROWN SUGAR	125 ML
1 TBSP	INSTANT COFFEE GRANULES	15 ML
4	9-INCH (23 CM) CIRCLES OF PARCHMENT PAPER	4

TO MAKE MERINGUES: TOAST ALMONDS; RESERVING SOME FOR DECORATION; CRUSH THE REMAINDER. BEAT EGG WHITES AND SALT UNTIL ALMOST STIFF. GRADUALLY ADD SUGAR; BEAT UNTIL GLOSSY PEAKS FORM. FOLD IN CRUSHED ALMONDS. SPREAD $\frac{1}{4}$ OF MERINGUE ON EACH PAPER CIRCLE. DECORATE 1 CIRCLE WITH RESERVED ALMONDS. PLACE ON 2 COOKIE SHEETS; BAKE AT 250°F (120°C) FOR 1 HOUR. TURN OFF OVEN AND LEAVE OVERNIGHT. DON'T PEEK!! NEXT DAY, REMOVE MERINGUES AND TAKE OFF PARCHMENT PAPER.

TO MAKE FILLING: WHIP CREAM. FOLD IN SUGAR AND COFFEE GRANULES. PLACE A MERINGUE ON A SERVING PLATE. SPREAD WITH $\frac{1}{3}$ OF FILLING. CONTINUE WITH REMAINING MERINGUES, FINISHING WITH DECORATED MERINGUE. REFRIGERATE AT LEAST 2 HOURS BEFORE SERVING. SERVES 8 TO 10.

CHOCOLATE MOCHA TORTE

7/8 CUP	SUGAR	220 ML
6	EGGS, SEPARATED	6
1/2 CUP	FINE WAFER CRUMBS (VANILLA OR GRAHAM)	125 ML
1/4 CUP	GRATED CHOCOLATE	50 ML
3/4 CUP	CHOPPED WALNUTS	175 ML
2 TBSP	BRANDY OR RUM	25 ML
1/2 TSP	DOUBLE ACTING BAKING POWDER	2 ML
1/2 TSP	CINNAMON	2 ML
1/4 TSP	CLOVES	1 ML
1/4 TSP	NUTMEG	1 ML

BEAT YOLKS, GRADUALLY ADDING SUGAR, THEN THE REMAINING DRY INGREDIENTS. WHIP WHITES UNTIL FLUFFY AND STIFF. FOLD INTO YOLK MIXTURE. BAKE IN 9-INCH (2.5 L) SQUARE PAN WITH REMOVABLE SIDES FOR 1 HOUR AT 325°F (160°C).

CHOCOLATE MOCHA TORTE ICING

16	LARGE MARSHMALLOWS	16
4 TBSP	INSTANT COFFEE	60 ML
1/3 CUP	WATER	75 ML
1 CUP	WHIPPING CREAM, WHIPPED	250 ML

MELT MARSHMALLOWS, COFFEE AND WATER, STIRRING CONSTANTLY, THEN COOL. FOLD WHIPPED CREAM INTO COOLED MARSHMALLOW MIXTURE. CUT TORTE INTO TWO LAYERS, FILLING TORTE. SAVE ENOUGH TO ICE THE REST OF THE TORTE.

SPRINKLE WITH GRATED CHOCOLATE, AND ADDITIONAL CHOPPED WALNUTS. SERVES 8 TO 12.

CHOCOLATE CHEESE TORTE

*THIS IS VERY RICH, VERY EXPENSIVE
BUT VERY, VERY GOOD!*

1 1/3 CUPS	GRAHAM WAFER CRACKER CRUMBS	325 ML
3 TBSP	SUGAR	45 ML
3 TBSP	UNSWEETENED COCOA POWDER	45 ML
1/3 CUP	BUTTER, MELTED	75 ML
4	PACKAGES (EACH 3 OZ/85 G) CREAM CHEESE	4
3/4 CUP	SUGAR	175 ML
2	EGGS	2
1 TBSP	COFFEE-FLAVORED LIQUEUR OR RUM	15 ML
1 TSP	VANILLA	5 ML
1	CARTON (8 OZ/250 ML) SOUR CREAM	1
1	SQUARE UNSWEETENED CHOCOLATE, GRATED	1
1 1/2 TSP	INSTANT COFFEE POWDER	7 ML
2 TBSP	BOILING WATER	25 ML
4	SQUARES SEMI-SWEET CHOCOLATE	4
4	EGGS, SEPARATED	4
1/3 CUP	SUGAR	75 ML
1 TBSP	COFFEE-FLAVORED LIQUEUR OR RUM	15 ML
1/2 TSP	VANILLA	2 ML
1/2 CUP	WHIPPING CREAM, WHIPPED	125 ML

PREHEAT OVEN TO 350°F (180°C). BLEND CRUMBS, SUGAR, COCOA AND BUTTER TOGETHER UNTIL WELL BLENDED. PRESS FIRMLY ONTO BOTTOM AND SIDE OF 9-INCH (23 CM) SPRINGFORM PAN. BAKE FOR 10 MINUTES. COOL WHILE PREPARING FILLING.

CONTINUED ON NEXT PAGE...

BEAT CREAM CHEESE IN A LARGE BOWL WITH ELECTRIC BEATER AT HIGH SPEED UNTIL LIGHT AND FLUFFY. GRADUALLY BEAT IN SUGAR. ADD 2 EGGS, ONE AT A TIME, BEATING WELL AFTER EACH ADDITION. ADD LIQUEUR AND VANILLA. TURN INTO BAKED CRUST. BAKE AT 350°F (180°C) FOR 30 MINUTES. COOL FOR 10 MINUTES ON WIRE RACK

GENTLY SPREAD SOUR CREAM OVER BAKED LAYER. SPRINKLE WITH GRATED CHOCOLATE. REFRIGERATE. DISSOLVE COFFEE IN BOILING WATER IN DOUBLE BOILER OVER HOT - NOT BOILING - WATER. ADD CHOCOLATE. STIR UNTIL MELTED AND BLENDED.

BEAT THE 4 EGG YOLKS UNTIL THICK. GRADUALLY BEAT IN SUGAR AND A SMALL AMOUNT OF CHOCOLATE MIXTURE. BEAT WELL. CONTINUE ADDING SMALL AMOUNTS OF CHOCOLATE MIXTURE TO EGG MIXTURE, UNTIL ALL HAS BEEN USED. ADD LIQUEUR AND VANILLA.

BEAT EGG WHITES UNTIL FLUFFY. GENTLY FOLD INTO CHOCOLATE MIXTURE. SPREAD OVER COOLED BAKED LAYER. REFRIGERATE UNTIL FIRM. WHEN READY TO SERVE LOOSEN SIDE OF PAN, REMOVE. PLACE CAKE ON SERVING PLATE. DECORATE WITH WHIPPED CREAM. SERVES 12.

MY WIFE MADE UFOS YESTERDAY - UNIDENTIFIED FRYING OBJECTS.

CHOCOLATE TORTE ROYALE

MERINGUE

2	EGG WHITES	2
1/2 TSP	VINEGAR	2 ML
	SALT	
1/2 CUP	SUGAR	125 ML
1/2 TSP	CINNAMON	2 ML

ADD SALT AND CINNAMON TO EGG WHITES AND BEAT UNTIL PEAKS FORM. GRADUALLY ADD SUGAR AND VINEGAR, BEATING WELL AFTER EACH ADDITION, UNTIL MERINGUE IS STIFF. SPREAD ON BROWN PAPER IN AN 8-INCH (20 CM) CIRCLE AND BAKE AT 275°F (140°C) FOR 1 HOUR.

TURN OVEN OFF, LET COOL IN OVEN FOR 2 HOURS.

FILLING

6 OZ	SEMI-SWEET CHOCOLATE	175 G
2	EGG YOLKS	2
1/4 CUP	WATER	50 ML
1 CUP	HEAVY CREAM	250 ML
1/4 CUP	SUGAR	50 ML
1/4 TSP	CINNAMON	1 ML
	CHOPPED PECANS	

MELT CHOCOLATE WITH WATER. SPREAD 2 TBSP (25 ML) OVER BOTTOM OF SHELL. TO REMAINING CHOCOLATE ADD BEATEN YOLKS, BLEND WELL AND CHILL UNTIL THICK. WHIP CREAM, SUGAR AND CINNAMON. FOLD INTO CHOCOLATE MIXTURE. SPREAD INTO SHELL AND CHILL. GARNISH WITH WHIPPED CREAM AND CHOPPED PECANS. SERVES 8.

SUPER CHOCOLATE CAKE

THIS IS DARN GOOD!

I CUP	WHITE SUGAR	250 ML
3 TBSP	BUTTER, ROOM TEMPERATURE	45 ML
I	EGG, BEATEN	I
1/2 CUP	COCOA, FILL WITH BOILING WATER TO MAKE I CUP OF (250 ML) LIQUID	125 ML
1/2 TSP	BAKING SODA	2 ML
1/2 CUP	BOILING WATER	125 ML
I CUP	FLOUR	250 ML
I TSP	BAKING POWDER	5 ML

CREAM TOGETHER SUGAR AND BUTTER; ADD EGG AND COCOA LIQUID. MIX SODA AND BOILING WATER. ADD THIS, FLOUR AND BAKING POWDER, MIX WELL. POUR INTO GREASED 9-INCH (2.5 L) SQUARE PAN (THE BATTER WILL BE THIN). BAKE AT 350°F (180°C) FOR 30 MINUTES, OR UNTIL A TOOTHPICK INSERTED IN CENTER COMES OUT CLEAN. (THIS CAKE DOUBLES WELL. BAKE IN A 13- X 9-INCH/3 L PAN OR A BUNDT PAN FOR 40 TO 50 MINUTES.) SERVES 8.

THE ONLY WAY TO GET OUT OF BED EVERY MORNING WITH A SMILE ON YOUR FACE IS TO GO TO BED AT NIGHT WITH A COAT HANGER IN YOUR MOUTH.

CHOCOLATE POUND CAKE

3 CUPS	SIFTED ALL PURPOSE FLOUR	750 ML
1/2 CUP	COCOA	125 ML
1/2 TSP	BAKING POWDER	2 ML
1/4 TSP	SALT	1 ML
1 CUP	BUTTER	250 ML
1/2 CUP	SOFT SHORTENING	125 ML
3 CUPS	SUGAR	750 ML
5	EGGS	5
1 1/4 CUPS	MILK	300 ML
2 TBSP	GRATED, UNSWEETENED CHOCOLATE	25 ML
1 TSP	VANILLA	5 ML

PREHEAT OVEN TO 350°F (180°C). LIGHTLY GREASE AND FLOUR A 10-INCH (4 L) TUBE PAN. SIFT FLOUR WITH COCOA, BAKING POWDER AND SALT. SET ASIDE. IN LARGE BOWL BEAT BUTTER, SHORTENING AND SUGAR FOR 5 MINUTES. ADD EGGS ONE AT A TIME, BEATING WELL AFTER EACH ADDITION. WITH MIXER AT LOW SPEED, BEAT IN FLOUR MIXTURE IN FOUR ADDITIONS, ALTERNATING WITH THE MILK IN THREE ADDITIONS, ENDING WITH THE FLOUR. ADD GRATED CHOCOLATE AND VANILLA. TURN BATTER INTO PREPARED PAN. BAKE 1 HOUR AND 15 TO 20 MINUTES OR TILL TESTER INSERTED IN CENTER COMES OUT CLEAN. LET COOL ON WIRE RACK FOR 10 MINUTES, TURN OUT AND LET COOL COMPLETELY. IF DESIRED, SERVE WITH WHIPPED CREAM AND SHAVED CHOCOLATE. SERVES 16 TO 20.

CHOCOLATE UPSIDE-DOWN CAKE

1¼ CUPS	CAKE OR REGULAR FLOUR	300 ML
¾ CUP	SUGAR	175 ML
2 TSP	BAKING POWDER	10 ML
¼ TSP	SALT	1 ML
½ CUP	BROKEN NUTS (OUCH!)	125 ML
1 OZ	BITTER CHOCOLATE	30 G
2 TBSP	BUTTER	25 ML
½ CUP	MILK	125 ML
1 TSP	VANILLA	5 ML

TOPPING

2 TBSP	COCOA	25 ML
½ CUP	BROWN SUGAR	125 ML
½ CUP	WHITE SUGAR	125 ML
1 CUP	BOILING WATER	250 ML
1 CUP	WHIPPING CREAM OR ICE CREAM	250 ML

SIFT FLOUR, ¾ CUP (175 ML) WHITE SUGAR, BAKING POWDER AND SALT TOGETHER. MELT CHOCOLATE AND BUTTER TOGETHER. MIX WITH MILK AND VANILLA. STIR INTO DRY INGREDIENTS. ADD NUTS AND BLEND THOROUGHLY. POUR INTO A WELL-GREASED LAYER CAKE PAN. NOW, MIX COCOA, BROWN SUGAR AND ½ CUP (125 ML) WHITE SUGAR. SPREAD OVER TOP OF CAKE BATTER. POUR BOILING WATER OVER ALL. BAKE IN MODERATE 350°F (180°C) OVEN FOR 1 HOUR. IT IS BEST SERVED SLIGHTLY WARM WITH WHIPPED CREAM. SERVES 8 TO 10.

GRASSHOPPER CAKE

A VERY SPECIAL DESSERT. THE CAKE CAN BE MADE AHEAD
AND FROZEN. ADD FILLING THE DAY OF SERVING.

CAKE

2	EGG WHITES	2
1/2 CUP	SUGAR	125 ML
1 3/4 CUPS	SIFTED CAKE FLOUR	425 ML
1 CUP	SUGAR	250 ML
3/4 TSP	BAKING SODA	4 ML
1 TSP	SALT	5 ML
1/3 CUP	OIL	75 ML
1 CUP	BUTTERMILK OR SOUR MILK (2 TBSP/25 ML VINEGAR TO 1 CUP/250 ML MILK)	250 ML
2	EGG YOLKS	2
2	SQUARES UNSWEETENED CHOCOLATE, MELTED	2

FILLING

1 TBSP	UNFLAVORED GELATIN	15 ML
1/4 CUP	COLD WATER	50 ML
1/3 CUP	GREEN CRÈME DE MENTHE LIQUEUR	75 ML
1/3 CUP	WHITE CRÈME DE CACAO LIQUEUR	75 ML
2 CUPS	WHIPPING CREAM (2 CARTONS)	500 ML

CAKE: PREHEAT OVEN TO 350°F (180°C). GREASE AND FLOUR
TWO 8-INCH (20 CM) ROUND PANS (AT LEAST 1 1/2-INCH/
4 CM DEEP). BEAT EGG WHITES UNTIL FOAMY. ADD 1/2 CUP
(125 ML) SUGAR, 1 TBSP (15 ML) AT A TIME, BEATING WELL
AFTER EACH ADDITION. BEAT UNTIL STIFF AND GLOSSY.
SIFT FLOUR, 1 CUP (250 ML) SUGAR, SODA AND SALT INTO

CONTINUED ON NEXT PAGE...

LARGE MIXING BOWL. ADD OIL, HALF OF THE BUTTERMILK ($1/2$ CUP/125 ML) AND BEAT ONE MINUTE AT MEDIUM SPEED. ADD REMAINING BUTTERMILK ($1/2$ CUP/125 ML), EGG YOLKS AND MELTED CHOCOLATE. BEAT ONE MINUTE MORE. FOLD IN EGG WHITES. BAKE 40 TO 45 MINUTES, OR UNTIL SPONGY. DON'T WORRY IF THE CAKE SEEMS DRY - ALL THAT FILLING WILL SOLVE EVERYTHING.

FILLING: ADD GELATIN TO COLD WATER AND SOAK 5 MINUTES. HEAT (BUT DO NOT BOIL) THE LIQUEURS. ADD GELATIN AND STIR TO DISSOLVE. COOL THOROUGHLY! BEAT THE WHIPPING CREAM UNTIL STIFF AND FOLD LIQUEUR MIXTURE INTO CREAM. CHILL FOR 15 MINUTES.

CUT EACH CAKE LAYER IN TWO (ANY ACCIDENTS ARE EASILY HIDDEN IN THE FILLING!). SPREAD FILLING BETWEEN ALL LAYERS AND COVER TOP AND SIDES. CHILL UNTIL SERVING. SERVES 10 TO 12.

MIDDLE AGE IS THAT TIME OF LIFE WHEN YOU CAN FEEL BAD IN THE MORNING WITHOUT HAVING HAD FUN THE NIGHT BEFORE.

LAZY DAISY CAKE

2	EGGS	2
I CUP	SUGAR	250 ML
I TSP	VANILLA	5 ML
I CUP	FLOUR	250 ML
I TSP	BAKING POWDER	5 ML
1/4 TSP	SALT	I ML
1/2 CUP	MILK	125 ML
I TBSP	BUTTER	15 ML

BEAT EGGS, SUGAR AND VANILLA UNTIL LEMON-COLORED.
SIFT FLOUR, BAKING POWDER AND SALT, ADD TO EGG
MIXTURE, MIXING BY HAND UNTIL COMBINED. HEAT (TO
BOILING) THE MILK AND BUTTER. ADD ALL AT ONCE
TO FIRST MIXTURE, BEATING ONLY UNTIL SMOOTH. BAKE
AT 350°F (180°C) FOR 30 MINUTES, IN 8-INCH (2 L) GREASED
SQUARE PAN. SERVES 8.

TOPPING

3 TBSP	MELTED BUTTER	45 ML
5 TBSP	BROWN SUGAR	75 ML
2 TBSP	CREAM	25 ML
1/2 CUP	COCONUT	125 ML

COMBINE ALL INGREDIENTS IN A PAN UNTIL MELTED.
SPREAD ON TOP OF BAKED CAKE AND BROWN UNDER
BROILER, WATCHING CAREFULLY THAT IT DOESN'T BURN.

DUTCH APPLE CAKE

2 CUPS	FLOUR	500 ML
1 TBSP	BAKING POWDER	15 ML
1/2 TSP	SALT	2 ML
3 TBSP	SUGAR	45 ML
1/4 CUP	BUTTER	50 ML
1	EGG	1
3/4 CUP	MILK	175 ML
2 TO 3 CUPS	SLICED APPLES	500 TO 750 ML
1/2 CUP	SUGAR, MIXED WITH 1 TSP (5 ML) CINNAMON	125 ML

SIFT THE FIRST FOUR INGREDIENTS TOGETHER. WORK IN THE BUTTER. BEAT EGG AND MILK AND STIR INTO DRY INGREDIENTS. SPREAD THE DOUGH IN SHALLOW GREASED 8-INCH (2 L) PAN. COVER WITH ROWS OF APPLES, PRESSING THE SHARP EDGES OF THE PIECES OF APPLES INTO DOUGH. SPRINKLE WITH SUGAR AND CINNAMON MIXTURE. BAKE 30 MINUTES AT 350°F (180°C). SERVE WARM WITH WHIPPED CREAM OR ICE CREAM. SERVES 6 TO 8.

MEMORY IS WHAT TELLS A MAN HIS WEDDING ANNIVERSARY WAS YESTERDAY.

APPLESAUCE SPICE CAKE

2½ CUPS	SIFTED FLOUR	625 ML
2 CUPS	SUGAR	500 ML
1½ TSP	SALT	7 ML
1½ TSP	BAKING SODA	7 ML
¼ TSP	BAKING POWDER	1 ML
1 TSP	CINNAMON	5 ML
½ TSP	GROUND CLOVES	1 ML
½ TSP	ALLSPICE	1 ML
1½ CUPS	APPLESAUCE	375 ML
½ CUP	SHORTENING	125 ML
½ CUP	WATER (SEE BELOW)	125 ML
2	EGGS	2
1 CUP	RAISINS	250 ML
½ CUP	CHOPPED WALNUTS OR PECANS	125 ML

PUT RAISINS AND SPICES IN A POT. ADD WATER TO 2 INCHES (5 CM) ABOVE RAISINS. BOIL FOR 20 MINUTES. COOL, THEN DRAIN, RESERVING LIQUID. ADD WATER TO LIQUID, IF NEEDED, TO MAKE ½ CUP (125 ML) OF LIQUID. IN BOWL, MIX TOGETHER FIRST 5 INGREDIENTS. ADD APPLESAUCE, SHORTENING AND RESERVED LIQUID. ADD EGGS; BEAT 2 MINUTES. STIR IN RAISINS AND NUTS. BAKE IN 2 LOAF PANS OR LARGE CAKE PAN AT 350°F (180°C) FOR 50 TO 60 MINUTES. KEEPS VERY WELL. SERVES 16.

HE HAS MONEY TO BURN AND SHE'S A PERFECT MATCH.

LEMONBERRY CAKE

18 OZ	UNSWEETENED FROZEN BLUEBERRIES, THAWED	511 G
1	PACKAGE 2-LAYER LEMON CAKE MIX	1
1 CUP	LEMON OR VANILLA YOGURT	250 ML
4	EGGS	4

GLAZE

1 CUP	ICING SUGAR	250 ML
4 TSP	MILK	20 ML

BLUEBERRY SAUCE

1 CUP	SUGAR	250 ML
2 TBSP	CORNSTARCH	25 ML
1 CUP	WATER	250 ML
3 TBSP	LEMON JUICE	45 ML
	WHIPPED CREAM	

RINSE AND DRAIN BERRIES, RESERVING LIQUID. COMBINE CAKE MIX, EGGS AND YOGURT, BEATING 2 MINUTES. FOLD IN HALF OF DRAINED BERRIES. BAKE IN GREASED 10-INCH (4 L) TUBE OR 10-INCH (3 L) BUNDT PAN AT 350°F (180°C) FOR 45 MINUTES, OR UNTIL DONE. DO NOT INVERT PAN, OR REMOVE, UNTIL CAKE IS COOL. MAKE GLAZE AND DRIZZLE OVER CAKE.

IN PAN, COMBINE SUGAR, CORNSTARCH, THEN THE WATER. BRING TO A BOIL AND COOK TWO MINUTES. ADD BLUEBERRIES AND JUICE. ADDITIONAL CORNSTARCH MAY BE ADDED IF A THICKER SAUCE IS DESIRED.

TO SERVE, REHEAT SAUCE AND POUR OVER CAKE SLICES ON SERVING PLATES, AND ADD A DAB OF WHIPPED CREAM TO EACH SERVING. SERVES 12 TO 16.

ARMENIAN ORANGE CAKE

FAST, SIMPLE AND ABSOLUTELY DELICIOUS.

CAKE

2 CUPS	BROWN SUGAR	500 ML
2 CUPS	FLOUR	500 ML
1/2 CUP	BUTTER	125 ML
1/2 TSP	SALT	2 ML
2 TSP	GRATED ORANGE ZEST	10 ML
1/2 TSP	ALLSPICE	2 ML
1 TSP	BAKING SODA	5 ML
1 CUP	SOUR CREAM	250 ML
1	EGG, SLIGHTLY BEATEN	1
1/2 CUP	CHOPPED MIXED NUTS (WALNUTS, CASHEWS, ALMONDS)	125 ML

TOPPING

1 CUP	WHIPPING CREAM	250 ML
2 TBSP	ICING (CONFECTIONER'S) SUGAR	25 ML
1 TSP	GRATED ORANGE ZEST	5 ML
2 TBSP	ORANGE JUICE OR GRAND MARNIER	25 ML

TO MAKE CAKE: PREHEAT OVEN TO 350°F (180°C). GREASE A 9-INCH (23 CM) SPRINGFORM PAN. IN A MEDIUM BOWL, COMBINE SUGAR, FLOUR, BUTTER, SALT, ORANGE ZEST AND ALLSPICE. BLEND WITH A PASTRY BLENDER UNTIL CRUMBLY. SPOON HALF INTO PAN. STIR SODA, SOUR CREAM AND EGG INTO REMAINING CRUMBS. POUR INTO PAN; SPRINKLE WITH NUTS. BAKE FOR 40-45 MINUTES; COOL. REMOVE SPRINGFORM AND SLIDE ONTO SERVING PLATE. SERVE WITH TOPPING. SERVES 8 TO 12.

CONTINUED ON NEXT PAGE...

TO MAKE TOPPING: WHIP CREAM UNTIL STIFF. STIR IN REMAINING INGREDIENTS. LET STAND FOR 1 HOUR TO LET FLAVORS BLEND.

THE HONEYMOON IS OVER WHEN THE DOG BRINGS HIM HIS SLIPPERS AND THE WIFE BARKS AT HIM.

STRAWBERRY ANGEL FOOD CAKE

THIS IS A LIGHT AND REFRESHING DESSERT.

1	ANGEL FOOD CAKE MIX	1
1	PACKAGE (3 OZ/85 G) STRAWBERRY JELL-O (RASPBERRY MAY BE USED)	1
1	PACKAGE (10 OZ/300 G) FROZEN STRAWBERRIES	1
1 CUP	WHIPPING CREAM	250 ML
1 CUP	WATER (BOILING)	250 ML

MAKE ANGEL FOOD CAKE. DISSOLVE JELL-O IN BOILING WATER. ADD SEMI-THAWED BERRIES. MIX WELL. PUT IN REFRIGERATOR WHEN THIS BEGINS TO SET BLEND IN WHIPPED CREAM. TEAR CAKE INTO BITE-SIZE PIECES AND ARRANGE IN ANGEL FOOD PAN. POUR BERRY MIXTURE AROUND SO THAT MIXTURE COVERS IT ALL. SET IN REFRIGERATOR FOR 24 HOURS. UNMOLD AND SERVE. ADD ADDITIONAL BERRIES AND WHIPPED CREAM. SERVES 8 TO 12.

THE BEACH IS A PLACE AT THE SEASHORE WHERE PEOPLE LIE ABOUT HOW RICH THEY ARE IN TOWN.

RHUBARB CAKE

EASY AND DELICIOUS SERVED WARM.

1½ CUPS	BROWN SUGAR	375 ML
½ CUP	BUTTER	125 ML
2	EGGS	2
1 CUP	SOUR MILK (2 TBSP/25 ML VINEGAR, 1 CUP/250 ML MILK)	250 ML
1 TSP	SODA	5 ML
1 TSP	SALT	5 ML
2¼ CUPS	FLOUR	550 ML
1 TSP	VANILLA	5 ML
1½ CUPS	RHUBARB, CHOPPED FINE	375 ML

TOPPING

| ½ CUP | BROWN SUGAR | 125 ML |
| 1 TSP | CINNAMON | 5 ML |

CREAM BROWN SUGAR AND BUTTER, ADD EGGS AND BEAT WELL. ADD SOUR MILK, SODA, SALT AND FLOUR. MIX WELL AND ADD VANILLA AND RHUBARB. POUR INTO 13- X 9-INCH (3 L) GREASED AND FLOURED PAN. MIX BROWN SUGAR AND CINNAMON AND SPRINKLE ON BATTER. BAKE AT 350°F (180°C) FOR 45 MINUTES. ADD A SCOOP OF ICE CREAM AND LISTEN TO THE ACCOLADES! SERVES 12 TO 16.

AN INTERMISSION AT A COLLEGE DANCE IS WHEN EVERYONE COMES INSIDE TO REST.

FRUIT COCKTAIL CAKE

A GREAT LAST MINUTE DESSERT. ONE FAMILY ALWAYS
TAKES THIS SAILING - NOW IT'S CALLED "FRUIT
COCKPIT CAKE".

CAKE

2	EGGS	2
1½ CUPS	SUGAR	375 ML
2 TSP	BAKING SODA	10 ML
½ TSP	SALT	2 ML
1	CAN (14 OZ/398 ML) FRUIT COCKTAIL WITH JUICE OR CRUSHED PINEAPPLE	1
2 CUPS	FLOUR	500 ML

SAUCE

¾ CUP	SUGAR	175 ML
½ CUP	MILK	125 ML
½ CUP	BUTTER	125 ML
1 TSP	VANILLA (OR 2 TBSP/25 ML RUM IS A SUPERB SUBSTITUTE!)	5 ML

TO MAKE CAKE: BEAT EGGS. ADD ALL INGREDIENTS, EXCEPT
FLOUR, AND MIX. ADD FLOUR AND MIX AGAIN. GREASE A
13- X 9-INCH (3 L) PAN OR A BUNDT PAN AND POUR IN MIXTURE.
BAKE AT 350°F (180°C) FOR 45 MINUTES.

TO MAKE SAUCE: HEAT SUGAR, MILK AND BUTTER IN
SAUCEPAN AND BRING TO A BOIL. REMOVE FROM HEAT AND
ADD VANILLA. POUR OVER HOT CAKE. (MAKES A LOT, BUT USE
ALL OF IT! THE CAKE WILL ABSORB IT.)

SERVE WARM WITH WHIPPED CREAM OR FROZEN VANILLA
YOGURT. KEEPS FOR SEVERAL DAYS REFRIGERATED (IF NO
ONE KNOWS IT'S THERE). SERVES 12 TO 16.

DATE TORTE

VERY RICH AND VERY BAD FOR YOU! WE LOVE IT!

I LB	PACKAGE PITTED DATES	500 G
I CUP	WALNUTS	250 ML
I TSP	BAKING POWDER	5 ML
I HEAPING TBSP	FLOUR	15 ML
3	EGGS	3
I TSP	VANILLA	5 ML
I CUP	SUGAR	250 ML

GRIND TOGETHER DATES AND WALNUTS. USE FOOD PROCESSOR OR MEAT-GRINDER. BEAT EGG YOLKS AND WHITES SEPARATELY. ADD BEATEN YOLKS TO DATE-WALNUT MIXTURE AND BLEND. MIX IN BAKING POWDER, FLOUR, SUGAR AND VANILLA. FOLD IN THE BEATEN EGG WHITES. BAKE IN GREASED 8-INCH (2 L) SQUARE PAN FOR APPROXIMATELY 40 MINUTES AT 365°F (185°C). SERVE WARM IN SQUARES TOPPED WITH WHIPPED CREAM OR ICE CREAM. SERVES 8 TO 12.

CONVERSATION OVERHEARD AT A BOY'S CAMP: "WE'RE GOING HOME TOMORROW. GUESS I BETTER RUMPLE MY PAJAMAS AND SQUEEZE OUT HALF MY TOOTHPASTE."

PRUNE CAKE

2 CUPS	SELF-RISING FLOUR	500 ML
2 CUPS	SUGAR	500 ML
1 TSP	CINNAMON	5 ML
1 TSP	NUTMEG	5 ML
1 TSP	ALLSPICE	5 ML
1 CUP	SALAD OIL	250 ML
2	EGGS	2
1	CAN (8 OZ/227 ML) PRUNES (PURÉED BABY FOOD)	1
1 CUP	CHOPPED PECANS	250 ML

COMBINE ALL INGREDIENTS, BEATING AT MEDIUM SPEED UNTIL BLENDED. DO NOT OVERMIX. POUR INTO 10-INCH (3 L) BUNDT PAN, WELL-GREASED AND LIGHTLY FLOURED. BAKE AT 350°F (180°C) FOR APPROXIMATELY 1 HOUR. SERVES 12 TO 16.

RUM CAKE

1	CHIFFON CAKE, READY-MADE	1
1 CUP	MAPLE SYRUP	250 ML
1/4 CUP	RUM	50 ML
	SHREDDED COCONUT OR CHOPPED NUTS	
	WHIPPED CREAM	

COMBINE MAPLE SYRUP AND RUM. ROLL CAKE IN SYRUP MIXTURE, THEN IN SHREDDED COCONUT OR CHOPPED NUTS. TOP EACH SERVING WITH WHIPPED CREAM FLAVORED WITH RUM. SERVES 8 TO 12.

KARROT'S CAKE

SO GOOD FOR YOUR EYESIGHT, NEVER MIND YOUR TASTE BUDS!

CAKE

3/4 CUP	CORN OIL	175 ML
1 CUP	SUGAR	250 ML
3	EGGS	3
1 1/2 CUPS	FLOUR	375 ML
1/2 TSP	SALT	2 ML
1 1/3 TSP	BAKING SODA	6.5 ML
1 1/2 TSP	CINNAMON	7 ML
2 CUPS	FINELY GRATED CARROTS (4-5)	500 ML

ICING

1	PACKAGE (8 OZ/250 G) CREAM CHEESE, ROOM TEMPERATURE	1
1/4 CUP	BUTTER, ROOM TEMPERATURE	50 ML
2 1/2 CUPS	ICING SUGAR	625 ML
2 TSP	VANILLA	10 ML

TO MAKE CAKE: BEAT TOGETHER OIL AND SUGAR. ADD EGGS, ONE AT A TIME, BEATING WELL AFTER EACH ADDITION. COMBINE DRY INGREDIENTS AND ADD TO EGG MIXTURE. BEAT ALL TOGETHER UNTIL WELL BLENDED. FOLD IN RAW CARROTS. BAKE 1 HOUR AT 300°F (150°C) IN A GREASED 13- X 9-INCH (3 L) PAN. (THIS CAN ALSO BE MADE IN A BUNDT PAN.)

TO MAKE ICING: SOFTEN CHEESE AND BUTTER; BEAT WELL. ADD SUGAR AND VANILLA AND BEAT AGAIN. SPREAD ON COOLED CAKE. SERVES 12 TO 16.

LIGHT CHRISTMAS CAKE

PREPARATION: A THREE-SIZED CHRISTMAS CAKE TIN SET MUST BE LINED, BOTTOMS AND SIDES, WITH BUTTERED BROWN PAPER. CUT THE PAPER TO SIZE. THE NIGHT BEFORE YOU MAKE THIS CAKE, POUR BOILING WATER OVER THE RAISINS, DRAIN AND DRY ON PAPER TOWELING. LEAVE THESE OVERNIGHT. THE FRUIT IN THE RECIPE IS FLOURED WITH 1/2 THE AMOUNT OF FLOUR CALLED FOR IN THE RECIPE.

1 CUP	BUTTER	250 ML
1 1/2 CUPS	WHITE SUGAR	375 ML
6	EGGS	6
1/2 CUP	ORANGE JUICE	125 ML
3 CUPS	REGULAR FLOUR, SIFTED	750 ML
1 TSP	BAKING POWDER	5 ML
1 TSP	SALT	5 ML
	JUICE AND ZEST OF 1 LEMON	
1/2 LB	RED GLACÉ CHERRIES	250 G
1/2 LB	GREEN GLACÉ CHERRIES	250 G
1/2 LB	CITRON PEEL	250 G
2	SLICES EACH RED AND GREEN PINEAPPLE, CUT UP	2
2 LBS	BLANCHED SULTANA RAISINS	1 KG
1/2 LB	BLANCHED ALMONDS	250 G

USE 1/2 OF THE FLOUR TO COVER CHERRIES, CITRON PEEL, PINEAPPLE, AND WELL-DRIED RAISINS. CREAM SUGAR AND BUTTER, ADD BEATEN EGGS, ORANGE AND LEMON JUICE, AND ZEST. ADD REMAINING FLOUR. MIX WELL. ADD FLAVORED FRUIT AND CHOPPED ALMONDS. BAKE AT 275°F (140°C) FOR 2 HOURS. TEST FOR DONENESS. STORE IN A COOL PLACE. MAKES 3 CAKES; EACH SERVES 10.

CHRISTMAS CHERRY CAKE

A DELICIOUS AND NEVER FAIL MOIST WHITE CAKE AND
HALF THE WORK OF A REGULAR CHRISTMAS CAKE!
FREEZES WELL.

1 CUP	WHITE SUGAR	250 ML
1 CUP	BUTTER	250 ML
2	EGGS, BEATEN	2
1/2 CUP	ORANGE JUICE	125 ML
2 CUPS	FLOUR	500 ML
1 TSP	BAKING POWDER	5 ML
12 OZ	SULTANA RAISINS	375 G
8 OZ	HALVED RED GLACÉ CHERRIES (OR USE HALF RED AND HALF GREEN CHERRIES)	250 G

CREAM BUTTER AND SUGAR. ADD BEATEN EGGS AND
ORANGE JUICE. SIFT FLOUR AND BAKING POWDER. RESERVE
1/3 CUP (75 ML) OF FLOUR MIXTURE AND TOSS WITH RAISINS
AND CHERRIES (THIS WILL KEEP THEM FROM SINKING
TO THE BOTTOM OF THE CAKE). ADD FLOUR MIXTURE TO
BATTER AND BLEND. ADD FLOURED RAISINS AND CHERRIES
TO DOUGH. BAKE IN A LARGE, GREASED, WAX PAPER-LINED
LOAF TIN AT 300°F (150°C) FOR 2 1/2 HOURS. DON'T SERVE
UNTIL SEVERAL DAYS OLD. WRAP IN PLASTIC OR FOIL WRAP
AND STORE IN A SEALED TIN. SERVES 16 TO 20.

IT IS MORE BLESSED TO GIVE "THEN" RECEIVE.

A "GRAND" CAKE

THIS RECIPE CAN BE MADE THE DAY AHEAD
IF COVERED AND REFRIGERATED.

CAKE

1 3/4 CUPS	FLOUR	425 ML
1 TSP	BAKING SODA	5 ML
1/2 TSP	BAKING POWDER	2 ML
1 TSP	SALT	5 ML
1/2 CUP	COCOA POWDER	125 ML
1/2 CUP	BUTTER, ROOM TEMPERATURE	125 ML
1 2/3 CUPS	GRANULATED SUGAR	400 ML
3	EGGS	3
1 TSP	VANILLA	5 ML
1 1/3 CUPS	WATER	325 ML
1/4 CUP	GRAND MARNIER	50 ML

FILLING

3/4 CUP	FROZEN ORANGE JUICE CONCENTRATE	175 ML
3/4 CUP	SUGAR	175 ML
1 TBSP	UNFLAVORED GELATIN	15 ML
	COARSELY GRATED PEEL OF 2 ORANGES	
1/4 CUP	GRAND MARNIER	50 ML
2 CUPS	WHIPPING CREAM	500 ML
3/4 CUP	ICING SUGAR	175 ML

TO MAKE CAKE: PREHEAT OVEN TO 350°F (180°C). GREASE
TWO 8-INCH (20 CM) ROUND CAKE PANS. LINE WITH WAXED
PAPER AND GREASE AGAIN. MEASURE FLOUR, BAKING SODA,
BAKING POWDER, SALT AND COCOA INTO A BOWL AND SIFT

CONTINUED ON NEXT PAGE...

TOGETHER. CREAM BUTTER USING ELECTRIC BEATER. GRADUALLY ADD SUGAR, BEATING UNTIL LIGHT AND FLUFFY. BEAT IN EGGS, ONE AT A TIME. ADD VANILLA. AT LOW SPEED, BEAT IN $\frac{1}{3}$ OF FLOUR MIXTURE, THEN $\frac{1}{2}$ OF THE WATER, BEATING ONLY UNTIL MIXED AFTER EACH ADDITION. BEAT IN ANOTHER $\frac{1}{3}$ FLOUR, REMAINING WATER AND REST OF FLOUR. POUR INTO PANS AND BAKE FOR 30-35 MINUTES, OR UNTIL CENTER OF CAKE SPRINGS BACK WHEN LIGHTLY TOUCHED. LET CAKES COOL 5 MINUTES, THEN TURN OUT. REMOVE WAXED PAPER AND COOL THOROUGHLY ON RACKS.

ONE TO 2 HOURS BEFORE ASSEMBLING, SLICE EACH CAKE IN HALF HORIZONTALLY TO MAKE 4 LAYERS. PLACE LAYERS CUT SIDE UP AND SPRINKLE EACH WITH 1 TBSP (15 ML) GRAND MARNIER.

TO MAKE FILLING: COMBINE JUICE, SUGAR AND GELATIN IN A SAUCEPAN; COOK OVER MEDIUM HEAT, STIRRING CONSTANTLY UNTIL SUGAR AND GELATIN ARE DISSOLVED, ABOUT 5 MINUTES. REMOVE FROM HEAT AND STIR IN ORANGE PEEL AND GRAND MARNIER. PRESS A SHEET OF WAXED PAPER ON SURFACE AND REFRIGERATE UNTIL COOL, ABOUT 20 MINUTES. WHIP CREAM UNTIL SOFT PEAKS FORM. GRADUALLY BEAT IN ICING SUGAR, THEN FOLD IN GRAND MARNIER MIXTURE.

TO ASSEMBLE: PLACE 1 LAYER OF CAKE, CUT SIDE UP, ON SERVING PLATE. SPOON ON $\frac{1}{4}$ OF FILLING AND SPREAD. TOP WITH ANOTHER LAYER AND CONTINUE UNTIL ALL ARE USED, ENDING WITH FILLING. REFRIGERATE IMMEDIATELY, LET SET AT LEAST 4 HOURS TO BLEND FLAVORS. SERVES 12.

TIA MARIA CAKE

1	LARGE ANGEL FOOD CAKE	1
1/2 CUP	TIA MARIA LIQUEUR	125 ML
2 TBSP	WHIPPING CREAM	25 ML
2 CUPS	WHIPPING CREAM	500 ML
2 TBSP	TIA MARIA LIQUEUR	25 ML
2 TBSP	ICING SUGAR	25 ML
6	ALMOND ROCA CHOCOLATE BARS	6

CUT CAKE INTO TWO LAYERS. PLACE EACH ON A PLATE. COMBINE 1/2 CUP (125 ML) TIA MARIA AND 2 TBSP (25 ML) CREAM. PRICK CAKE ALL OVER WITH SKEWER - BOTH LAYERS. DRIZZLE TIA MIXTURE OVER ALL PARTS OF EACH LAYER; BOTTOM AND TOP. COVER WITH SARAN WRAP AND CHILL SEVERAL HOURS. TWO HOURS BEFORE SERVING, WHIP 2 CUPS (500 ML) OF CREAM AND FOLD IN 2 TBSP (25 ML) TIA MARIA AND THE ICING SUGAR. ICE CAKE, INCLUDING LAYERS. CRUSH ALMOND ROCA AND TOSS OVER TOP AND SIDES OF CAKE. CHILL UNTIL SERVING TIME. SERVES 10 TO 12.

ONCE WOMEN WORE BATHING SUITS DOWN TO THEIR ANKLES, THEN DOWN TO THEIR KNEES, THEN DOWN TO THEIR HIPS. THIS YEAR NO ONE IS EVEN THAT SURE THEY'LL WEAR THEM DOWN TO THE BEACH!

PASTRY SHELLS

FOR ENTRÉES OR APPETIZERS

I CUP	COLD WATER	250 ML
1/2 CUP	BUTTER	125 ML
4	EGGS (ROOM TEMPERATURE)	4
1/2 TSP	SALT	2 ML
I CUP	SIFTED FLOUR	250 ML

COMBINE WATER, BUTTER AND SALT IN A PAN. BRING TO A BOIL, STIRRING CONSTANTLY, AND ADD FLOUR. REMOVE FROM HEAT. STIR INTO A SMOOTH BALL. RETURN TO HEAT, AT MEDIUM TEMPERATURE, AND BEAT FOR I MINUTE. COOL APPROXIMATELY 5 MINUTES. BEAT IN EGGS ONE AT A TIME, STIRRING THOROUGHLY AFTER EACH ADDITION. COVER AND LET STAND IN COOL PLACE UNTIL COOL. PLACE 1/2 TSP (2 ML) DOUGH FOR EACH SHELL AT INTERVALS ON GREASED COOKIE SHEET. BAKE AT 425°F (220°C) FOR ABOUT 30 MINUTES. WHEN BAKED, PRICK THE TOP OF EACH SHELL TO ALLOW AIR TO ESCAPE. LEAVE IN OVEN, HEAT TURNED OFF, FOR 10 MINUTES. COOL. MAY BE FROZEN.

TO SERVE, SPLIT SHELLS AND FILL. MAKES 40 TO 50 SHELLS.

GRAHAM CRACKER CRUMB CRUST

1¼ CUPS	GRAHAM CRUMBS	300 ML
¼ CUP	BROWN SUGAR	50 ML
⅓ CUP	MELTED BUTTER OR MARGARINE	75 ML
½ TSP	CINNAMON (OPTIONAL)	2 ML

MIX TOGETHER AND PRESS INTO 8- OR 9-INCH (20 OR 23 CM)
PIE PLATE. BAKE AT 300°F (150°C) FOR 5 TO 8 MINUTES.
COOL. MAKES ONE 8- OR 9-INCH (20 OR 23 CM) PIE SHELL.

CHOCOLATE WAFER CRUMB CRUST

1¼ CUPS	CRUSHED CHRISTIE CHOCOLATE WAFERS (USE BLENDER OR ROLL WITH ROLLING PIN ON WAXED PAPER)	300 ML
⅓ CUP	MELTED BUTTER OR MARGARINE	75 ML

MIX TOGETHER AND PRESS INTO 8- OR 9-INCH (20 OR 23 CM)
PIE PLATE. BAKE AT 300°F (150°C) FOR 5 TO 8 MINUTES.
COOL. MAKES ONE 8- OR 9-INCH (20 OR 23 CM) PIE SHELL.

*STATISTICS PROVE THAT MORE AND MORE PEOPLE
ARE MARRYING AT AN EARLY URGE.*

PEPPERMINT ICE CREAM PIE

1	PACKAGE (6 OZ/170 G) SEMI-SWEET CHOCOLATE CHIPS	1
2 TBSP	BUTTER, SOFTENED	25 ML
2 TBSP	POWDERED SUGAR	25 ML
1 QUART	PEPPERMINT ICE CREAM, SOFTENED	1 L
	CHOCOLATE SHAVINGS FOR TOPPING	

LINE A 9-INCH (23 CM) PIE PLATE BY PRESSING A 12-INCH (30 CM) SQUARE OF HEAVY ALUMINUM FOIL ON BOTTOM, SIDES AND OVER RIM. SPRINKLE CHIPS EVENLY ON FOIL LINER. PUT IN 250°F (120°C) OVEN FOR 5 MINUTES, ABSOLUTELY NO LONGER. BLEND BUTTER INTO MELTED CHOCOLATE. ADD POWDERED SUGAR; BLEND AGAIN UNTIL MIXTURE THICKENS SLIGHTLY. SPREAD MIXTURE THINLY OVER BOTTOM AND UP SIDES OF FOIL LINER. REFRIGERATE 30 MINUTES FOR CHOCOLATE SHELL TO HARDEN. PEEL FOIL FROM SHELL AND RETURN SHELL TO PIE PLATE. FILL WITH ICE CREAM; DECORATE WITH SHAVED CHOCOLATE. STORE IN FREEZER UNTIL READY TO SERVE. SERVES 6 TO 8.

COFFEE ICE CREAM PIE

2 TO 3 TBSP	BUTTER	25 TO 45 ML
3/4 CUP	SHREDDED COCONUT	175 ML
1/2 QUART	COFFEE ICE CREAM, SOFTENED	500 ML

SPREAD BUTTER EVENLY ON BOTTOM AND SIDE OF 9-INCH (23 CM) PIE PLATE. SPRINKLE SHREDDED COCONUT OVER TOP AND PRESS EVENLY INTO BUTTER. BAKE AT 300°F (150°C) FOR 15 TO 20 MINUTES UNTIL BROWN. COOL. PUT ICE CREAM IN SHELL AND PUT IN FRIDGE TO SET. TOP WITH BUTTERSCOTCH SAUCE. SERVES 6 TO 8.

SAUCE

1 CUP	LIGHT CREAM	250 ML
2 TBSP	BUTTER	25 ML
3/4 CUP	BROWN SUGAR	175 ML
1 TBSP	CORN SYRUP	15 ML

MIX IN HEAVY POT OVER LOW HEAT STIRRING FREQUENTLY UNTIL MIXTURE IS SMOOTH AND THICK. COOL. LIGHTLY BURN SLIVERED ALMONDS IN SMALL AMOUNT OF BUTTER, SPRINKLE OVER TOP. THIS MAY BE FROZEN FOR LATER USE. YOU MAY WISH TO TOP WITH WHIPPING CREAM.

SMALL PORTIONS ARE SUFFICIENT!

LINCOLN CENTER DELICATESSEN CHOCOLATE ICEBOX PIE

1	BAKED 8-INCH (20 CM) PIE SHELL	1
3/4 CUP	ICING SUGAR	175 ML
1/4 CUP	BUTTER	50 ML
1/4 CUP	SEMI-SWEET CHOCOLATE (2 SQUARES)	50 ML
1/2 TSP	VANILLA	2 ML
3	EGGS	3
1 CUP	WHIPPING CREAM	250 ML
	CHOCOLATE SHAVINGS (SEMI-SWEET HERSHEY BAR IS BEST)	

CREAM SUGAR AND BUTTER. MELT CHOCOLATE IN DOUBLE BOILER AND BEAT INTO MIXTURE USING ELECTRIC BEATER. ADD VANILLA. ADD EGGS, ONE AT A TIME, BEATING EACH EGG THOROUGHLY AT HIGH SPEED (2 TO 3 MINUTES EACH EGG). POUR MIXTURES INTO BAKED COOLED PIE SHELL. REFRIGERATE UNTIL SERVING TIME.

TOP WITH WHIPPED CREAM AND GARNISH WITH CHOCOLATE CURLS. (A SEMI-SWEET HERSHEY BAR AT ROOM TEMPERATURE WORKS BEST.) SERVES 6.

MOHAMMED'S WIVES: PROPHET SHARES.

CHOCOLATE MUD PIE

CRUST

1	PACKAGE (8½ OZ/241 G) CHOCOLATE WAFERS	1
½ CUP	BUTTER	125 ML

FILLING

3 CUPS	COFFEE ICE CREAM, SOFTENED	750 ML

NEXT LAYER

⅓ CUP	COCOA	75 ML
⅔ CUP	SUGAR	150 ML
⅓ CUP	WHIPPING CREAM	75 ML
3 TBSP	BUTTER	45 ML
1 TSP	VANILLA	5 ML

GARNISH

2	SQUARES SEMI-SWEET CHOCOLATE, AT ROOM TEMPERATURE	2

CRUST: CRUSH CHOCOLATE WAFERS INTO FINE CRUMBS. IN A SMALL SAUCEPAN OVER LOW HEAT, MELT BUTTER. IN A 9-INCH (23 CM) PIE PLATE, COMBINE CRUMBS AND BUTTER AND PRESS MIXTURE TO BOTTOM AND SIDES OF PAN. BAKE AT 375°F (190°C) FOR 10 MINUTES. COOL CRUST COMPLETELY ON WIRE RACK. CAREFULLY SPREAD ICE CREAM ONTO CRUST. FREEZE 1½ HOURS.

NEXT LAYER: IN LARGE SAUCEPAN OVER MEDIUM HEAT, COOK COCOA, SUGAR, WHIPPING CREAM AND BUTTER UNTIL MIXTURE IS SMOOTH AND BOILS. REMOVE FROM HEAT AND STIR IN VANILLA. COOL MIXTURE SLIGHTLY

CONTINUED ON NEXT PAGE...

THEN POUR OVER ICE CREAM. RETURN PIE TO FREEZER FOR AT LEAST 1 HOUR.

TOPPING: IN SMALL BOWL, BEAT WHIPPING CREAM AT MEDIUM SPEED WITH SUGAR AND VANILLA UNTIL SOFT PEAKS FORM. MOUND ONTO PIE AND GARNISH WITH CHOCOLATE CURLS. SERVES 10.

TIP: USE A VEGETABLE PEELER TO MAKE CHOCOLATE CURLS.

CHOCOLATE MINT PIE

1	9-INCH (23 CM) CRUMB PIE SHELL	1
2	SQUARES SEMI-SWEET CHOCOLATE	2
1 CUP	ICING SUGAR	250 ML
½ CUP	BUTTER	125 ML
2	EGGS	2
1 TSP	VANILLA	5 ML
1 TSP	PEPPERMINT	5 ML
	WHIPPED CREAM	
	CHOCOLATE CURLS	

CREAM BUTTER AND SUGAR. MELT CHOCOLATE SLOWLY OVER LOW HEAT. ADD CHOCOLATE, BEATEN EGGS TO BUTTER MIXTURE AND BEAT AT HIGH SPEED UNTIL FLUFFY. ADD VANILLA AND PEPPERMINT. POUR INTO COOLED SHELL. REFRIGERATE FOR 24 HOURS BEFORE SERVING. SERVE WITH WHIPPED CREAM AND GARNISH WITH CHOCOLATE CURLS. SERVES 6 TO 8.

GRASSHOPPER PIE

1¼ CUPS	CHOCOLATE WAFER CRUMBS	300 ML
1/4 CUP	SUGAR	50 ML
1/3 CUP	BUTTER	75 ML

MIX ALL INGREDIENTS AND PRESS INTO BOTTOM AND SIDES OF A 9-INCH (23 CM) PIE PLATE. BAKE IN OVEN AT 400°F (200°C) FOR 5 MINUTES.

1 TBSP	UNFLAVORED GELATIN	15 ML
1/2 CUP	SUGAR	125 ML
PINCH	SALT	PINCH
1/2 CUP	COLD WATER	125 ML
3	EGGS, SEPARATED	3
1/4 CUP	CRÈME DE MENTHE	50 ML
1/4 CUP	CRÈME DE CACAO	50 ML
1 CUP	WHIPPING CREAM	250 ML

IN DOUBLE BOILER MIX GELATIN, 1/4 CUP (50 ML) SUGAR AND SALT. ADD WATER AND EGG YOLKS. STIR WELL UNTIL GELATIN IS DISSOLVED AND MIXTURE THICKENS SLIGHTLY. REMOVE FROM HEAT. STIR IN LIQUEURS. CHILL, STIRRING OCCASIONALLY UNTIL MIXTURE THICKENS SLIGHTLY. BEAT EGG WHITES STIFF. GRADUALLY ADD REMAINING SUGAR, BEAT UNTIL VERY STIFF. FOLD IN GELATIN MIXTURE. FOLD IN WHIPPED CREAM. TURN INTO SHELL. CHILL FOR 2 HOURS IN FREEZER OR OVER NIGHT IN REFRIGERATOR. SERVES 6 TO 8.

RUM CREAM PIE

USE TWO 8-INCH (20 CM) PIE SHELLS (PASTRY, GRAHAM WAFER OR CHOCOLATE WAFER)

6	EGG YOLKS	6
1 CUP	SUGAR	250 ML
1 TBSP	GELATIN	15 ML
1/2 CUP	COLD WATER	125 ML
2 CUPS	CREAM, WHIPPED	500 ML
1/2 CUP	RUM	125 ML

BEAT THE EGG YOLKS WITH THE SUGAR UNTIL LIGHT AND FLUFFY. IN A SAUCEPAN SOAK GELATIN IN WATER AND BRING TO A BOIL. ADD TO THE EGG MIXTURE AND COOL. ADD RUM TO WHIPPED CREAM AND FOLD INTO EGG MIXTURE. POUR INTO COOLED PIE SHELLS. SPRINKLE WITH SHREDDED CHOCOLATE. SERVE AFTER CHILLING FOR SEVERAL HOURS. SERVES 12 TO 16.

NEWLYWED COOKING TURKEY SUPPER HEARS A KNOCK ON THE OVEN DOOR. SHE OPENS THE DOOR, AND THE TURKEY SAYS: "LOOK, LADY, EITHER TURN ON THE OVEN OR GIVE ME BACK MY FEATHERS. IT'S COLD IN HERE!"

PECAN PIE

3	EGGS	3
I CUP	WHITE SYRUP (KARO)	250 ML
1/8 TSP	SALT	0.5 ML
I CUP	SUGAR	250 ML
I TSP	VANILLA	5 ML
I CUP	WHOLE PECANS	250 ML
I	9-INCH (23 CM) PIE SHELL (UNCOOKED)	I

BEAT EGGS. ADD SYRUP, SALT, SUGAR AND VANILLA. BEAT UNTIL WELL MIXED. ADD PECANS. POUR INTO PIE SHELL. BAKE AT 450°F (230°C) FOR 10 MINUTES. REDUCE TO 350°F (180°C) FOR A FURTHER 30 MINUTES. SERVE WITH WHIPPED CREAM OR ICE CREAM, IF DESIRED. IF YOU HAVE A FROZEN PIE SHELL ON HAND, THIS PIE CAN BE WHIPPED UP IN MINUTES. TERRIFIC FOR THOSE UNEXPECTED GUESTS – AND YOU ALWAYS THOUGHT IT WAS SO DIFFICULT! SERVES 6 TO 8.

A HIGHBROW IS A PERSON WHO CAN LISTEN TO THE "WILLIAM TELL OVERTURE" WITHOUT THINKING OF THE LONE RANGER!

SOCIAL APPLE BETTY

EVERYONE LOVES THIS OLD ENGLISH RECIPE. BE SURE TO SERVE IT WARM WITH WHIPPING CREAM OR ICE CREAM.

6	APPLES, PEELED, SLICED	6
	CINNAMON TO TASTE	

CRUST

1/2 CUP	BUTTER, AT ROOM TEMPERATURE	125 ML
I CUP	BROWN SUGAR	250 ML
3/4 CUP	FLOUR	175 ML

FILL A SMALL CASSEROLE 2/3 FULL WITH SLICED APPLES, ADDING THE CINNAMON TO TASTE. IF THE APPLES ARE TART, YOU MAY WANT TO ADD SOME SUGAR.

TO MAKE CRUST: CREAM BUTTER AND BROWN SUGAR. ADD FLOUR AND MIX TO A CRUMBLY MIXTURE. SPRINKLE MIXTURE OVER APPLES AND PAT FIRMLY INTO A CRUST. BAKE AT 350°F (180°C) FOR 40 MINUTES. SERVES 6.

LIME PARFAIT PIE

2	PACKAGES (EACH 3 OZ/85 G) LIME JELL-O	2
2 CUPS	BOILING WATER	500 ML
2 TBSP	GRATED LIME ZEST	25 ML
1/3 CUP	LIME JUICE	75 ML
1 QUART	VANILLA ICE CREAM	1 L
1	CHOCOLATE WAFER CRUMB CRUST (PAGE 320)	1

DISSOLVE JELL-O IN BOILING WATER. STIR IN LIME ZEST AND JUICE. ADD ICE CREAM TO JELL-O IN A BLENDER OR LARGE BOWL WITH A MIXER AT HIGH SPEED, WHIPPING UNTIL MELTED. CHILL UNTIL MIXTURE BEGINS TO SET, THEN PILE INTO CRUST. CHILL UNTIL FIRM. TOP WITH WHIPPED CREAM AND COCONUT TO SERVE. SERVES 8.

RECIPE FOR A REAL SPONGE CAKE - YOU BORROW ALL THE INGREDIENTS!

BUTTER TARTS

THESE ARE EXCEPTIONAL! FOR THESE USE FROZEN SHELLS OR YOUR OWN PASTRY RECIPE.

1 CUP	WHITE SUGAR	250 ML
1 CUP	SEEDLESS RAISINS	250 ML
2	EGGS	2
1 TSP	VANILLA	5 ML
1/3 CUP	BUTTER	75 ML
4 TBSP	CREAM OR HALF-AND-HALF	60 ML
1/2 CUP	BROKEN WALNUTS	125 ML

BEAT EGGS. COMBINE WITH REMAINING INGREDIENTS EXCEPT NUTS, AND BOIL AT MEDIUM HEAT FOR 3 MINUTES. ADD NUTS. FILL UNBAKED TART SHELLS AND BAKE FOR 15 MINUTES AT 375°F (190°C). MAKES FILLING FOR 24 TARTS.

SHORTBREAD TARTS WITH CHEESE 'N' FRUIT OR LEMON FILLING

SO PRETTY TO LOOK AT – MORE FUN TO EAT!

SHORTBREAD TARTS

I CUP	BUTTER	250 ML
½ CUP	ICING SUGAR	125 ML
I½ CUPS	FLOUR	375 ML
I TBSP	CORNSTARCH	15 ML

MIX INGREDIENTS IN MIXER. DON'T ROLL, BUT PAT INTO I½-INCH (4 CM) TART TINS WITH YOUR FINGERS TO FORM SHELLS. PRICK THE BOTTOMS WITH A FORK AND BAKE 20 MINUTES AT 300°F TO 325°F (150°C TO 160°C). AFTER 10 MINUTES, PRICK BOTTOMS AGAIN AS SHELLS PUFF UP. THIS RECIPE DOUBLES WELL AND THEY FREEZE BEAUTIFULLY. MAKES ABOUT 3 DOZEN.

CHEESE 'N' FRUIT FILLING

8 OZ	CREAM CHEESE, SOFTENED	250 G
I	CAN (10 OZ/284 ML) SWEETENED CONDENSED MILK	I
⅓ CUP	LEMON JUICE	75 ML
I TSP	VANILLA	5 ML

IN A LARGE BOWL BEAT CHEESE UNTIL FLUFFY. GRADUALLY BEAT IN MILK. STIR IN LEMON JUICE AND VANILLA. CHILL SEVERAL HOURS. KEEPS WELL IN REFRIGERATOR. FILL TARTS AND DECORATE WITH SMALL PIECES OF KIWI AND STRAWBERRIES.

CONTINUED ON NEXT PAGE...

LEMON FILLING

½ CUP	FRESH LEMON JUICE	125 ML
I TBSP	GRATED LEMON ZEST	15 ML
I CUP	SUGAR	250 ML
3	EGGS, WELL BEATEN	3
½ CUP	BUTTER, ROOM TEMPERATURE	125 ML

PUT JUICE AND ZEST IN DOUBLE-BOILER. WHISK IN SUGAR, EGGS AND BUTTER AND BLEND WELL. PLACE OVER GENTLY BOILING WATER AND WHISK CONSTANTLY UNTIL MIXTURE BECOMES CLEAR AND THICKENS. COOL. KEEPS WELL IN THE REFRIGERATOR.

RUM MINCEMEAT FILLING

I	BOTTLE PREPARED MINCEMEAT	I
¼ CUP	RUM, OR TO TASTE	50 ML

COMBINE MINCEMEAT AND RUM IN SAUCEPAN AND HEAT UNTIL WARM.

ANYBODY WHO CAN SWALLOW AN ASPIRIN AT A DRINKING FOUNTAIN DESERVES TO GET WELL.

STRAWBERRY LEMON ANGEL TARTS

THIS IS A DELIGHTFULLY COOL DESSERT AND
CAN BE MADE SEVERAL DAYS AHEAD.

4	EGG WHITES	4
1/4 TSP	CREAM OF TARTAR	1 ML
1 CUP	SUGAR	250 ML

BEAT EGG WHITES AND CREAM OF TARTAR UNTIL STIFF.
ADD SUGAR VERY GRADUALLY, BEATING THOROUGHLY AFTER
EACH ADDITION, APPROXIMATELY 20 MINUTES IN ALL.
GREASE COOKIE SHEETS WITH SHORTENING OR PAM AND
SPOON MERINGUE TO FORM 3-INCH (7.5 CM) SHELLS,
BUILDING UP SIDES WITH BACK OF SPOON. BAKE 20 MINUTES
AT 250°F (120°C), THEN AT 300°F (150°C) FOR 40 MINUTES.
TURN OFF HEAT, OPEN OVEN DOOR AND LET SHELLS
STAND FOR AT LEAST 40 MINUTES. IF MAKING AHEAD,
STORE IN CARDBOARD SHIRT-BOX IN COOL DRY PLACE.
SEE BELOW FOR FILLING.

FILLING

4	EGG YOLKS	4
1/3 CUP	SUGAR	75 ML
1/4 TSP	SALT	1 ML
3 TBSP	LEMON JUICE	45 ML
1 TBSP	LEMON PEEL	15 ML
1 CUP	WHIPPING CREAM OR 1 PACKAGE WHIPPED TOPPING	250 ML
	FRESH STRAWBERRIES	

CONTINUED ON NEXT PAGE...

COMBINE ALL INGREDIENTS EXCEPT WHIPPED CREAM AND STRAWBERRIES IN TOP OF DOUBLE BOILER. BRING TO A BOIL AND SIMMER 2 MINUTES. COOL COMPLETELY. ADD WHIPPED CREAM. THIS MAY BE STORED FOR SEVERAL DAYS.

TO SERVE, SPOON FILLING IN EACH SHELL AND CHILL UP TO 8 HOURS. GARNISH WITH FRESH STRAWBERRIES AND EXTRA WHIPPED CREAM, IF DESIRED. SERVES 8.

HINT: WHEN BEATING EGG WHITES, ALWAYS WHIP THEM IN A GLASS BOWL OR IN A POT THAT HAS BEEN CLEANED IN SUDSY WATER TO REMOVE ALL TRACES OF GREASE. NEVER BEAT EGG WHITES IN PLASTIC BOWLS.

A MAN USUALLY FEELS BETTER AFTER A FEW WINKS, ESPECIALLY IF SHE WINKS BACK.

APPLE ROLL

THE MEN IN YOUR LIFE WILL LOVE THIS.

| I CUP | BROWN SUGAR | 250 ML |
| I CUP | HOT WATER | 250 ML |

COMBINE AND HEAT UNTIL A SYRUP.

I CUP	FLOUR	250 ML
2 TSP	BAKING POWDER	25 ML
1/2 TSP	SALT	2 ML
2 TBSP	SHORTENING	25 ML
1/3 CUP	MILK	75 ML

MIX AND ROLL INTO RECTANGULAR SHAPE.

2	APPLES, PEELED AND SLICED	2
PINCH	BROWN SUGAR	PINCH
PINCH	CINNAMON	PINCH
	WHIPPING CREAM, WHIPPED	

SPRINKLE PASTRY WITH SUGAR AND CINNAMON. SPREAD APPLES ON TOP. ROLL UP AND SLICE I INCH (2.5 CM) THICK. PUT CUT SIDE DOWN IN BAKING DISH. DOT WITH BUTTER AND POUR SYRUP OVER. BAKE IN 350°F (180°C) OVEN FOR 30 MINUTES OR UNTIL BROWN ON TOP. SERVE WITH WHIPPED CREAM. SERVES 8.

"A GOSSIP" – THE KNIFE OF THE PARTY.

APRICOT SMOOCH

A BEAUTIFULLY LIGHT, REFRESHING DESSERT TO SERVE AT BRIDGE OR AFTER A HEAVY MEAL. IT CAN ALSO BE MADE AHEAD AND FROZEN.

1/2 CUP	CRUSHED VANILLA WAFERS	125 ML
1/2 CUP	SOFT BUTTER	125 ML
1/2 CUP	ICING SUGAR	125 ML
1	EGG	1
1 CUP	WHIPPING CREAM, WHIPPED	250 ML
1/2 TSP	ALMOND EXTRACT OR APRICOT LIQUEUR	2 ML
1/4 TSP	VANILLA	1 ML
3	SMALL CANS JUNIOR STRAINED APRICOTS (BABY FOOD)	3
	CHOPPED NUTS TO COVER TOP	

GREASE 8-INCH (2 L) SQUARE PAN. SPRINKLE WITH HALF THE CRUMBS. BEAT BUTTER AND SUGAR TOGETHER. ADD EGG AND FLAVORINGS. BEAT WELL. SPREAD OVER CRUMBS WITH THE BACK OF A WET SPOON. COVER WITH APRICOTS. COVER ALL WITH WHIPPED CREAM AND SPRINKLE WITH REMAINING CRUMBS AND CHOPPED NUTS. FREEZE. REMOVE FROM FREEZER ONE HOUR BEFORE SERVING. SERVES 6 TO 8.

BRANDIED PEACHES

1	CAN (28 OZ/796 ML) PEACH HALVES	1
2 TBSP	SYRUP FROM PEACHES	25 ML
4 TBSP	BUTTER	60 ML
1/2 CUP	BROWN SUGAR	125 ML
1/4 TSP	CINNAMON	1 ML
1/4 CUP	BRANDY	50 ML

DRAIN PEACHES, RESERVING 2 TBSP (25 ML) OF SYRUP. PLACE IN SHALLOW BAKING DISH. COMBINE ALL INGREDIENTS AND SPOON OVER PEACHES. BAKE AT 350°F (180°C) FOR 25 TO 30 MINUTES, BASTING OCCASIONALLY.

SERVE OVER VANILLA ICE CREAM, OR WITH HEAPING TEASPOON OF SOUR CREAM IN EACH CENTER. GARNISH WITH NUTMEG. SERVES 4 TO 6.

"TEA KETTLE": A MARVELOUS APPLIANCE. I'D LOVE TO SEE YOU SING WITH YOUR NOSE FULL OF BOILING WATER!

PEACH FLAMBÉ

8	PEACH HALVES, RESERVING JUICE	8
1 TBSP	BUTTER	15 ML
	JUICE OF 2 ORANGES	
3 OZ	BRANDY	90 ML
1½ OZ	GRAND MARNIER	45 ML
1½ OZ	SLIVERED ALMONDS	45 G
⅓ CUP	SUGAR	75 ML
1½ OZ	KIRSCH	45 ML
	JUICE OF 1 GRAPEFRUIT	
	JUICE OF 1 LEMON	
8	SCOOPS LEMON SHERBET	8

BROWN THE SUGAR, STIRRING CONSTANTLY, UNTIL CARAMELIZED. ADD BUTTER, PEACH JUICE AND LIQUEURS. REMOVE FROM HEAT AND FLAME. ADD JUICES OF LEMON, GRAPEFRUIT AND ORANGES, COOKING FOR ABOUT 3 MINUTES. ADD PEACH HALVES, WARM AND SERVE OVER SHERBET. SERVES 8.

A BOY IS GROWN WHEN HE'D RATHER STEAL A KISS THAN SECOND BASE.

BLUEBERRY DELIGHT

YOU MAY ALSO USE STRAWBERRY OR RASPBERRY PIE FILLING. THIS IS A LIGHT, REFRESHING DESSERT.

2 1/2 CUPS	GRAHAM WAFER CRUMBS	625 ML
1/2 CUP	BUTTER	125 ML
1 TBSP	SUGAR	15 ML
	BLUEBERRY PIE FILLING	
1 CUP	WHIPPING CREAM, WHIPPED	250 ML
1 1/2 CUPS	ICING SUGAR	375 ML

BLEND FIRST THREE INGREDIENTS TOGETHER AND PUT IN 13- X 9-INCH (3 L) PAN. BAKE AT 350°F (180°C) FOR 10 MINUTES. BLEND WHIPPED CREAM AND ICING SUGAR TOGETHER AND POUR MIXTURE ON COOLED WAFER CRUST. POUR CANNED BLUEBERRY FILLING ON TOP AND CHILL UNTIL READY TO SERVE. MAY BE SERVED WITH A SMALL DAB OF WHIPPED CREAM ON TOP. SERVES 12.

CHAOS IS SIX WOMEN PLUS ONE LUNCHEON CHECK.

FRESH STRAWBERRY DELIGHT

ONE OF THE EASIEST SUMMER DESSERTS YOU'LL EVER FIND. GREAT FOR CASUAL ENTERTAINING AND CHILDREN ARE WILD ABOUT IT.

STRAWBERRIES

SOUR CREAM

BROWN SUGAR OR POWDERED MAPLE SUGAR

WASH AND HULL STRAWBERRIES. SET IN LARGE SERVING BOWL. ADD SOUR CREAM TO A SMALL BOWL AND BROWN SUGAR TO ANOTHER BOWL. USING A FORK, DIP STRAWBERRIES INTO SOUR CREAM AND THEN INTO BROWN SUGAR. EVERYONE DOES THEIR OWN – ABSOLUTELY DELICIOUS!

THE STORK IS TOO OFTEN HELD RESPONSIBLE FOR CIRCUMSTANCES THAT MIGHT BETTER BE ATTRIBUTED TO A LARK.

STRAWBERRY CRÊPES

CRÊPES

1	EGG	1
1¼ CUPS	MILK	300 ML
1 TBSP	MELTED BUTTER	15 ML
1¼ CUPS	SIFTED FLOUR	300 ML
½ TSP	SALT	2 ML

STRAWBERRY CRÊPE GLAZE

4 CUPS	STRAWBERRIES	1 L
3	FIRM, RIPE BANANAS	3
¾ CUP	WATER	175 ML
2 TBSP	CORNSTARCH	25 ML
½ CUP	SUGAR	125 ML
⅓ CUP	CURAÇAO	75 ML

CRÊPES: BEAT EGG, MILK, BUTTER, FLOUR AND SALT UNTIL SMOOTH. LIGHTLY GREASE CRÊPE PAN OR SMALL SKILLET WITH OIL OR PAM. HEAT SKILLET; REMOVE FROM HEAT AND POUR IN ¼ CUP (50 ML) OF BATTER, TILTING PAN TO COVER BOTTOM QUICKLY. RETURN TO HEAT, BROWNING ON ONE SIDE ONLY, AND COOL ON PAPER TOWEL. MAKE 7 MORE CRÊPES. STACK BETWEEN WAX PAPER. CRÊPES MAY BE FROZEN.

STRAWBERRY CRÊPE GLAZE: CRUSH 2 CUPS (500 ML) OF STRAWBERRIES IN SAUCEPAN, ADD WATER AND BRING TO A BOIL. SIMMER FOR 2 MINUTES. SIEVE. IN SAME SAUCEPAN, COMBINE SUGAR AND CORNSTARCH. ADD SIEVED BERRIES, STIRRING CONSTANTLY, UNTIL MIXTURE BUBBLES. REMOVE FROM HEAT AND ADD CURAÇAO.

CONTINUED ON NEXT PAGE...

RESERVE 1 CUP (250 ML) OF GLAZE. STIR 1 CUP (250 ML) SLICED BERRIES INTO REMAINING GLAZE AND SPREAD 3 TBSP (45 ML) ON UNBROWNED SIDE OF EACH CRÊPE, PLACING THEM IN CHAFING OR SERVING DISH. ADD LAST CUP OF HALVED STRAWBERRIES AND SLICED BANANAS, POURING REMAINING GLAZE OVER ALL. COVER AND KEEP WARM TILL SERVING TIME. SERVES 8.

ONLY ONE PERFECT WOMAN EVER EXISTED – THE WOMAN YOUR HUSBAND COULD HAVE MARRIED.

FRESH STRAWBERRY PUFF PANCAKE

1/4 CUP	BUTTER OR MARGARINE	50 ML
3	EGGS	3
1 1/2 CUPS	MILK	375 ML
1/2 CUP	SUGAR	125 ML
3/4 CUP	FLOUR	175 ML
1/4 TSP	SALT	1 ML
1	SMALL BASKET FRESH STRAWBERRIES	1

PLACE BUTTER IN 9-INCH (23 CM) OVENPROOF FRYING PAN, CAKE PAN OR PIE PLATE. PUT PAN IN 425°F (220°C) OVEN UNTIL BUTTER MELTS AND BUBBLES (ABOUT 10 MINUTES). MEANWHILE, BEAT TOGETHER THE EGGS, MILK, 6 TBSP (90 ML) SUGAR, FLOUR AND SALT UNTIL SMOOTH.

REMOVE PAN FROM OVEN AND IMMEDIATELY POUR MIXTURE INTO THE HOT PAN. RETURN TO OVEN AND BAKE AT 425°F (220°C) FOR 30 MINUTES OR UNTIL EGGS ARE PUFFED AND BROWNED.

SPRINKLE BERRIES WITH REMAINING SUGAR AND SPOON INTO CENTER OF THE PANCAKE, WHEN DONE. SERVE IMMEDIATELY, CUT INTO WEDGES. SERVES 6.

CHERRIES JUBILEE

I LB	DARK RED CHERRIES, OR I LARGE CAN DRAINED	500 G
I TBSP	GRATED LEMON ZEST	15 ML
¼ CUP	WHITE SUGAR	50 ML
⅛ TSP	CINNAMON	0.5 ML
¼ CUP	KIRSCH OR CURAÇAO	50 ML
I TBSP	CORNSTARCH	15 ML
3 TBSP	SUGAR	45 ML
½ CUP	BRANDY	125 ML
	VANILLA ICE CREAM	

MARINATE CHERRIES WITH FIRST FOUR INGREDIENTS FOR 24 HOURS.

IN CHAFING DISH BLEND CORNSTARCH WITH CHERRIES, STIRRING UNTIL IT THICKENS. SPRINKLE WITH SUGAR AND ADD BRANDY.

FLAME AND SERVE AT ONCE OVER ICE CREAM. FLAME AT THE TABLE TO ADD A SPECIAL TOUCH. SERVES 6 TO 8.

YOU'RE MIDDLE-AGED IF YOU CAN REMEMBER WHEN RADIOS PLUGGED IN, AND TOOTHBRUSHES DIDN'T.

CARDINAL'S LIME SPECIAL

THESE MERINGUES MAY BE MADE AHEAD AND STORED IN A COOL DRY PLACE.

5	EGGS	5
1/4 TSP	CREAM OF TARTAR	1 ML
1 CUP	SUGAR	250 ML
1/4 TSP	PISTACHIO FLAVORING	1 ML
4 TBSP	LIME JUICE	60 ML
2 TSP	GRATED LIME ZEST	10 ML
1/2 CUP	SUGAR	125 ML
1 CUP	WHIPPING CREAM	250 ML

SEPARATE 4 OF THE EGGS AND BEAT WHITES UNTIL STIFF. ADD CREAM OF TARTAR. ADD SUGAR A TABLESPOON AT A TIME CONTINUING TO BEAT. ADD PISTACHIO FLAVORING AND BEAT MIXTURE FOR 20 MINUTES IN ALL.

USE 2 WELL GREASED COOKIE SHEETS. WITH 8-INCH (20 CM) PIE PLATE DRAW CIRCLES ON COOKIE SHEETS. SPREAD MIXTURE ON CIRCLES, BUILDING UP SIDES WITH SPOON. BAKE AT 275°F (140°C) FOR 20 MINUTES. TURN OVEN UP TO 300°F (150°C) AND BAKE 40 MINUTES LONGER. COOL COMPLETELY.

NOW, BEAT EGG YOLKS AND FIFTH EGG UNTIL THICK. BEAT IN LIME JUICE, ZEST AND SUGAR. COOK IN DOUBLE BOILER UNTIL THICK, STIRRING OCCASIONALLY. COOL. LOOSEN CRUSTS.

WHIP CREAM AND SPREAD 1/4 OVER EACH CRUST, THEN 1/2 OF THE FILLING ON EACH. TOP WITH REMAINING WHIPPED CREAM. PLACE CRUSTS, ONE ON TOP OF THE

CONTINUED ON NEXT PAGE...

OTHER, RIGHT SIDE UP. CHILL 24 HOURS. SERVES 6 TO 8.

NOTE: LEMON JUICE AND ZEST MAY BE SUBSTITUTED FOR LIME BUT USE ALMOND FLAVORING FOR THE PISTACHIO FLAVORING IN THE MERINGUES.

MELON IN RUM SAUCE

THIS LIGHT SUMMER DESSERT IS MOST APPETIZING SERVED IN A LARGE GLASS BOWL.

1	CANTALOUPE	1
1	HONEYDEW MELON	1
1/4	SMALL WATERMELON	1/4
1 CUP	FRESH OR FROZEN BLUEBERRIES (DRAIN WELL IF FROZEN)	250 ML

CUT MELON INTO BALLS AND ADD BERRIES; CHILL.

SAUCE

2/3 CUP	SUGAR	150 ML
1/3 CUP	WATER	75 ML
1 TSP	LIME ZEST	5 ML
6 TBSP	LIME JUICE	90 ML
1/2 CUP	LIGHT RUM	125 ML

MIX SUGAR WITH WATER IN SAUCEPAN; BRING TO BOIL, THEN REDUCE HEAT AND SIMMER FOR 5 MINUTES. ADD LIME ZEST AND LET COOL TO ROOM TEMPERATURE. STIR IN LIME JUICE AND RUM. POUR OVER FRUIT AND CHILL SEVERAL HOURS. SERVES 6 TO 8.

PINEAPPLE SLICE

2½ CUPS	GRAHAM WAFER CRUMBS (SAVE ½ CUP/125 ML FOR TOPPING)	625 ML
1 CUP	BUTTER	250 ML
1½ CUPS	ICING SUGAR	375 ML
2	UNBEATEN EGGS	2
1	CAN (14 OZ/398 ML) CRUSHED PINEAPPLE, DRAINED	1
1 CUP	WHIPPING CREAM, WHIPPED	250 ML

COMBINE WAFER CRUMBS AND ½ CUP (125 ML) BUTTER, PAT INTO 8-INCH (2 L) SQUARE PAN AND BAKE FOR 10 MINUTES AT 375°F (190°C), COOL.

CREAM ½ CUP (125 ML) BUTTER WITH ICING SUGAR, AND ADD EGGS ONE AT A TIME, BEATING WELL AFTER EACH ADDITION. SPOON ONTO CRUST. WHIP CREAM, THEN FOLD IN PINEAPPLE. POUR OVER EGG MIXTURE AND SPRINKLE WITH CRUMBS. REFRIGERATE FOR 1 HOUR BEFORE SERVING.

MAY BE SERVED WITH AN EXTRA SPOONFUL OF CRUSHED PINEAPPLE ON EACH SLICE. SERVES 6 TO 8.

THERE COMES A TIME IN A MAN'S LIFE WHEN A YEN IS ONLY JAPANESE MONEY.

MEXICAN WEDDING CAKE

1 CUP	SOFT BUTTER	250 ML
1/2 CUP	SUGAR	125 ML
1/2 TSP	SALT	2 ML
2 CUPS	SIFTED FLOUR	500 ML
1 1/2 CUPS	GROUND ALMONDS	375 ML
2 TSP	VANILLA	10 ML

MIX WELL AND REFRIGERATE FOR 1 HOUR. ROLL INTO SMALL BALLS. BAKE AT 325°F (160°C) FOR 15 MINUTES. ROLL IN ICING SUGAR WHILE HOT. MAKES ABOUT 4 DOZEN.

THE ONLY THING WORSE THAN BEING OLD AND BENT
IS BEING YOUNG AND BROKE.

BRANDY SNAPS

A FUSSY HOUR OF PREPARING THE SHELLS WILL PROVIDE YOU WITH A TOP-NOTCH COMPANY DESSERT, WHICH MAY BE PREPARED AND FROZEN DAYS IN ADVANCE.

1/2 CUP	BUTTER	125 ML
1/2 CUP	SUGAR	125 ML
1/3 CUP	DARK MOLASSES	75 ML
1/2 CUP	FLOUR	125 ML
PINCH	SALT	PINCH
1 TSP	GROUND GINGER	5 ML
1 TSP	LEMON JUICE	5 ML
1/2 TSP	VANILLA	2 ML

HAVE READY ROLLING PIN, BROOM HANDLE OR LONG EMPTY CARDBOARD GIFT WRAP TUBE OR TIN FOIL TUBES. SET OVEN AT 350°F (180°C). MELT THE BUTTER, SUGAR AND MOLASSES IN A PAN, STIRRING UNTIL THE BUTTER IS MELTED. COOL SLIGHTLY. SIFT FLOUR, SALT AND GINGER INTO THE BUTTER MIXTURE, STIRRING WELL, AND ADDING LEMON JUICE AND VANILLA LAST. COOL. ONTO A WELL GREASED COOKIE SHEET, DROP THE MIXTURE HALF A TEASPOON AT A TIME, ALLOWING ONLY 5 OR 6 TO EACH LARGE COOKIE SHEET. THESE WILL SPREAD ON THE SHEET DURING BAKING INTO THIN WAFERS IDEALLY 3 TO 4 INCHES (7.5 TO 10 CM) IN DIAMETER.

BAKE FOR 7 OR 8 MINUTES, OR UNTIL EACH WAFER BUBBLES ALL OVER AND IS BROWNED. IMMEDIATELY SEPARATE WAFERS WITH A SPATULA AND COOL FOR 1/2 A MINUTE. WORKING RAPIDLY, REMOVE FROM COOKIE SHEET

CONTINUED ON NEXT PAGE...

AND ROLL AND SHAPE, BUBBLED SIDE OUT, AROUND BROOM HANDLE, CARDBOARD TUBING OR ANY SIMILAR OBJECT.

ALLOW TO COOL IN THIS POSITION UNTIL IT WILL REMAIN IN ROLLED POSITION. YOU MAY FIND IT PREFERABLE TO LEAVE THE SHELL PARTIALLY OPEN SO THAT IT IS EASIER TO FILL. IF THEY HARDEN BEFORE THEY ARE ROLLED, RETURN TO THE OVEN FOR A FEW MOMENTS. MAKES ABOUT 2 DOZEN.

THESE SHELLS MAY BE FROZEN AT THIS POINT AND FILLED JUST BEFORE SERVING WITH WHIPPED CREAM LACED WITH BRANDY.

OR... SLIGHTLY THAW VANILLA ICE CREAM, ADD $\frac{1}{4}$ TO $\frac{1}{2}$ CUP (50 TO 125 ML) BRANDY, AND WHIP TILL SMOOTH. FREEZE. AFTER SHELLS HAVE COOLED COMPLETELY, FILL EACH WITH THE BRANDIED ICE CREAM AND RETURN TO FREEZER UNTIL SERVING TIME. TO SERVE, ARRANGE ON SERVING PLATE, GARNISH EACH WITH BRANDIED WHIPPED CREAM AND NUTS. FOR THE FINAL TOUCH, WARM SOME BRANDY, AND AT THE TABLE, POUR OVER ALL BRANDY SNAPS AND FLAME.

CUCUMBER PATCH: DILLIES OF THE FIELD.

CRÈME DE MENTHE DESSERT

1	REGULAR PACKAGE OREO BISCUITS, CRUSHED	1
1	LARGE PACKAGE MARSHMALLOWS	1
1 CUP	MILK	250 ML
2 CUPS	WHIPPED CREAM	500 ML
6 TBSP	CRÈME DE MENTHE	90 ML

MELT MARSHMALLOWS IN DOUBLE BOILER WITH MILK. COOL. WHIP THE CREAM AND ADD TO COOLED MARSHMALLOWS. FOLD IN CRÈME DE MENTHE.

PLACE HALF OF THE CRUMBS IN A 13- X 9-INCH (3 L) PAN. COVER WITH MIXTURE. ADD REMAINDER OF THE CRUMBS TO TOP. REFRIGERATE OVERNIGHT. SERVES 12 TO 16.

NOTE: YOU MAY ALSO USE CRUSHED CANDY CANES INSTEAD OF CRÈME DE MENTHE, MAKING IT PINK.

"SWIMMING POOL": A SMALL BODY OF WATER COMPLETELY SURROUNDED BY NEIGHBORS.

Mrs. Larson's Bars (page 282)
Fantastic Fudge Brownies (page 287)

Verna's Chocolate Squares (page 284)

Cheesecake Cupcakes (page 289)

Lemonberry Cake (page 305)

PEPPERMINT CANDY DESSERT

*THIS DESSERT IS VERY RICH – SO GO EASY
ON THE SIZE OF THE SERVING.*

2 CUPS	VANILLA WAFER CRUMBS	500 ML
1/4 CUP	MELTED BUTTER	50 ML
1/2 CUP	BUTTER	125 ML
1 1/2 CUPS	ICING SUGAR	375 ML
3	EGGS, SLIGHTLY BEATEN	3
3	SQUARES UNSWEETENED CHOCOLATE, MELTED	3
1 1/2 CUPS	WHIPPING CREAM, WHIPPED	375 ML
1	PACKAGE MINIATURE MARSHMALLOWS	1
1	CRUSHED PEPPERMINT CANDY STICK	1

MAKE A CRUST OF WAFER CRUMBS AND MELTED BUTTER.
PAT INTO 13- X 9-INCH (3 L) PAN AND REFRIGERATE. CREAM
TOGETHER SUGAR AND 1/2 CUP (125 ML) BUTTER, THEN
ADD EGGS AND CHOCOLATE. BEAT WELL THEN SPOON
OVER CRUST, REFRIGERATE. COMBINE WHIPPED CREAM
AND MARSHMALLOWS, AND SPOON OVER CHOCOLATE
LAYER. WHEN SERVING, SPRINKLE CRUSHED PEPPERMINT
CANDY STICK OVER TOP. SERVES 12 TO 16.

MARSHMALLOW COFFEE DESSERT

½ LB	MARSHMALLOWS	250 G
½ CUP	STRONG COFFEE	125 ML
1 CUP	WHIPPING CREAM, WHIPPED	250 ML
	VANILLA WAFERS	

CUT MARSHMALLOWS WITH SCISSORS IN 4 PIECES AND POUR HOT COFFEE OVER THEM. WHEN COOL, ADD WHIPPED CREAM. LINE PIE PLATE WITH VANILLA WAFERS AND POUR IN MIXTURE. SPRINKLE CRUSHED WAFERS ON TOP. REFRIGERATE UNTIL SERVING TIME. SERVES 8.

IF OWLS ARE SO SMART, HOW COME THEY DON'T GET OFF THE NIGHT SHIFT?

MOCHA TORTE DESSERT

DELICIOUS AND SO LOVELY TO LOOK AT! A GREAT CHANGE FOR THAT 40TH BIRTHDAY!

1	CHOCOLATE CAKE MIX	1

MOCHA CREAM FILLING

1/2 CUP	SEMI-SWEET CHOCOLATE CHIPS	125 ML
2 TBSP	HOT WATER	25 ML
2 TBSP	INSTANT COFFEE POWDER	25 ML
1/4 CUP	GRANULATED SUGAR	50 ML
1 1/4 CUPS	WHIPPING CREAM	300 ML

PREPARING CAKE ACCORDING TO PACKAGE INSTRUCTIONS. BAKE IN TWO 8-INCH (20 CM) ROUND CAKE PANS THAT HAVE BEEN GREASED AND LINED WITH CIRCLES OF WAXED PAPER. BAKE AND COOL, THEN TURN OUT ON WIRE RACKS. WITH A KNIFE, SPLIT EACH LAYER INTO TWO.

FILLING: COMBINE CHOCOLATE CHIPS, WATER, COFFEE POWDER AND SUGAR IN SMALL, HEAVY SAUCEPAN. HEAT, STIRRING UNTIL SMOOTH, AND COOL. WHIP CREAM UNTIL IT STARTS TO THICKEN; ADD CHOCOLATE MIXTURE AND WHIP UNTIL STIFF. SPREAD BETWEEN LAYERS AND ON TOP OF TORTE. CHILL AT LEAST ONE HOUR. DECORATE WITH SHAVED CHOCOLATE. SERVES 10 TO 12.

CHOCOLATE ROLL

5	EGGS	5
1/2 TSP	CREAM OF TARTAR	2 ML
1 CUP	SUGAR	250 ML
1/4 CUP	FLOUR	50 ML
3 TBSP	COCOA	45 ML
1 TSP	VANILLA	5 ML
2 CUPS	WHIPPING CREAM, WHIPPED	500 ML

SEPARATE EGGS. BEAT WHITES WITH THE CREAM OF TARTAR UNTIL STIFF. GRADUALLY BEAT IN 1/2 CUP (125 ML) OF SUGAR. SIFT REMAINING SUGAR, COCOA AND FLOUR. BEAT YOLKS UNTIL THICK. FOLD FLOUR MIXTURE INTO YOLKS. ADD VANILLA (THIS WILL BE VERY STIFF). CAREFULLY FOLD YOLK MIXTURE INTO BEATEN WHITES.

PREHEAT OVEN TO 325°F (160°C). LINE COOKIE SHEET (15-1/2- X 10 1/2-INCH/39 X 26 CM) WITH WAX PAPER. GREASE AND FLOUR. SPREAD BATTER EVENLY ON PAN. BAKE FOR 20 MINUTES. COOL 5 MINUTES AND TURN ONTO TOWEL SPRINKLED WITH ICING SUGAR. PEEL OFF WAX PAPER AND ROLL CAKE WITH TOWEL. COOL. WHIP CREAM AND SPREAD ON UNROLLED CAKE. ROLL AGAIN.

SERVE WITH FOAMY BUTTER SAUCE (PAGE 370) OR FUDGE SAUCE (PAGE 371). FOR VARIATION, ADD 2 TBSP (25 ML) RUM OR YOUR FAVORITE LIQUEUR TO THE WHIPPED CREAM. SERVES 8.

CHOCOLATE POTS DE CRÈME

SHORTCUT METHOD FOR THAT FAMOUS DESSERT.

I	PACKAGE (6 OZ/170 G) SEMI-SWEET CHOCOLATE CHIPS	I
2 TBSP	SUGAR	25 ML
PINCH	SALT	PINCH
I	EGG	I
I TSP	VANILLA	5 ML
I ½ TO 2 TSP	DARK RUM OR I TSP (5 ML) POWDERED INSTANT COFFEE	7 TO 10 ML
¾ CUP	MILK	175 ML
	WHIPPED CREAM, FOR TOPPING	

COMBINE CHOCOLATE, SUGAR, SALT, EGG, VANILLA AND RUM IN BLENDER. HEAT MILK JUST TO BOILING. POUR OVER OTHER INGREDIENTS. COVER AND BLEND I MINUTE. POUR IMMEDIATELY INTO CHOCOLATE POTS OR RAMEKINS. CHILL AT LEAST I HOUR. SERVE WITH WHIPPED CREAM. SERVES 4.

ON A TENNIS PLAYER'S T-SHIRT: "NEVER FALL IN LOVE WITH A TENNIS PLAYER. TO HIM, LOVE MEANS NOTHING!"

CHOCOLATE MOCHA MOUSSE

I	PACKAGE (7 OZ/200 G) CHOCOLATE WAFERS	I
1/4 CUP	MELTED BUTTER	50 ML
I CUP	BOILING WATER	250 ML
4 TSP	INSTANT COFFEE	20 ML
I	PACKAGE (11 OZ/313 G) MARSHMALLOWS	I
I CUP	WHIPPING CREAM	250 ML

MELT MARSHMALLOWS IN THE TOP OF A DOUBLE BOILER. ADD INSTANT COFFEE TO BOILING WATER AND STIR INTO MARSHMALLOWS. CHILL AT LEAST ONE HOUR. RESERVE 14 CHOCOLATE WAFERS AND CRUSH REST OF PACKAGE. SET ASIDE I TBSP (15 ML) CRUSHED WAFERS FOR TOPPING. ADD BUTTER TO REMAINING WAFER CRUMBS AND PRESS INTO BOTTOM OF SPRINGFORM PAN. PLACE THE 14 WAFERS AROUND EDGE OF PAN. WHIP CREAM. REMOVE COFFEE MIXTURE FROM FRIDGE AND WHIP. FOLD CREAM AND COFFEE MIXTURE TOGETHER AND POUR INTO PAN. ADD TOPPING AND CHILL. SERVES 6.

"YOU GAVE AWAY MY SECRET."
"I DID NOT, I EXCHANGED IT FOR ANOTHER."

ICEBOX PUDDING

LIGHT AND DELICIOUS. A FAMILY FAVORITE FOR AT LEAST THREE GENERATIONS - WHICH IS PROBABLY WHY IT'S CALLED ICEBOX PUDDING!

½ CUP	GRAHAM WAFER CRUMBS	125 ML
I CUP	WHIPPING CREAM	250 ML
3	EGGS, SEPARATED	3
I CUP	SUGAR, DIVIDED	250 ML
I TBSP	UNFLAVORED GELATIN	15 ML
	JUICE OF I LEMON	
	JUICE OF I ORANGE	
¼ CUP	GRAHAM WAFER CRUMBS	50 ML

SPREAD ½ CUP (125 ML) GRAHAM WAFER CRUMBS IN BOTTOM OF AN 8½ X 4½-INCH (1.5 L) LOAF PAN. WHIP CREAM UNTIL STIFF. IN ANOTHER BOWL, BEAT EGG WHITES UNTIL STIFF. GRADUALLY ADD ½ CUP (125 ML) SUGAR AND CONTINUE BEATING. IN A LARGE BOWL, BEAT EGG YOLKS WITH REMAINING SUGAR UNTIL LEMON COLORED. SOFTEN GELATIN IN LEMON AND ORANGE JUICES AND ADD TO YOLK MIXTURE. GENTLY FOLD IN EGG WHITES. FOLD IN WHIPPED CREAM AND POUR INTO LOAF PAN. SPRINKLE WITH REMAINING GRAHAM WAFER CRUMBS. FREEZE AT LEAST 4 HOURS OR OVERNIGHT.

AT LEAST I HOUR BEFORE SERVING, LOOSEN EDGES AND INVERT ONTO SERVING PLATE. LEAVE IN REFRIGERATOR. SERVES 6 TO 8.

LEMON PUDDING

AN OLD FAMILY FAVORITE! THE TOP TURNS TO
CAKE AND THE BOTTOM TURNS TO SAUCE.
SERVE WARM WITH WHIPPED CREAM.

2 TBSP	FLOUR	25 ML
I CUP	SUGAR	250 ML
2 TBSP	BUTTER	25 ML
2	EGGS	2
I CUP	MILK	250 ML
	JUICE AND GRATED ZEST OF I LEMON	

MIX FLOUR AND SUGAR IN SHALLOW CASSEROLE DISH.
CREAM BUTTER INTO MIXTURE. SEPARATE EGGS. BEAT
YOLKS AND MILK TOGETHER. ADD TO MIXTURE IN
CASSEROLE DISH AND BEAT UNTIL SMOOTH. ADD LEMON
JUICE AND ZEST. BEAT EGG WHITES UNTIL STIFF. FOLD
INTO MIXTURE. SET CASSEROLE IN DISH OF HOT WATER.
BAKE 35 TO 40 MINUTES AT 350°F (180°C). BROWN LIGHTLY
UNDER BROILER. SERVES 5.

I LOVE PLAYING THE VIOLIN, ESPECIALLY WHEN I AM
DEPRESSED; IT HELPS ME KEEP MY CHIN UP.

DANISH RUM SOUFFLÉ

AN ALL-TIME FAVORITE – PARTICULARLY WITH THE MEN. MAKE IT THE DAY BEFORE!

4	EGG YOLKS	4
½ CUP	SUGAR	125 ML
¼ CUP	DARK RUM	50 ML
1 TBSP	UNFLAVORED GELATIN	15 ML
¼ CUP	COLD WATER	50 ML
½ PINT	WHIPPING CREAM	250 ML
4	EGG WHITES	4
½ CUP	SUGAR	125 ML
½ PINT	WHIPPING CREAM, FOR TOPPING	250 ML
	HERSHEY'S SEMI-SWEET CHOCOLATE BAR, ROOM TEMPERATURE	

BEAT EGG YOLKS AND ½ CUP (125 ML) SUGAR IN A LARGE BOWL UNTIL LEMON-COLORED. ADD RUM AND BEAT. DISSOLVE GELATIN IN COLD WATER AND SET IN SLIGHTLY LARGER BOWL OF HOT WATER TO KEEP GELATIN MIXTURE LIQUID. BEAT CREAM UNTIL STIFF. BEAT EGG WHITES UNTIL STIFF AND GRADUALLY ADD ½ CUP (125 ML) SUGAR. ADD GELATIN MIXTURE TO YOLK MIXTURE. FOLD WHIPPED CREAM INTO YOLK MIXTURE. FINALLY, FOLD IN EGG WHITES. POUR INTO CRYSTAL BOWL OR INDIVIDUAL SHERBET DISHES. CHILL 4 TO 6 HOURS OR OVERNIGHT. JUST BEFORE SERVING, TOP WITH WHIPPED CREAM AND POTATO PEELER CURLS OF CHOCOLATE. SERVES 8.

ENGLISH TRIFLE

1	SPONGE CAKE, STALE	1
1	PACKAGE (20 OZ/570 G) FROZEN RASPBERRIES OR STRAWBERRIES	1
1/2 CUP	MEDIUM SHERRY	125 ML
1 CUP	WHIPPED CREAM	250 ML
	TOASTED ALMONDS	
	MARASCHINO CHERRIES	
	SHERRY CUSTARD (SEE BELOW)	

CUT SPONGE CAKE INTO SLICES AND ARRANGE IN A LAYER IN THE BOTTOM OF A LARGE GLASS SERVING BOWL. SPOON A LAYER OF SEMI-THAWED FRUIT OVER CAKE. SPOON A LAYER OF SHERRY CUSTARD OVER FRUIT AND REPEAT LAYERS FINISHING WITH A LAYER OF CUSTARD. POUR 1/4 CUP (50 ML) SHERRY OVER ALL AND REFRIGERATE 2 HOURS. POUR REMAINING SHERRY OVER ALL, INSERTING A SILVER KNIFE TO THE BOTTOM IN SEVERAL PLACES SO THE SHERRY WILL SOAK THROUGH. ALLOW TO MELLOW IN FRIDGE FOR AT LEAST 24 HOURS. JUST BEFORE SERVING, WHIP CREAM AND SPREAD OVER THE TOP. DECORATE WITH ALMONDS AND CHERRIES. SERVES 10 TO 12.

SHERRY CUSTARD FOR ENGLISH TRIFLE

4	EGG YOLKS	4
1/2 CUP	GRANULATED SUGAR	125 ML
PINCH	SALT	PINCH
1 TBSP	FLOUR	15 ML
1/2 TO 1 CUP	MEDIUM SHERRY	125 TO 250 ML
4	EGG WHITES, BEATEN STIFF	4

CONTINUED ON NEXT PAGE...

IN TOP PART OF DOUBLE BOILER, COMBINE EGG YOLKS, SUGAR, SALT, FLOUR AND SHERRY. COOK OVER HOT WATER AND STIR CONSTANTLY UNTIL MIXTURE THICKENS, ABOUT 7 MINUTES. REMOVE FROM HEAT IMMEDIATELY AND FOLD IN STIFFLY BEATEN EGG WHITES. THIS IS NOW READY TO BE ADDED TO ENGLISH TRIFLE RECIPE AS DESCRIBED ON PAGE 362.

FOOD PRICES ARE CHANGING OUR WHOLE WAY OF LIFE. NOW PARENTS TELL THEIR CHILDREN, "EAT YOUR DESSERT OR YOU WON"T GET YOUR MEAT."

ANGEL FOOD FLAN

THIS CAKE IS MADE ENTIRELY FROM MIXES WHICH IS GREAT FOR TWO REASONS - IT NEVER FAILS AND YOU CAN KEEP THE INGREDIENTS INDEFINITELY. IT ALSO TASTES TERRIFIC!

I	PACKAGE ANGEL FOOD CAKE MIX	I
I½ CUPS	MILK	375 ML
I	PACKAGE VANILLA PUDDING MIX (THE KIND YOU COOK)	I
I	ENVELOPE DREAM WHIP	I
½ CUP	MILK	I25 ML
½ TSP	ALMOND EXTRACT	5 ML

TOPPING

I	CAN (IO OZ/284 ML) MANDARIN ORANGES, DRAINED	I
½ CUP	TOASTED SLIVERED ALMONDS	I25 ML

PREHEAT OVEN TO 375°F (I90°C). PREPARE ANGEL CAKE MIX AS DIRECTED. PUSH BATTER INTO UNGREASED PAN. YOU MAY USE EITHER A I3- X 9-INCH (3 L) OR A IO-INCH (4 L) TUBE PAN. (KEEP IN MIND THAT THIS CAKE WILL REALLY RISE DURING BAKING AND IF YOU HAVE SOME BATTER LEFT OVER, COOK IT IN ANOTHER PAN AND USE FOR ANOTHER DESSERT.)

CUT THROUGH BATTER WITH A KNIFE TO REMOVE AIR. SPREAD SMOOTH. BAKE ON LOWEST OVEN RACK 30 TO 40 MINUTES. INVERT CAKE TO COOL. LET HANG 2 HOURS.

(IF USING IO-INCH/4 L TUBE PAN, DOUBLE FILLING RECIPE.)

CONTINUED ON NEXT PAGE...

FILLING: PREPARE VANILLA PUDDING AS DIRECTED, USING 1½ CUPS (375 ML) MILK. COVER SURFACE OF PUDDING WITH WAX PAPER TO PREVENT SCUM FROM FORMING. CHILL. PREPARE DREAM WHIP AS DIRECTED USING ½ CUP (125 ML) MILK AND ½ TSP (2 ML) ALMOND EXTRACT. BEAT CHILLED PUDDING UNTIL LIGHT. FOLD IN DREAM WHIP. LOOSEN AND TURN OUT CAKE. IF 13- X 9-INCH (3 L), CUT IN HALF. IF IN TUBE PAN, CUT INTO TWO LAYERS. SPREAD FILLING BETWEEN LAYERS, RESERVING ENOUGH TO FROST ENTIRE CAKE. DECORATE WITH MANDARIN ORANGES AND TOASTED ALMONDS. SERVES 12.

NOTE: FOR A FIRMER FILLING, ADD 1 TSP (5 ML) CORNSTARCH TO DREAM WHIP.

A LOSER IS A WINDOW WASHER ON THE 44TH FLOOR
WHO STEPS BACK TO ADMIRE HIS WORK!

QUICK FROZEN DESSERT

3 TBSP	BUTTER, MELTED	45 ML
1½ CUPS	GRAHAM WAFER CRUMBS	375 ML
1 PINT	VANILLA ICE CREAM	500 ML
1 TSP	CINNAMON	5 ML

COMBINE MELTED BUTTER AND CRUMBS AND PAT INTO BOTTOM OF CAKE PAN. BEAT VANILLA ICE CREAM AND ADD CINNAMON. SPREAD OVER CRUST, SPRINKLE WITH ADDITIONAL CRUMBS AND FREEZE UNTIL FIRM. SERVES 6 TO 8.

BUTTER BRICKLE DESSERT

2 CUPS	FLOUR	500 ML
½ CUP	OATMEAL	125 ML
½ CUP	BROWN SUGAR	125 ML
1 CUP	BUTTER	250 ML
1 CUP	CHOPPED PECANS	250 ML
1	JAR CARAMEL SAUCE	1
1 PINT	VANILLA ICE CREAM	500 ML

MELT MARGARINE. ADD FLOUR, OATMEAL, BROWN SUGAR AND PECANS. PAT THIN ON A LARGE COOKIE SHEET AND BAKE AT 400°F (200°C) FOR 15 MINUTES. CRUMBLE WHILE HOT AND SPREAD HALF ON BOTTOM OF 9-INCH (2.5 L) SQUARE PAN. DRIZZLE ½ JAR OF CARAMEL TOPPING OVER CRUMBS. SPREAD THE ICE CREAM OVER TOP, THEN PUT THE REMAINING CRUMBS ON ICE CREAM AND DRIZZLE REST OF CARAMEL SAUCE ON TOP. FREEZE. SERVES 8 TO 12.

FLUFFY ICING

WONDERFUL FOR KIDS' CAKE. IT MAKES GOBS!

I CUP	WHITE SUGAR	250 ML
1/4 TSP	CREAM OF TARTER	I ML
I	EGG WHITE	I
1/2 TSP	VANILLA	2 ML
1/2 CUP	BOILING WATER	125 ML

PLACE ALL INGREDIENTS IN LARGE BOWL, ADDING BOILING WATER LAST. BEAT ON HIGH WITH ELECTRIC MIXER FOR 10 MINUTES. MAKES ENOUGH ICING FOR A LARGE ANGEL FOOD CAKE OR 2 OR 3 CAKE LAYERS. FOOD COLORING MAY BE ADDED FOR COLOR.

ISLA'S ICING

THIS ICING NEVER GETS HARD.
IT'S REALLY GREAT ON SPICE CAKE.

4 TBSP	SOFT BUTTER	60 ML
6 TBSP	ICING SUGAR	90 ML
2 TSP	MILK (I SAID TEASPOONS)	10 ML
2 TSP	WATER	10 ML

BEAT IN MIXER AT HIGH SPEED FOR 5 MINUTES, UNTIL FLUFFY. MAKES ENOUGH FOR A 9-INCH (23 CM) SQUARE CAKE.

WHEN YOUR DAUGHTER MARRIES, DON'T THINK OF IT AS LOSING A DAUGHTER; THINK OF IT AS GAINING A BATHROOM!

CREAMY VANILLA FROSTING

2 TBSP	SHORTENING	25 ML
1/2 TSP	SALT	2 ML
1 TSP	VANILLA	5 ML
1 1/2 CUPS	ICING SUGAR	375 ML
2 TBSP	MILK	25 ML
	CINNAMON TO TASTE	

MIX SHORTENING, SALT, VANILLA AND 1/2 CUP (125 ML) SUGAR. ADD MILK AND THE REST OF THE SUGAR. MAKES ABOUT 3/4 CUP (175 ML).

LEMON BUTTER

FOR CAKE FILLINGS AND TARTS

5	EGGS, WELL BEATEN	5
1 CUP	BUTTER	250 ML
1 CUP	SUGAR	250 ML
4	LEMONS	4

MELT BUTTER AND SUGAR. GRATE LEMON ZEST, SQUEEZE JUICE. ADD TO BUTTER MIXTURE, THEN POUR IN EGGS, BEATING WELL OVER MEDIUM HEAT UNTIL THICK. MAKES ABOUT 2 1/2 CUPS (625 ML).

"SUNBURN": GETTING WHAT YOU BASKED FOR.

DELUXE SAUCE

(FOR ANGEL CAKES)

½ CUP	BUTTER	125 ML
½ CUP	FLOUR	125 ML
½ CUP	SUGAR	125 ML
PINCH	SALT	PINCH
I CUP	MILK	250 ML
2	EGG YOLKS	2
2	EGG WHITES	2
2 TBSP	SUGAR	25 ML
	ZEST OF I ORANGE	
I CUP	WHIPPING CREAM, WHIPPED	250 ML
I TSP	VANILLA OR ORANGE JUICE	5 ML
I	PREPARED ANGEL FOOD CAKE	I

MELT BUTTER IN DOUBLE BOILER, STIRRING IN FLOUR AND ½ CUP (125 ML) SUGAR AND SALT. ADD MILK, AND COOK FOR 10 MINUTES. REMOVE FROM HEAT AND BEAT IN EGG YOLKS. ALLOW TO COOL COMPLETELY. BEAT IN STIFFLY BEATEN EGG WHITES AND 2 TBSP (25 ML) SUGAR. ADD WHIPPED CREAM, ORANGE PEEL AND FLAVORING. SPOON OVER CAKE. REFRIGERATE UNTIL SERVING TIME. SERVES 8 TO 12.

FLUFFY LEMON CREAM TOPPING

8 OZ	CREAM CHEESE, SOFTENED	250 G
1/2 CUP	SIFTED CONFECTIONERS POWDERED SUGAR	125 ML
1/4 CUP	LIGHT CREAM	50 ML
1/2 TSP	LEMON EXTRACT	2 ML

BLEND CREAM CHEESE, SUGAR, CREAM AND LEMON EXTRACT TOGETHER IN A SMALL BOWL. CHILL SLIGHTLY AND SERVE ON WARM GINGERBREAD. MAKES ABOUT 1 1/2 CUPS (375 ML).

FOAMY BUTTER SAUCE

1/2 CUP	BUTTER	125 ML
1	EGG	1
1 CUP	ICING SUGAR	250 ML

COMBINE ALL INGREDIENTS IN TOP OF DOUBLE BOILER. COOK, STIRRING UNTIL IT FORMS A SMOOTH SAUCE. MAKES ABOUT 3/4 CUP (175 ML).

SERVE WARM OVER CHOCOLATE ROLL.

WHERE DO BAD LITTLE GIRLS GO? BAD LITTLE GIRLS GO ALMOST EVERYWHERE THEY WANT TO.

FUDGE SAUCE

1 TBSP	BUTTER	15 ML
1	SQUARE UNSWEETENED CHOCOLATE (1 OZ/30 G)	1
1/3 CUP	BOILING WATER	75 ML
1 CUP	SUGAR	250 ML
2 TBSP	CORN SYRUP	25 ML
1/2 TSP	VANILLA	2 ML

MELT BUTTER AND CHOCOLATE IN MEDIUM SAUCEPAN. ADD BOILING WATER. BRING MIXTURE TO BOIL. ADD SUGAR AND SYRUP. BOIL, STIRRING, FOR 5 MINUTES. ADD VANILLA AND STIR. MAKES ABOUT 1 CUP (250 ML).

SERVE JUST WARM OVER CHOCOLATE ROLL.

IT'S AN ILL WIND THAT BLOWS THE MINUTE YOU LEAVE THE BEAUTY PARLOR.

Library and Archives Canada Cataloguing in Publication

The complete Best of Bridge cookbooks, volume 1: All 350 recipes from The Best of Bridge and Enjoy!

Includes index.

Includes: The Best of Bridge: royal treats for entertaining and Enjoy!: more recipes from the Best of Bridge.

ISBN-10: 0-7788-0206-X (v.1)
ISBN-13: 978-0-7788-0206-8 (v.1)

1. Cookery.

TX714.C6423 2008   641.5   C2008-902452-4

INDEX